D1042033

THE Solution

THE Solution

Conquer Your Fear, Control Your Future

Lucinda Bassett

New York / London
www.sterlingpublishing.com

STERLING and the distinctive Sterling logo are registered trademarks of Sterling Publishing Co., Inc.

Library of Congress Cataloging-in-Publication Data Available

2 4 6 8 10 9 7 5 3 1

Published by Sterling Publishing Co., Inc.
387 Park Avenue South, New York, NY 10016

Distributed in Canada by Sterling Publishing
c/o Canadian Manda Group, 165 Dufferin Street,
Toronto, Ontario, Canada M6K 3H6

Manufactured in the United States of America

Sterling ISBN 978-1-4027-7988-6

For information about custom editions, special sales, premium and corporate purchases, please contact Sterling Special Sales Department at 800-805-5489 or specialsales@sterlingpublishing.com.

CONTENTS

DEDICATION

This book is dedicated to all the people

who have used my life's skills

to improve their own.

You are why I continue to do what I do.

FOREWORD

by Daniel Amen, MD

Author of *Change Your Brain, Change Your Body*

Lucinda Bassett has helped millions of people around the globe conquer stress, anxiety, and depression. Her message has survived the test of time because it is relevant, extremely effective, and easy to understand and implement. Now, with her new book, *The Solution,* she continues to changes people's lives for the better.

As a psychiatrist and brain enhancement expert, I started looking into Lucinda's work a number of years ago because several of my patients had taken her home study course. I noticed quickly that she and I were aligned in our attitudes since she was teaching people many of the lessons that I had introduced to them in therapy. My research has shown me that learning effective mental health principles at home can be very effective in overcoming issues related to stress, anxiety, and depression. Clear focus, correcting negative thought patterns, eliminating self-limiting beliefs, learning how to manage anxiety and stress, and overcoming obstacles are keys to a healthy life, yet nowhere in school do we learn these essential tools. This is why Ms. Bassett's work is so valuable and crucial for finding happiness and fulfillment in our world today.

Given the challenging economy, the constant bombardment of negative media messages, the large number of two-parent working families, and countless other stresses, many people feel at the end of their rope. For these reasons, I love *The Solution: Conquer Your Fear, Control Your Future* because it is a road map to sanity and a healthy life. In this innovative book, Lucinda once again uses her talents as an expert in self-help and personal empowerment to teach people how to conquer their fears, worries, anxieties, and insecurities in order to create the life they want. The lessons, questionnaires, action assignments, and anecdotes are all geared toward recognizing what Lucinda calls "your Core Story" as she encourages people to use their inherent childhood weaknesses, challenging life experiences, and early trauma to create strength and power and increase their self-esteem.

In this book, Lucinda offers brand-new ways to embed these concepts into your mind. There is some insightful and creative work involved in the process, since all meaningful change requires effort. But if you persist, you are well on your way to a clearer mind, a healthier body, a more positive attitude, and an optimistic and clear perspective on your life's potential. That really is what we all want.

INTRODUCTION

Recently I was in a marketing meeting explaining the concept of this book, *The Solution,* to the creative team. They were expecting a two-minute "elevator pitch," where I describe why my book is compelling, unique, and life-changing. Instead, I began by explaining the power and significance of the "Core Story" theory and "re-active living."

"We all have a Core Story," I began, "and our life is all about how we react as a result of early programming and life experiences." Then I asked the people in the meeting a few questions:

"How were you raised? What messages did you receive growing up, verbal and nonverbal? What did you see your parents doing? Were they worriers? Overreactors? Did anyone abandon you, scare you, or sabotage you? Did you go through anything you'd prefer to deny or hide? What were the messages you received about money, responsibility, love, and relationships? How did your family members deal with stress, anxiety, and change?"

I went on to explain that our Core Story is what molded each of us into who we have become. While genetics play a significant part, so does the environment along with all that we endured in our childhood and young adulthood, both good and bad. The point is, I told them, the way in which we handled these early challenges has shaped our current belief systems, which we have the power to change.

Our current beliefs that were programmed during childhood and adolescence have created automatic re-active attitudes and actions that determine how we spontaneously respond to everything from a stressful event to an anticipated concern, from an unhealthy relationship to a dissatisfying career. Because of these Core Story beliefs and the subsequent re-active responses that go with them, we may be making unproductive and even destructive choices. This book is about learning how to stop these negative behavioral cycles so we can feel better, have a happier, more successful life, and, more importantly, so we don't pass them on to our children.

One of the men in the meeting was so enthusiastic about the Core Story theory that he wanted to share part of his own Core Story with me. "My mother had to drive for fifteen minutes over three bridges to get to the grocery store," he said. "Then several years ago, the city erected a new bridge near her house that allowed her to cross just one bridge to get to the store, shortening her trip by at least ten minutes. But when I drove to the store with her, she took the old route. 'Why are you going this old way,' I asked her, 'when the new route would save you time?'

"'Well, I've never gone that way,' she said. 'What if I don't like it? This way is familiar and I'd rather just stick to what I know. Never do something you haven't done, Steven, because you may not like it.'"

Steven sat there shaking his head in disbelief. "I understand why it was difficult for me to take risks and try new things in my life," he said. "I wasn't a good risk-taker and now I know why."

Someone else shared a part of her Core Story, and then someone else did, too. Before I knew it, everyone understood at a profound level one of the most important concepts in this book:

Our Core Story made us who we are today, both bad and good. And the good news is that we can use our Core Story to positively transform our lives.

So how about you? What's your Core Story? What is holding you back and keeping you stuck, justifying your misery, your lack, your fear or dysfunction? What past belief or experience is fueling your neediness, insecurity, or inability to take risks? Possibly you had a particularly challenging experience in your past that you would rather not remember, thinking nothing good could come from recalling such pain. But there is a purpose for the pain. You will come to understand why you struggled so much and what you are going to do with your pain by reading this book.

Maybe you had a great childhood with very little turmoil, but you struggle to find passion in your life. Maybe you find it hard to deal with challenge and change, or maybe you can't seem to find balance or peace of mind. Maybe you just don't know what it would take to make you happy. The answers and solutions are in this book. The Core Story is important but it is only the beginning. I'll help you figure out what kind of worrier you are. Everyone worries to some extent, so I'll be sharing the following information in a way that is easy to access and understand for everyone:

- Great worriers make fabulous goal-setters.
- Anxiety and fear can be transformed into ways of thinking and responding that will make you happy, successful, and satisfied.
- When you take an honest look at your past and your Core Story, you can begin to change your present moment so you feel relaxed, confident, and peaceful.
- It is possible to define where you want to go and create an effective plan for getting there.

I wrote this book because we are living in stressful times. People feel anxious and vulnerable. If this is you, you really need to take back your power that was inherent within you—until you unwittingly gave it away. When the power within is intact, nothing can make you insecure because you have yourself. Most of us, however, never learned the skill of self-empowerment. We learned instead to look outside ourselves for power and reinforcement. But when you give the outside world or another person your power, you are vulnerable. It's a false sense of security because it can be taken from you.

A LOOK INSIDE THE BOOK

This book was designed to help you take back your power so you can find your inner confidence and strength—an inner strength so powerful and irrefutable that nothing can take it from you. The process begins with your thoughts. You will find empowering affirmations at the end of a number of chapters. At first glance, these personal affirmations may seem hard to believe or relate to because you are most likely unfamiliar with empowerment thinking, especially at a level that helps you manifest your goals and dreams.

However, once you have finished each chapter, the affirmations will make more sense to you because you have implemented the skills and concepts here, and you just might find that you actually believe them to be true about yourself and your potential.

The Solution is divided into two parts.

In **Part One: The Problem,** you'll look closely at who you've become as a result of your Core Story and your life experiences. You will begin to understand why you sabotage yourself and you'll learn how to stop doing it. You'll begin to see the potential of your life and your future *because* of what you've been through and who you've become—not *in spite* of it.

Part Two: The Solution is full of exciting new concepts for change that will motivate you to look at life from a whole new perspective. You'll learn to establish a sense of lasting personal security as you deepen your understanding about the importance of healthy detachment. In short, you will become a power thinker. Now, that's something worth passing on to your children!

Every chapter reinforces the importance of going from being a re-active person, out of control, doing what comes naturally and impulsively, and getting the same negative results, to becoming a pro-active person who thinks and responds in ways that get positive results. This is the number one skill of highly successful people and it will be a skill that you will "own" by the end of this book. How?

The Solution is full of Pro-Active Action Assignments, Pro-Active Attitude Adjustments, and self-evaluations, created to change the way you think and respond. You will learn to reprogram your brain and patterns of behavior in ways that may at times seem abrupt and shocking. But as is the case with a good exercise plan, you will know as you work your way through that you are getting results. As the saying goes, *No pain, no gain.*

HOW TO USE THIS BOOK

Start by opening your mind to the fact that you can be or do anything you choose. It isn't too late, you aren't too old, too young, or too dysfunctional. The truth is that you are full of potential and you are available for good energy, good people, and good things to come to you.

There are twenty-one Pro-Active Action Assignments scattered throughout the book in various chapters, so I suggest you do one action assignment a day for twenty-one days until the process is complete. The Pro-Active Attitude Adjustments at the end of each chapter are to be pondered and internalized as you move through the book until they become a natural part of your reprogrammed way of thinking. In a relatively short period of time, you will begin to notice a change in the way you think about yourself. You will clearly see where you need to change in order to become stronger, healthier, and more whole as a human being. You will feel a surge of confidence and independence that, although unfamiliar, will be exciting.

SHINE YOUR LIGHT

Who am I to tell you how to transform yourself from someone who can't cope, who can't see the light at the end of the tunnel, into someone who can't stop giving off light inside the tunnel and out?

Simple. I've done it. I've been through extreme loss, challenge, and change of the worst kind, and I'll share some of my stories with you. I have also helped millions of people from all walks of life and in all parts of the world overcome anxiety, stress, and depression. That is my mission: to show people the way and even the will, when there isn't one.

I have found my power, even in the most difficult of times. If I can do it, so can you. Let me show you how. It is an honor and a privilege to share this book with you.

—Lucinda Bassett

1

THE Problem

CHAPTER ONE

What Is Your Core Story?

The period of greatest gain in knowledge and experience is the most difficult period in one's life.

—Dalai Lama

There's an old Cherokee legend in which an elder is sitting with his grandchildren, telling them a story. "In every life," he says, "there's a terrible fight, a fight between two wolves. One is evil. He is fear, anger, envy, greed, arrogance, self-pity, resentment, sadness, and deceit. The other wolf is good. He is joy, serenity, humility, confidence, generosity, truth, gentleness, and compassion."

One of the children asks, "Grandfather, which one will win?"

The elder looks the child in the eye and says, "The one you feed."

Which one will you feed? It's time to take control of your thoughts and reactions to situations with a new set of skills. These skills will not only improve your present life experience, but also help you define a positive, secure future.

ANYTHING IS POSSIBLE

The fact that you're reading this book tells me that you are ready, right now, to make a commitment to yourself to put aside all false beliefs about yourself and your potential. It's time to open your heart, your mind, and your eyes to all the possibilities that lie before you. How do you do that? By believing in your inherent right to success and happiness.

Below are examples of great power thinkers who were *not* voted most likely to succeed in high school or college. In fact, many of them dropped out of high school and never attended college. And still they became hugely successful because of their attitudes and passions. Using various types of motivation—including worry, fear, and insecurity—they were able to positively transform their negative Core Story beliefs (to be detailed later in the chapter) into positive ones. Most of all, they succeeded because of their ability to think from a position of empowerment. Wouldn't you be proud to be included in this list?

Famous, Rich, Successful People Who Were High School and/or College Dropouts

Andre Agassi: Tennis player, winner of eight Grand Slam titles. Quit school in the ninth grade and turned tennis pro at sixteen.

Paul Allen: Billionaire cofounder of Microsoft, founder of Xiant software, owner of Seattle Seahawks and Portland Trailblazers. Dropped out of Washington State to start up Microsoft with Bill Gates.

Tom Anderson: Cofounder of MySpace. High school dropout.

Richard Branson: Billionaire founder of Virgin Music, Virgin Atlantic Airways, and other Virgin enterprises. Dropped out of high school at sixteen.

James Francis Byrnes: U.S. Representative, U.S. Senator, Supreme Court justice, U.S. secretary of state, South Carolina governor. Dropped out of St. Patrick's Catholic School at fourteen to apprentice in a law office. Didn't attend college or law school.

James Cameron: Oscar-winning director, producer, screenwriter. Dropped out of California State University. Took up street racing while working as a truck driver and a high school janitor. Built models for Roger Corman's New World Pictures.

Winston Churchill: British prime minister, historian, artist. Rebellious by nature; flunked the sixth grade. Applied to the Royal Military Academy at Sandhurst; had to take the entrance exam three times. Never attended college.

Simon Cowell: Millionaire, TV producer, judge on *American Idol, Britain's Got Talent,* and *The X Factor.* Dropped out of high school at sixteen. Member of Forbes 2008 Celebrity 100.

James M. Cox: Newspaper publisher, three-term governor of Ohio, presidential nominee in 1920. Founded Cox Enterprises. Never finished high school.

Charles Culpeper: Multimillionaire owner and CEO of Coca Cola. High school dropout.

John Paul DeJoria: Billionaire cofounder of John Paul

Mitchell Systems hair care products, founder of Patron Spirits Tequila. Dropped out of high school and joined the U.S. Navy. Did odd jobs and lived in his car before landing an entry-level marketing job with *Time* magazine.

Michael Dell: Founder of Dell Computers. Billionaire, among top ten wealthiest Americans. Founded his company in his college dorm room. Dropped out of University of Texas to run the company.

Clint Eastwood: Oscar-winning actor, director, producer. Attended half a dozen schools and excelled at none. Enrolled at Los Angeles City College, never graduated. Bagged groceries, delivered papers, fought forest fires, dug swimming pools. Worked as a steelworker and logger.

Larry Ellison: Billionaire cofounder of Oracle software company. Dropped out of University of Chicago and University of Illinois.

Bill Gates: Billionaire cofounder of Microsoft, one of the richest men in the world, philanthropist. Dropped out of Harvard after his second year. He noted, “I realized the error of my ways and decided I could make do with a high school diploma.”

David Geffen: Billionaire founder of Geffen Records, cofounder of DreamWorks. Dropped out of University of Texas after one year. Flunked out of Brooklyn College. Began in the mail room at William Morris Agency.

Daniel Gilbert: Psychology professor, Harvard University. High school dropout.

John Glenn: Astronaut, U.S. Senator. Did not finish college in Ohio.

Tom Hanks: Oscar-winning actor, youngest person to receive American Film Institute’s Lifetime Achievement Award. Did not attend college.

Louise Hay: Author of *You Can Heal Your Life,* founder of Hay House Publishing, one of the founders of the self-help movement. Suffered from an impoverished, abusive childhood; never attended college.

Peter Jennings: News anchor at ABC. Failed the tenth grade and dropped out of high school at sixteen.

Ray Kroc: Multimillionaire founder of McDonald's. High school dropout.

Cathy Lanier: Chief of Police of Washington, DC. Was a fourteen-year-old pregnant high school dropout.

Doris Lessing: Novelist. Dropped out of school at fourteen. Won the Nobel Prize for Literature in 2007.

Wolfgang Puck: Millionaire chef, owner of fine restaurants and eighty Express Bistros. Quit school at age fourteen.

Rachael Ray: Emmy Award–winning TV cooking show host and author of several highly successful cookbooks; has no formal training as a chef and never attended college.

Tony Robbins: Motivational self-help guru, best-selling author, personal growth trainer to many celebrities, major corporations, political figures. Never attended college.

J.K. Rowling: Author of the best-selling Harry Potter novels, first billionaire author. No college.

Alfred E. Smith: Governor of New York, presidential candidate. Left school at fourteen to help his family after his father died. Later joked that he received his "FFM" degree from the Fulton Fish Market in New York City.

Steven Spielberg: Billionaire movie director and producer, cofounder of DreamWorks. Rejected by the best film schools, enrolled in and then dropped out of California State University.

Anna Wintour: Editor in chief, *Vogue* magazine. Did not attend college.

This is just a small sample of people who did not complete their formal education and ended up being highly successful. Hopefully, reading this list opens your mind to the realization that anything is possible and that there are no limitations. I'm not putting down formal education. We all understand its importance and value. But the truth is that education or the lack thereof may have little to do with success and even less to do with limitations.

Our limitations are self-imposed, often programmed during childhood, and they remain with us for a lifetime. But these same "core" beliefs can be used as motivation to achieve great things. You just need a few good role models to inspire you and teachers who have been there, done that, and can show you how to believe in yourself.

We all want to feel secure about our lives, our finances, and our future. Opportunities are everywhere and, contrary to public opinion, they knock more than once. They actually knock so hard, they can knock you over. But all too often, you aren't paying attention when they arrive, or you're intimidated and too afraid to embrace them. You must remember that success is not a random event. Rather, it arises as a direct result of circumstances meeting attitude and preparation. Once you believe in yourself and have a positive plan of action, you can tap into a limitless potential of opportunity and success.

Begin now to believe that anything is possible. Begin now to change the person you are into the person you can become. You are about to embark on an exciting journey of self-discovery.

CORE STORY

In order to begin your journey to the New You, you must become intimately familiar with your Core Story. In his insightful book *It's Not About the Money,* author Brent Kessel describes a Core Story as the deepest held beliefs about yourself you carry in your subconscious mind. Your Core Story, then, is the foundation upon which you built the messages that you tell yourself *about* yourself—what you can and cannot do, what you must and must not do, and what you are *really* like from the inside out.

Kessel goes on to say that the power of the subconscious mind is so strong that, despite your considerable efforts to improve your situation on the outside, very little changes on the inside. In the real world, he says, the unconscious mind holds you back, even while you are desperate to forge a new and different relationship with yourself.

Your Core Story may be your excuse for why you never made it, your justification for why your life isn't what you want it to be and you don't even realize it. You may blame your Core Story for your present difficulty, why you don't have what you want, and why you've never gone after your dreams. You may see it as the reason for your inability to make healthy commitments or maintain healthy relationships. You may see it as the very thing holding you back or it may be affecting your decisions in ways you are completely unaware of. Worst of all, you may be passing these limiting Core Story beliefs on to your children.

But your Core Story can become a catalyst for success beyond your wildest dreams. The very challenges and struggles that you faced during childhood and into adulthood can become the motivations that are shaping you today and guiding you to your mission in life. In order to achieve this mission, you must look intimately and honestly at your Core Story, understand how it has affected you, and make the conscious decision to use it for your benefit. You must decide right now to break the cycle of Core Story beliefs that may be affecting you negatively.

◆ ◆ ◆ ◆ ◆

To understand what a Core Story really is, read this example:

SHE WAS NOT YOUR AVERAGE, FAIR-SKINNED, MIDWESTERN eight-year-old. She was a little bit chubby, her lips were too big for her face, and she was "different" looking—which did not go over well in a small town in Ohio. She looked ethnic with her dark hair, dark eyes, and warm brown skin. Was she Indian, Italian, or maybe Hispanic? She didn't have the luxury of knowing, because her father had been adopted and had no clue as to his nationality or family history. The one thing she was certain about, however, was that alcoholism was prominent in her father's gene pool.

She would lie in bed in her pale green bedroom just off the kitchen on many a fear-filled night, waiting to hear him coming home. He would stumble in, cursing to himself, rattling the pots and pans while attempting to fix himself something to eat. He sometimes managed to make food; other times, he just passed out. And sometimes he just got mean. What would he do this time? Should she be afraid? Should she have hidden the knives just in case? Knives were one of her greatest fears and obsessions.

Life in general was very difficult back then as she hid in her tiny green bedroom, shaking with fear. Did daddy have a gun? Would he hurt mommy? She remembered the police dragging him down the sidewalk one night as she ran after them, screaming at them to leave her daddy alone. Holidays were the worst since they gave her father an excuse to drink. He never had money for birthday or Christmas presents because he drank it all away. She had trouble making friends because everyone knew her father was an alcoholic—everyone except him. She never knew what she would find if she invited a friend home. Would her dad be passed out or would he be obnoxious and belittle her in front of her friends?

She lived in an old house beside a railroad track at the end of a dead-end street. Her dad had bought it for $7,000 in 1962, as a peace offering to her mom, promising her a new life. Things would get better, he assured her. He would get better, too. She loved him in spite of himself; the whole family did because when he was sober, life was good. He had inbred class and when he was in his right mind, he bought her mother fine chocolates on Valentine's Day and took the family out to restaurants he couldn't afford.

On a good day, she ran errands with her father. He whistled when he was happy and she remembered the sulfur smell when he struck a match to light his cigarette. But she also remembered the refrigerator getting shoved over on its side as she and her siblings rushed out barefoot into the snow, heading for a neighbor's house because "daddy was mad and had brought home a gun."

She found comfort in her mother's arms, but all too often, she was the one doing the comforting. Her mother was a strong, sensitive woman who loved her husband very much. But the little girl lost count of how many times she heard her mom crying in the night. How often did her brothers try to protect their mother and bring their father to his senses, one more time? The family's life revolved around her father and his drinking.

During that time, everything was a struggle and she heard over and over that people from her "type of family" didn't get very far. Was her dead-end street an indication of her future? She often listened to the train whistle before she fell asleep, wishing she could hop on the train and run away, speeding toward a better, safer life.

She envied her friends' fine families and what she considered their perfect lives. She fantasized becoming "somebody" and doing "something big" one day, something that mattered. She knew she could comfort people and make them feel better. After all, she had been doing just that in her family for a long time. But little did she know that comforting people would play such a major role in her adult life.

That little girl was me.

My powerful Core Story is very important because it is the reason I am who I am today. Take a moment now to think about your own Core Story. It doesn't matter if you remember it vaguely or in perfect detail. It doesn't matter if your story was good, bad, or a bit of each. Take a moment to think about what you remember most.

Day 1

Pro-Active Action

ASSIGNMENT

Write a brief summary of your Core Story as you believe it to be. Choose a quiet place and concentrate on this task for a minimum of twenty minutes. Just begin. Write. Share your Core Story with me.

HOW MY CORE STORY MADE ME WHO I AM TODAY

Once you have examined your Core Story as I did, you'll begin to see how your foundation turned you into the person you are today. In my case, because of my Core Story, I understand pain, embarrassment, and fear. I know the feelings of inadequacy and humiliation and I know all about fear of abandonment—that constant edgy sensation that something bad is about to happen and you feel you can't cope. In the light of these feelings, I can understand why some people believe that good things don't last, that something or someone will surely ruin it. I know how it feels when people talk about you behind your back, and I am intimately familiar with low self-esteem.

As a result, I don't wrap up any of my seminars until the last needy person feels validated and supported. I can't walk away when someone is devastated; I must reach out instead. I immediately stick up for anyone being picked on because I'm wired to fight for the underdog, since I *was* one. I respond without a second thought when people are in struggle and despair. I do what I can to help them find hope, even when it seems elusive.

As a young adult, I blamed my problems on my father's alcoholism. Yes, his behavior affected me negatively and created a great deal of difficulty and insecurity, but his weakness also contributed to my strength. I had to develop enough character and compassion to get through it all, which paved the way for my current "mission" and the life I live today. As a result, I teach others to be compassionate with people who struggle with addiction and illness because I know that my father was basically a good man until the terrible disease of alcoholism took over. As a result of being the one who often found the light at the end of the tunnel for my own family, I am able to show that light to others in their darkest hour. When people say they have no self-esteem or confidence because of their childhoods, I encourage them to dream again and to reclaim their identities *because* of their past, not in spite of it. I know how to guide them because I have been there.

My Core Story was filled with obstacles and challenges. Many are, and the story of Iyanla Vanzant is another example.

Iyanla Vanzant

IYANLA VANZANT, AN AFRICAN AMERICAN GIRL, LOST HER mother when she was three. She was raised by her grandmother in an atmosphere laden with abuse by an uncle who raped her when she was nine. Although she received no encouragement, Iyanla got good grades in school, but at sixteen, she became pregnant by a schoolmate who was also violent. Married at eighteen to an abusive husband, she had three children by the time she was twenty-one. When she finally managed to leave her husband, she had sustained several black eyes, three fractured ribs, a broken jaw, a displaced uterus, and what she considers worst of all—the death of her personhood. One day, in a fit of depression, she attempted suicide but was unsuccessful.

After Iyanla was released from the hospital psychiatric ward, she and her three children went on welfare for the next eight years as she educated herself, much to the protest of family members. Despite their criticism, she attended Medgar Evers College and, three and a half years later, graduated summa cum laude with a bachelor's degree in public administration. Gone were her days on welfare as she landed a good job.

Three years after she graduated, Iyanla earned a law degree from City University in New York. After twenty years of studying spirituality and personal empowerment, she chose the spiritual route, through which she offered a blend of ancient-based contemporary wisdom and common sense. Later she would become a public defender.

Today, Iyanla writes and lectures on her healing journey from despair to self-reliance as she leads her readers in and out of what she calls the "dark experiences" of life. Out of her troubled past, she has emerged a winner, committed to her eclectic message of divine power and self-determination. She takes her audiences by the hand and guides them down the path of self-discovery, self-help, self-empowerment, and self-love. She stresses that any social and self-improvement is made possible only by "tapping the power within."

Iyanla's *Faith in the Valley,* the companion book to her best-selling *Acts of Faith,* has inspired thousands of black women to seriously consider how their own behavior may be causing them problems. In *Faith in the Valley,* she says, "Black women, like many others, have found it difficult to accept that life is more than hopping from one mountaintop experience to another. Somehow we forget there is a valley between every mountain. Eventually we [must] do the work it takes to get out of those dark experiences." She reminds us that these valleys are purposeful, that the highs and lows, the light and dark, balance out and each experience is necessary to appreciate the other.

Perhaps most impressive of all, Iyanla does not see herself as a victim, neither to that childhood rape nor to her abusive marriage. She is simply happy to be off welfare and to have had a successful career as a public defender, spiritual counselor, best-selling author, and doting grandmother.

The point here is that until you understand your Core Story, whatever it is, and how it made you who you are today, your foundation will reflect only your unconscious beliefs about yourself, real or imagined, positive or negative. When you delve into your subconscious beliefs about your lot in life, whether you believe you deserve to be happy or sad, successful or unsuccessful, only then do you have the chance to change the story that is replaying over and over in your head and determining how you go through your life.

This might seem like a scary process for some of you, but you don't need to be afraid. None of us likes to drum up unpleasant memories, old hurts and wounds from the past, but remember: *What you don't feel, you can't heal.* If you really want to move beyond the confines of old stories and limiting belief systems, the first step is to take a cold hard look at what you have unconsciously been carrying around with you. Once you identify your Core Story, you will have the power to change it.

QUESTION, QUESTION, QUESTION

The idea is to question your assumptions and beliefs about yourself in order to understand your Core Story. Once you know where you got these false beliefs and feelings of insecurity, you can begin to make different choices in order to regain the freedom and healthy self-esteem that may have been lost due to your earliest experiences. Question your story and then question some more. Delve as deeply as you can so you can enjoy the freedom, success, and happiness that you may have abandoned along the way. After all, these things are your birthright.

In order to get in touch with the details of your Core Story and how it has made you who you are, fill out the following questionnaire. As you answer the questions, think about how the answers have affected you as an adult:

YOUR CORE STORY QUESTIONNAIRE

1. When you think about your past, what is your first memory?
2. How do you recall your father's and mother's personalities and behaviors?
3. Does recalling them make you anxious, happy, or angry?
4. Which of their personality traits did you take on, positive and negative?
5. Did they listen and spend quality time with you?
6. What Core Story fears are fueling your present life? Where do they come from? Do you fear abandonment, being alone, death and dying, or commitment?
7. Were you confused about who you were or thought you should be when you were growing up?
8. What were you taught was most important in life? Negative and positive.
9. Were you a rebel or did you go along with the status quo?
10. Were you taught to share or hoard?
11. Did you feel isolated or connected to family and friends?
12. Did you have a good, strong family upbringing? Or was it the opposite?
13. Was your childhood unhealthy or dysfunctional? How did this affect you as an adult?
14. Did you have examples of healthy, loving relationships or the opposite?
15. Were you taught financial responsibility or irresponsibility?
16. Do you recall great family talks and open affection, or the opposite?
17. Did you get support for your dreams, outside activities, and school efforts?
18. Did you enjoy family holidays?
19. How did your family express emotions like anger, worry, and depression?

20. Where did success and failure fit into your family's core beliefs?
21. Can you see how your Core Story created your emotional foundation?
22. How does your Core Story define who you are now?

Sit with the above questionnaire for a few moments. Ponder it. Honest answers to the above questions will help you interpret your Core Story. Are you still using any of these false beliefs today, to justify your lack? Do you see how your personal experience can justify your right to success, safety, a sense of control, and positive motivation? Let me remind you again that some uncomfortable feelings will almost certainly arise in you when you review your Core Story. Don't judge them or think it's wrong to feel that way. Simply observe and accept them as part of the process of reinventing yourself by rewriting the story of your new and empowered life.

RE-ACTIVE VS. PRO-ACTIVE

In my work, I've noticed that people tend to be re-active in life rather than pro-active as a result of their Core Story predetermining their responses. In other words, you spontaneously (often impulsively) react to life in your usual, predetermined ways. For example, if you typically react with anger, you will get angry. It is the same with worry, anxiety, and blame. You just don't think it through, you don't have a plan, and you end up frustrated, angry, anxious, depressed, out of control, and victimized.

The difference is easy to discern. When you are re-active, you are being negative and impulsive and you get the same negative results you've always gotten. These immediate, familiar re-active responses are tied directly to your Core Story. But when you operate from a pro-active attitude, you are being positive, effective, and moving toward change, growth, and a healthier future. A pro-active response can be learned; it is something you can choose. Responding pro-actively is one of the most prominent traits of successful, happy people. To learn how pro-active thinking can help you respond with pro-active behavior, look at the following examples:

Imagine you have a deadline for a sales report that is keeping you up at night.

- The **re-active response** to this anxiety is to tell yourself, "I can't sleep. I'll never make that deadline. If I don't, they'll fire me. If I do and it isn't good enough, they'll *still* fire me. Either way, I'm in big trouble."
- The **pro-active response** is, "The deadline I'm facing is too short. I need to speak to my boss and let him know that I need a little extra time to make the report really good. I am valuable and I do a great job here. My boss will be understanding and give me the extra time I need."

"I'm worried about my boyfriend not calling me. I wonder what he's feeling."

- The **re-active response** is, "I guess my boyfriend is mad at me. It must be my fault. What if he leaves me?"
- The **pro-active response** is, "I must put my worrying about this into a healthier, less needy perspective and get busy. If I don't hear from him, it's okay to call eventually and check in, without coming off as insecure. But it's important to remember that I can fill my own security needs. I don't need him. Whether I hear from him or not, I'll be okay."

"I'm worried about the pain in my stomach. I've had it for several days."

- The **re-active response** is, "What if there's something seriously wrong with me, like stomach cancer? What if I get sick and can't take care of myself?"
- The **pro-active response** is, "Most likely this is nothing serious and I'm overreacting. But it's a good idea to see the doctor to put my mind at ease. Then I'll know if I need to do something

and what I should do. I'll probably find out it's nothing and I can stop worrying."

"The economy is awful. I wonder if my job is secure."

- The **re-active response** is, "What if I lose my job and end up going bankrupt and losing everything? I need to worry."
- The **pro-active response** is, "I'm not the only one struggling and feeling insecure right now. Who do I need to talk to in order to reassure myself about my job? What plan can I put in place in place so I feel prepared in case I need to find other employment? What friend can help me put this concern into perspective?"

Responding pro-actively versus re-actively is a very important part of this book. I will be referring to it often throughout the chapters as well as providing you with pro-active action assignments that will help you change your behaviors to embrace the concept. In addition, you must begin to *think* from a pro-active perspective. At the end of each chapter, you'll be asked to adjust your re-active thoughts into pro-active attitudes. Learning to behave and respond like this will absolutely change your life.

Day 2

Pro-Active Action

ASSIGNMENT

Start a pro-active journal. It can be a simple pad of paper that you keep on your desk or by your bed. Journaling will become an insightful process for change and manifestation throughout this book. At least once a day, write down some of your thoughts and responses to the questions and assignments in this book.

Begin now by writing down several true, empowering statements that relate to your Core Story beliefs, statements that can help you turn your Core Story responses to the above questionnaire into a pro-active way of seeing the situation, in order to create strength, motivation, and opportunity.

Here are some examples of turning your Core Story responses (perceived as negative) into pro-active responses to build your character and give you the skills to achieve your goals:

- Because I was the middle child and I felt neglected, I've learned to be independent and a great negotiator.
- Because my father was never around, I understand the importance of being there for my kids. I've decided to make good parenting choices.
- Because my mother was an alcoholic, I'm sensitive to those who struggle with this disease. I handle my issues in a healthy way.
- I've had so many losses in my life, I'm grateful to be alive. I am open to taking risks because I know that life is a short and precious gift.

Can you see how many wonderful opportunities are available to you when you reframe what you previously thought of as negative? By shifting your perspective just a little, you will be able to view the situation in a new light. What you once considered a disadvantage, you will now recognize as an asset that can support you in creating the kind of life that your heart desires.

Take a good look at your re-active responses. No matter how difficult or traumatic your Core Story is, it is extremely important to put a new twist on your responses. Then you'll be able to view your Core Story as the sum total of the person you are, as well as the path to the person you can become. It's time to stop the cycle of negativity, not just for yourself, but so you can avoid passing a negative legacy on to your children.

STOPPING THE CYCLE

When I was a fourteen, years before I moved out West, I visited my sister, Donna, and her husband, who had moved from Ohio to northern California. With money they'd saved over a few years, they purchased a lovely, modest new home with brand-new furniture. This was a far cry from our old brown house where we grew up with tattered chairs and peeling paint. I'll never forget walking into Donna's home and looking around in awe. We never had nice things like Donna had. I didn't think that "people like us" *could* ever have nice things.

I specifically remember her eggshell leather sofa, soft as butter, in the middle of the living room. *Wow,* I thought to myself as I sank into the most comfortable sofa on earth, *if she can do this, maybe I can, too. We may have been raised in a poor family, but that doesn't mean we can't have nice things now.*

Donna set the trend for my brothers and me. She showed us that it could be done, that we could stop the poverty and the have-not cycle that was holding us back. Since then, we have all found success at different times in our lives and in different ways. We've had our sibling rivalries from time to time, of course, but Donna showed us the way. Instead of feeling envious and resenting what she had, we used her success as motivation for ending the poverty consciousness cycle in which we were raised.

Stopping the cycle can help you appreciate your whole self, because this is who you are. You don't need to apologize or make excuses for who you are "not." Instead, use your past to fashion a future exactly how you want it to be. If you don't know how that future will look as yet, that's okay. We'll be defining this further in a future chapter.

Once you've gotten in touch with your Core Story, you can change it into something beautiful, no matter how difficult it was. The idea is to see your story as rungs of a ladder that will lead you to your life's goals, whether they are professional, personal, spiritual, or financial. Once you define them for yourself, then you can regain your empowerment and strength. You may have been the most fortunate child in the world who received nothing but support and compassion, or you may have been abused, neglected, or humiliated. However it unfolded, you can let your past work *for* you instead of *against* you. But always remember that it's a choice.

Will you use your story as a prison cell in which you are held captive, an excuse for not getting what you want, a justification for being unhappy, depressed, and utterly dysfunctional? Or will you use what you have been through to build character, personal power, and inner strength? Will you use it as motivation to have a good life from this moment on? As always, the choice is yours.

Re-Active to Pro-Active Attitude Adjustments

1. **RE-ACTIVE:** I am holding onto and using my Core Story beliefs for disempowerment, self-sabotage, and justification for my lack.
   PRO-ACTIVE: I am using my Core Story experiences as motivation and justification for my success and happiness.

2. **RE-ACTIVE:** I blame others and my past for my insecurities, lack of success, lack of options, and bad behavior.
   PRO-ACTIVE: I am taking responsibility for my life, my behavior, and my future. I understand that past people and situations have helped mold who I am today, in ways that have bolstered my strength and character while securing me a better future.

3. **RE-ACTIVE:** I am using my Core Story beliefs to make limited decisions that keep me trapped in my past.
   PRO-ACTIVE: The decisions I am making are healthy and empowering, increasing self-confidence and belief in myself. This is leading me to a better future.

You are strong and powerful. You are capable of controlling your emotions in the most difficult times. You see opportunities where most people see only problems. You understand that challenge and change create opportunities for growth. You also understand that difficult times can lead to incredible opportunities to change your life.

You are able to be your own safe person. You are in good hands—your own. You can connect to experiences that are healthy and detach from experiences that are unhealthy and you truly know the difference. You are able to attract positive people and you know when you need to walk away from an unhealthy experience or person. When you are faced with a difficult situation, you don't back down or operate from a place of fear. You think clearly, form an effective plan of action, and take steps to take control. You come out of it not only with strength, but also with possibilities and an optimistic attitude.

Life is full of challenge and uncertainty, but you have been through challenge before and it has helped to define who you are today. You are confident, capable, and full of potential. You have clarified your dreams and you are doing what you want to do. You recognize the presence of universal and personal power in your life. Opportunities are everywhere, new doors are opening, and all sorts of wonderful things are happening.

CHAPTER TWO

A World of Worry

Only in quiet waters things mirror themselves undistorted. Only in a quiet mind is an adequate perception of the world.

—Hans Margolius

Here's the good news. Great worriers make fabulous goal-setters and achievers. After all, worriers like you are focused, determined, and set on a particular outcome. You have a powerful imagination, you think in minute detail, and you are extremely creative and a futuristic thinker. This is the same set of skills it takes to succeed. So if you're a world-class worrier, you can also be a world-class achiever. All you need to do is change the focus of your attention from worrying to achieving great things.

But that isn't you right now. You might be thinking, *What if the test results come back positive for a terminal disease? How will I deal with that? I don't think I could. I'm afraid to die. What about my kids? Who will take care of them? Will I live long enough to see them grow up? How much pain will I be in? What if it's cancer? Will our insurance cover it? What if I lose my hair? What if I die?*

I know that for many, the scenario I just painted has increased your anxiety. You may be thinking, "I want to feel better, not worse." Of course you want to feel better, but if you trust this process, it will lead you to the other side where you can find the solution to your obsessive worrying. This is how anxiety-ridden people excel at being great worriers. They take their worry and run with it. All the "what-ifs" come into play—the same things that a successful person does. Even Donald Trump, a self-made real estate developer and designer of a billion-dollar empire, has had his ups and downs, which provided him with tremendous opportunities for worry. Let's see how he dealt with them.

Donald Trump

Born in New York City in 1946, Donald Trump, one of five children, learned his deal-making and entrepreneurial skills from his father, Frederick. But Frederick died when Donald was eleven, forcing the boy to step up and start running the family business at an early age. And so Donald began by constructing and operating 24,000 affordable nursing units in Brooklyn, Queens, and Staten Island. From that beginning, he built an empire.

In the late 1980s, Trump's empire was estimated as worth $1 billion, making his real estate organization one of the world's most powerful. He planned to erect a billion-dollar commercial project in Los Angeles featuring a 125-story office building. But Trump, known in Manhattan as "the P.T. Barnum of finance," was a controversial figure. Despite his reputation, his wealth, and his skills at "closing the deal," he could not overcome a real estate market that was beginning a steep downward trend. After so much success, Trump suddenly faced bankruptcy when he could not make his massive loan payments of over $2 billion. It was no longer possible for him to convince the banks to believe in what they called his "risky" investments.

After losing some of his real estate holdings to creditor banks, Trump was forced to trade part of his empire in order to restructure his debts. His expertise in investing came into question as his worth plummeted from $1.7 billion to $500 million. He found this period to be extraordinarily challenging, but rather than wasting time and energy worrying, he turned to his talents, experience, personality, and name, which were still valued. Remaining optimistic in the face of disaster, he secured favorable loan terms, negotiated bond obligations, and sold off his unprofitable holdings.

With a firm commitment to pro-active thinking and responding, Trump managed to bounce back with the aid of the current bankruptcy laws that favor debtors. Always maintaining a professional decorum, he presented himself as someone still at the top of his game in spite of his situation, which appeared bleak. There was simply no time or place for worrying in Donald Trump's world! That was not his modus operandi. Because of his pro-active attitude, his creditors were willing to broker deals with him as he appointed a CFO for his company, he lived on a budget for a while, and he standardized his operations. Now, with his business on a tight rein, he was offered a bailout that lowered his debt interest while he held onto his casinos, rail yard, residences, and his partial interest in the Plaza Hotel.

Talk about moving forward instead of worrying! Talk about a pro-active approach to a negative situation with the potential for a negative outcome! By the early 1990s, Trump was reportedly worth about $900 million, a number that soared to almost $2 billion by 1997. He continues to make money to this day, no matter the climate of the economy or attitudes of the world at large. Simply put, Trump does not and never has operated from a re-active base of fear.

THE STATE OF THE WORLD

There is always something to fear and worry about. The world is, and always has been, full of these opportunities. But these days, we are facing challenges on a daily basis due to overexposure to news and the media, which we access everywhere—television, radio, computers, and even on our cell phones! We are forced to watch the world around us become destabilized. A quick look at the state of the world will show you how many things there are to worry about. The economy is different than it was a few years ago, and almost everyone is feeling vulnerable and worried. Here are a few reasons:

- The American Psychological Association reports that 73 percent of all Americans point to money as the primary factor affecting their stress levels.
- Along with the subprime mortgage meltdown, foreclosures are driving down the value of surrounding properties, shrinking sources of retirement wealth for baby boomers.
- Unemployment is very high.
- Consumer spending is on the decline because people don't know what tomorrow will bring.
- The stock market continues to swing wildly, mostly in negative territory.

We are living in stressful times. That's true. But we have been here before, many times. And there is always something to worry about. So how do you feel safe? If you let the outside world determine your feelings of safety or justify your worrying, you will never feel safe. Now is the time to take control of your emotions and stop letting the outside world define who you are. Remember, you can't control the outside world. Think Donald Trump. You can only control how you choose to respond and react to it.

Once you grasp this potent concept, you will enjoy a renewed sense of safety and stability that can never be taken away from you, regardless of what you previously perceived as the source of your worries and concerns. This new sense of security generates from within you—the place where your ultimate power lies.

WHAT IS WORRY?

The dictionary describes worry as *persistent torment, torture, the destroying of one's peace of mind.* Perhaps the most apt definition for our purposes is *over-concern for something impending or anticipated, causing painful mental distress and agitation.*

The following behavioral and emotional symptoms indicate that you are a good worrier, or, more appropriately put, a chronic worrier, which is both bad and good. It's bad because you can make yourself sick with worry. It's good because you can use your worry skills to achieve great things. See how you relate to the list below:

Chronic worriers

- feel overwhelmed, moody, agitated, and irritable
- learned how to worry from their core family
- worry about their core family
- are addicted to worry and feel unable to break the cycle
- beat themselves up for compulsive worrying
- try to control themselves, other people, and everything around them
- feel in control only when they're trying to solve their worry problems
- obsess and ruminate about the same problems, never finding peace or resolution

- complain constantly and feel helpless and victimized by their lives
- suffer from headaches, ulcers, upset stomachs, and sleeping disorders
- view the glass as half-empty instead of half-full
- are focused on the negative and tend to see everything as a catastrophe
- suffer from panic, anxiety, and/or post-traumatic stress syndrome, resulting in the fight or flight response
- have regrets about the past and fear of the future
- have a hard time enjoying the present moment
- find it hard to stay focused in order to complete the simplest of tasks
- procrastinate and are afraid to take action or make decisions, in case they don't have the perfect solution
- suffer from social anxiety, resulting in nervousness and self-consciousness
- fear being judged, being rejected, or failing
- worry about how others see them
- worry about themselves or a family member having a serious illness or dying
- worry about finances or some other impending doom about to befall them
- isolate themselves and feel unloved, unwanted, and misunderstood
- are overwhelmed by hopelessness and despair
- feel weak, pathetic, and powerless over their lives
- experience a decreased interest in sex and other pleasures
- constantly escape reality through addictive behaviors such as alcohol abuse, drug abuse, gambling, and overspending
- worry they will never find love and are destined to be alone forever

As you can see, when you worry, you are caught up in a mental state of overconcentration, overanalysis, and unhealthy anticipation. You're so creative, you predict elaborate worst-case scenarios, most of which never happen. This brings to mind the famous Mark Twain quote about worry: "I have known a great many troubles, but most of them never happened."

Can you see how being consumed with worry robs you of your happiness, drains your energy, and creates depression and anxiety as well as anger and agitation? It certainly isn't productive. But remember, you have the power to change it! With the tools you are learning in this book, you *will* find the solution to your World of Worry.

The worst part of worrying is that it can literally make you sick. Do you know anyone (maybe it's you) who worries to the point of an upset stomach, ulcers, heartburn, or migraine headaches? Worry can be relentless; people seek relief in a glass of wine, comfort food, or a tranquilizer. They want to turn it off badly, but they don't know how.

It's very important to understand that most of us have *learned* the art of worry. The more you practice anything, the better you get at it, whether it's anger, blame, worry, compassion, patience, or self-love. While these states are not inherent, they are generally something you learned from your core family. Did your mother worry constantly? What about your father? Did he use anger to express worry or did he self-medicate with alcohol? Even though men often worry alone while women usually share these emotions with family or a friend, we all feel the symptoms of anxiety, fear, and depression. The point is to transform worry into healthy thinking and manifestation. Yes, this is possible!

WORRY INVENTORY

We all worry, because worrying is a part of human nature, but do you worry excessively? Do you know how to turn worry off when you are overwhelmed? Take a look at how much you worry by filling out the following inventory.

1 – RARELY	2 – OCCASIONALLY	3 – SOMETIMES	4 – OFTEN

1. Were your parents worriers? ____
2. Did you worry as a child? ____
3. Do you feel plagued by worrisome thoughts? ____
4. Do you worry even when (or especially when) things are going well? ____
5. Do your friends say that you worry too much? ____
6. Do you think you worry too much? ____
7. Do your worries overwhelm most of your other thoughts? ____
8. Do you worry about what other people think of you? ____
9. Do your worries get in the way of your decision-making? ____
10. Do you obsess about the past? ____
11. Do you worry about the future? ____
12. Do you worry about being abandoned by friends or family members? ____
13. Do you obsess about your health? ____
14. Do you obsess about death and dying? ____
15. Do you develop physical symptoms in response to worry? ____
16. Do you worry about money? ____
17. Do you drink alcohol or use medications to try to ease the pain of worry? ____
18. Do you spend time ruminating on your decisions? ____
19. When you are alone, is worry your most dominant pastime? ____
20. Do you think it is unrealistic to feel secure? ____
21. Are you tortured by a sense that things you do are wrong or not good enough? ____

22. Are your daydreams filled with worst-case scenarios? ____
23. Do you look for what's wrong before you look for what's right? ____
24. Do you worry about disappointing others? ____
25. Do you have the same worries and concerns over and over again? ____
26. Do you think others are out to take advantage of you? ____
27. Do you avoid confrontation so you won't anger people? ____
28. Do you set standards for yourself that you cannot live up to? ____
29. Are you frightened about what is coming in the mail? ____
30. Do you worry that vacations will not meet your expectations? ____
31. Do you worry that people are judging you? ____
32. Do you worry about embarrassing yourself? ____
33. Do you worry about your thought process? ____
34. Do you ruin a fun evening by worrying about future problems? ____
35. Is it hard for you to relax mentally or physically? ____
36. Does your obsessive worrying make it hard to focus? ____
37. Do you feel nervous and anxious? ____
38. Do you have a hard time sleeping due to excessive worrying? ____
39. Do you dominate conversations by talking about worry? ____
40. Are you offended when people dismiss your worries as irrational? ____

SCORING
0 – 25: You are a manageable worrier. *26 – 50: You are a mild worrier.* *51 – 80: You are a moderate worrier.* *81 – over 100: You are a significant worrier.*

WHAT TYPE OF WORRIER ARE YOU?

Now that you know how dedicated to worry you really are, you need to figure out what you can and cannot change that is causing you worry, and act accordingly. Once you accept what is in front of you, you can stop worrying, you can become pro-active, and you can let go.

But since we are all different, we all worry differently. While some people are concerned about being criticized, others worry about being left by a loved one or not living up to their personal standards of perfection. To discover what kind of worrier you are, review the following personality styles of worriers. As you read though them, keep in mind that many people fall into several types at the same time. Identifying your own particular worry model or models will help you understand why you respond to situations as you do, what worries you the most, and why certain things affect you so strongly. It will also show you why other people react in ways that are different from yours.

As you identify with some of the characteristics in the descriptions below, be kind to yourself. This is not an opportunity to beat yourself up or hide your head in shame. It is simply a way to recognize some of your past habitual patterns of behavior so you can learn how to change them. Remember, ***Knowledge is power.***

Avoidant: You have low self-esteem and are overly sensitive to criticism. You're a people pleaser, craving reassurance from others rather than yourself. You worry about not being good enough and not being able to trust other people. You open up to others only after trust has been established. You are hypersensitive to rejection, uncomfortable in social situations, and unwilling to take social risks. Your timidity and fear of criticism keep you isolated and alone with your worries.

Dependent: You feel needy and clingy in your relationships. You worry about being abandoned by your partner. You are devoted and loyal and you do whatever it takes to keep the connection going. You worry about being alone and unable to function without somebody else to take care of you emotionally. You put others' needs ahead of your own to ensure you are needed and will not be left.

Passive-Aggressive: You worry about confrontation and speaking your truth directly to another person. You resist meeting the wishes and needs of your spouse, boss, or friends by procrastinating, feigning forgetfulness, or being stubborn, inefficient, and indifferent. You have mixed feelings about doing your share or being responsible to others. You swear you'll do something but you don't necessarily follow through. You worry about being overwhelmed, unappreciated, and controlled by others.

Compulsive: You worry about work and productivity. You keep lists and tight schedules, and you have high standards for yourself and your coworkers. You are reliable, honest, and overly devoted to work. You worry about deadlines and you are so focused on perfection and order that a lack of flexibility can interfere with your productivity and efficiency. You refuse to delegate because you feel that others cannot meet your standards.

Social: On the surface you appear worry-free. You are charming and fun to be with. You thrive on excitement, adventure, and taking risks. You sometimes break the rules to get what you want, maybe hurting other people in the process, which comes at a price—a nagging feeling in the pit of your stomach that your impulsiveness will finally catch up with you and get you into trouble.

Narcissistic: You feel superior to others and believe you deserve special attention and admiration. You worry about maintaining an appearance of perfection in your status and position in the world. You worry that others will see chinks in your armor and cracks in your perfect veneer. You worry they'll see your flaws and no longer admire you or put you on a pedestal. You are genuinely amazed to discover that you offended someone by being insensitive to their needs, since you need to be seen as noble and honorable.

Histrionic: You are exciting and glamorous. Everyone is attracted to you and seduced by your charismatic personality. You are emotional and theatrical: you enjoy attracting attention to yourself in imaginative ways. You worry about holding other people's attention and you constantly attract drama into your life to keep people interested. You fear losing your physical energy and sparkle.

Neurotic: You are consumed by intense, ongoing worry, characterized by episodes of anxiety and panic. You are high-strung, irritable, and edgy, always waiting for the crisis to occur. You rarely feel safe, positive, or relaxed, sometimes turning to tranquilizers or alcohol for relief. You have anxious energy and you need to keep active to distract yourself from worrying.

Depressive: Your worry is focused on feelings of doom, hopelessness, aloneness, isolation, and sadness. You feel misunderstood; your worry causes you great concern, emotional pain, and suffering to the point that normal functioning is difficult. You are antisocial and nonproductive, even self-destructive. You sleep or eat too much, and you self-medicate with alcohol or prescription medications.

Hypochondriac: Your worry is focused on your health. You go from one real or imagined health concern to another, certain you are at risk for a major illness or disease. You run to doctors constantly, or you avoid doctors for fear they will "find something." You are consumed with thoughts of death and dying, or fear of some looming, undiagnosed, horrible disease.

Catastrophic: Your worry is overblown and all-encompassing. You suffer from "the sky is falling" syndrome, certain the worst-case scenario will happen and that the world is coming to an end. Your life seems impossible to manage, there is no solution, and you know it will destroy you and everything around you. You are certain you cannot handle the outcome which, in your mind, will be extreme. You make bad decisions based in fear and you have difficulty relaxing and sleeping.

Victim: You worry that things are out of your control. You believe there is no answer, you have no power, someone is out to get you, and no one cares or understands. You don't trust people; you feel victimized, taken advantage of, cheated, and abused. You are so adamant that there are no answers that you find ways to justify your worry, which is usually someone else's "fault." Your victim attitude justifies your inability to stop the worry, fueling the fire even more.

Obsessive: Your worry is occupational, a full-time job, as you constantly worry about everything. You attach worry to every thought and you can't get away from it. You overanalyze, scrutinize, and dissect every possible scenario, repeating the various outcomes in your head. You unabashedly tell your worries to others, repeating yourself, using the same exact words, and discussing the same scenarios, in a vain attempt to find temporary relief.

ANTICIPATION

When you worry, you are anticipating what is going to happen as you try to think ahead. So why do you imagine the worst thing happening rather than the best? I call this "negative anticipation" or "anticipatory anxiety"—another way to describe worrying. And like worry, anticipation is a skill that can work for you instead of against you.

Setting a goal involves a form of anticipation, but you are expecting good things to happen rather than bad things. Positive anticipation is exhilarating—the exact opposite of anticipatory worry.

When my family and I made the decision to move from Ohio to California, for instance, everyone came out of the woodwork to tell us how foolish we were. "California's too expensive," they said. "There are earthquakes and fires. You'll hate it out there. It's too far away and it's going to fall into the ocean anyway."

It was easy for me to visualize all that catastrophe, but I decided to replace those thoughts with what I wanted to happen. How about warm weather, palm trees, and opportunities? In fact, many of my best opportunities have come from living where I could network and meet people. If I'd listened to the catastrophic concerns of others, I wouldn't be where I am today. Instead, I choose to worry pro-actively and anticipate the positive.

The lesson here is to anticipate good things and get really excited about them. You choose your thoughts, so why not choose empowering ones that motivate you and make you feel like anything is possible? Anticipation is a great start in believing that you actually can have what you want, whatever it is, while worry will keep everything you want at bay. Worry will enable you to justify all sorts of reasons why you shouldn't take risks and go after your dreams. You'll be so busy worrying, you won't have time to make good things happen in your life.

> **Day 3**
>
> **Pro-Active Action**
>
> ASSIGNMENT
>
> Take a moment right now to anticipate what you want in your life. Choose one specific goal, something you truly believe you can achieve, and imagine it is already done. Let your imagination soar as you anticipate how reaching this goal could change your life. Take a few minutes to write it down in your journal.

FAMOUS WORRIERS

Let's look at a couple of famous people who used their intense worry skills to achieve excellence, not only in their personal lives, but also in the world.

The first example is scientist Sir Isaac Newton. Labeled "mad" because of his quirky personality traits, he was a confirmed hypochondriac. But he didn't worry only about his health. He also worried about fitting in, death, and sin. Driven by so much worry energy, he was inspired to search for answers, which produced, among other things, his mastery of calculus as well as the universal laws of medicine and gravity. His penchant for overanalysis and scrutiny and his powerful intellect were catalysts for his discoveries. One of the leading scientists of all time and president of the Royal Society of London, Sir Isaac Newton was knighted. Despite his hypochondria, which never went away, he lived to the age of eighty-five.

Now, let's look at psychiatrist Sigmund Freud, a revolutionary genius, arguably one of the most brilliant men in the world, who lived his life filled with angst. It is a known fact that Freud obsessed about his sex life, he was overly concerned about money, he felt combative with his rivals, and he was overly credulous when it came to opposing medical theories. His personal fears, worries, and obsessions, especially those related to his past, motivated Freud to study human development and eventually to develop his revolutionary theories, including the theory of the subconscious, the Oedipus complex, free association, and dream theory.

These two extraordinary men used their worry energy productively although they were unaware they were doing so. If they'd realized it, they most certainly would have built a scientific theory around the concept, considering who they were. I call it "worry reversal," a way to consciously use the creative energy and techniques of worry—creativity, imagination, analysis, and futuristic thinking—to accomplish your goals.

THE NEGATIVE EFFECTS OF WORRY

After addressing worry issues with people for twenty years, I would estimate that the average person spends approximately twenty hours a week worrying. Even when you're doing other things, worry clouds hang over you, consuming your thoughts and weakening your ability to function at full capacity. But imagine using those twenty hours to create a positive, powerful plan of action that could change the course of your life.

Think about focusing on one particular goal for twenty hours a week. How much weight could you lose? What kind of romantic relationship could you find? What quality of education could you achieve with that much time dedicated to one dream or goal? What kind of business could you build and what kind of focus and positive attention could you give your children?

Above and beyond what you can achieve in the material world when you transform worry into positive creation, you also need to think about your health. Constant worry will damage your body, so you need to avoid the stress responses that come with chronic worry. Even if you think you're handling stress well, worry is taking a toll on your body and your mind. Maybe you're having physical symptoms such as headaches or stomachaches that you're not associating with worrying. The story below is a good example of how constant worry can hurt you in ways you haven't thought about.

Ellen

A WOMAN NAMED ELLEN WORKED WITH ME IN SALES SOME years ago. She was a lively, positive, vivacious person who generally saw the glass half-full. Even when her husband lost his job and her mother passed away in the space of a couple of months, Ellen told everyone she was doing fine.

Then one day at lunch, she opened up to me about a physical problem she was having. It seemed she had developed a twitch in her muscles over which she had no control. "You know how it feels when your eye twitches?" she asked me.

I did.

"Well, that's what's happening to me but it's all over my body," she said. "It's in my legs, my arms, my lips, anywhere and everywhere. It all starts twitching and I'm scared I have some kind of neurological disease."

"Why don't you go see a doctor?" I asked her.

"No," she moaned. "What if he finds something wrong with me? I couldn't handle that right now, with all the other stuff I'm dealing with."

As the twitching continued, Ellen went through her own private hell, obsessing over being seriously ill but refusing to see a doctor. Finally, months later, she gave in and made an appointment with her GP. The doctor ran some tests and, much to Ellen's relief, found nothing tangible; she was diagnosed with stress.

Relieved that she was not ill, Ellen began to make some changes. She started exercising, she practiced conscious relaxation techniques, and she talked openly with her husband about her financial concerns. She encouraged him to take a mild antidepressant at least temporarily, and they began to go out together and have some fun. As soon as his attitude changed, he landed a terrific job. Was that a coincidence? I don't think so.

It didn't take long for Ellen's twitching problem to subside, a poignant demonstration of what unconscious fear and worry can do to the body. Stress and anxiety, both offshoots of worry, are often associated with heart disease, cancer, stomach problems, migraines, hair loss, acne, and a host of other concerns. This is why the skill of worry reversal is so miraculous. When you master it, you will improve the quality of your life with a major dose of preventive medicine that will feed your emotional well-being.

FIVE STEPS TO WORRY REVERSAL

Worry reversal is the simple skill of turning your worry around. In other words, it's about using your creativity, anticipation, vivid imagination, and analytical mind to come up with effective methods of thinking through your worries and concerns. Then you can create a plan of action to address them in a pro-active way. Eventually, this process will become second nature to you and will be as simple as the examples below.

1. Instead of worrying about your health, why not go see a doctor?
2. Instead of worrying about being financially destitute, why not create a financial plan that will guide you along the way?
3. Instead of worrying about being lonely, how about checking in with a close group of friends and making a social date or joining a dating service?
4. Instead of seeing your future as a pipe dream, why not talk to someone who is already doing what you want to do and take steps to make it happen for you?
5. Instead of worrying about what's coming or not coming, the skill of worry reversal can put the steering wheel back in your hands. Take a look at the following five steps of worry reversal.

STEP ONE: Define Your Fears

You can't fix what you don't understand. Categorize your areas of worry and concern in order of priority. Ask yourself, "Which of these worries do I have control over?" Then cross out the ones you cannot affect. Now ask yourself, "Are these worries valid, reasonable, rational, realistic?" Cross out the ones that aren't. Read the remaining list of worries. Ask yourself, "Can I look at this with less personal involvement? What is the opposite of this worry? What would I like to see happen that might help me alleviate it or even create something positive from it?"

STEP TWO: Take a Time-Out

When something makes you worry, you'll react the same way you've always reacted. It's a habit by now. To change your impulsive reactive response to worry, take a ten-minute to twenty-four-hour time-out to reevaluate the situation before you react. Then you can come up with a response that will best meet your needs.

During this break, ask yourself, "What do I really want to happen here? Why am I so worried? What am I afraid of? What end result would be most productive for me and anyone else involved?" A break in the action can help you cool down enough to see what's in front of you. You may be surprised to find that after twenty-four hours, you don't really care anymore. If you still *do* care, your analysis of the problem will greatly increase your chances of handling it in a mature and responsible way.

Here, I also include a concept I call "planned worry time." Set aside a certain amount of time, preferably in the evening, to assess your worries and create a pro-active plan for addressing them. That means you agree *not* to worry at any other time until your planned thirty minutes of worry time. When you push worries out of your mind and decide to deal with them later, you'll probably forget some of the things that were bothering you.

STEP THREE: Create a Plan of Action

When you worry, you desperately hope that the negative thing you're worried about *will not* happen. But worrying is not preventing. You have to switch your focus from what you *don't* want to what you *do* want. Ask yourself, "What needs to happen right now to eliminate my fears and build a sense of security?" Once you know what you need to do, set a goal and do it. For example, if you're worried about running out of money, determine what you need to feel more in control of your finances.

Here are six steps to create your plan of action:

- Review your worries and clarify how to approach them.
- Talk to an expert in your field of concern for educated advice or information.
- Take control of your own and your family's problems in a reasonable, responsible way and let go of what you cannot control.
- Formulate a timeline that gives you a long-term sense of control.
- Be open to change and challenge.
- Ask for help when you need it.

STEP FOUR: Use Your Fear as a Motivator

Worry creates an adrenaline response that can make you feel depressed, anxious, obsessive, and unable to sleep. When you're caught up in this knot of anticipation, you can't function. But if you focus that energy outward, by getting on the computer or making a few calls or writing out a "to-do" list, the tiniest baby step will help you feel in control. Write, write some more, and talk to the experts. Use your creative energy not to worry, but rather to solve problems.

STEP FIVE: Think Outside the Box

Here is a classic puzzle that will demonstrate the topic of this chapter.

Try to connect the nine dots with four lines without lifting your pencil from the paper. If you find it tough, don't worry. Very few people solve this puzzle quickly, but once it's done, you'll be surprised at how easy it actually is.

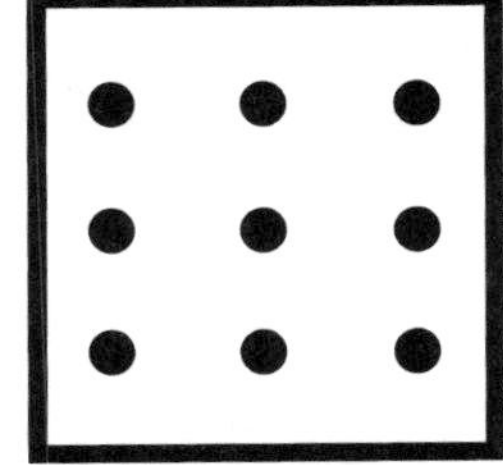

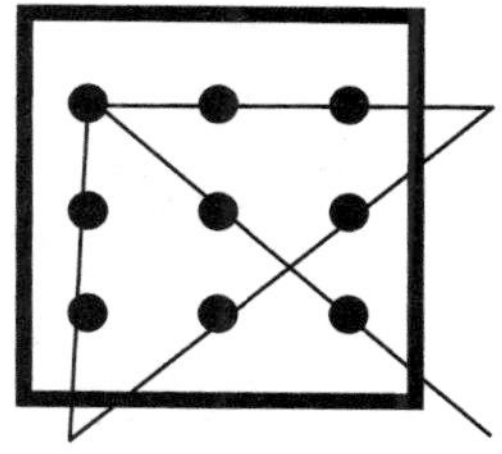

We have all found ourselves in comparable boxes at one time or another. It doesn't matter whether we tried to find the solution calmly and logically, or if we ended up running around frantically and scaring ourselves to death. We were still thinking in the same way we always thought, so we got the same results. The trick is to step *totally* outside the box, open your mind, and look for a solution that's completely fresh and new. Yes, it's scary, but it's also exciting since it can lead to unique opportunities.

A good example is my nephew, Charlie, who moved to China a few years ago. Initially, he was worried—about being so far from home, fitting in, adjusting to the food and the culture, learning a different language. He'd had no interest in learning a foreign language when he was in school. But now he had a fantastic job offer to run a bungee-jumping business in Macau. He thought it would be an interesting and exciting opportunity so he took the risk.

He moved to Macau and he learned to speak Mandarin, one of the most complicated languages in the world, because he needed to. Now, when you call his voice mail, it sounds like you've reached a Chinese businessman. He also has come to appreciate a whole new culture and culinary experience. He loves it there, and he recently became engaged to a local girl. In short, his life has changed for the better because he stepped outside the box, out of his comfort zone, and embarked on something exciting and brand-new on every level.

Just like Charlie, you never know when you might be thrown into a situation that will push you into learning a new set of thinking and skills. Do you want to be ruled by worry and make decisions based in fear? Or would you rather open your mind like my nephew did, think outside the box, and embark on experiences that could change the course of your life? Charlie is thriving today because he was willing to embrace a new set of thoughts and ideas.

These steps may seem overwhelming at first. You might be telling yourself that you don't have the time or the energy. But if you want different results, you'll have to change what you've been doing so far. So step out of your box, embrace the new and unfamiliar, and open up to a new world of opportunities.

Re-Active to Pro-Active Attitude Adjustments

1. **RE-ACTIVE:** I use my imagination, futuristic analytical thinking, and my creativity to worry about the future—to the point of making myself sick.
   PRO-ACTIVE: I recognize this behavior as negative and begin to change it. I use these same traits and skills to solve problems, set goals, and create a plan of action so I can gain a sense of control over my worrisome issues.

2. **RE-ACTIVE:** I waste precious time and destroy the present moment with obsessive worry.
   PRO-ACTIVE: I enjoy the present, being in the moment, and detaching from my worries. I am letting them go completely until my planned worry time.

3. **RE-ACTIVE:** I worry and obsess about one thing after another, feeling out of control and anxious.
   PRO-ACTIVE: I am setting aside a specific time of day to worry pro-actively. I am using this time to create a plan of action so I can respond in a realistic, pro-active way.

You are in control of your thoughts. You energize only those thoughts that bring out the best in you. Your mind is aligned with positive ideas. You are bright, cheerful, lively, and enthusiastic about the possibilities that life has to offer. You enjoy the present moment, plan positively for the future, and leave the past to the past. As a result, you have a peaceful body and mind, and you give off a sense of ease, self-confidence, and assurance. Your thoughts are organized and beneficial for you as well as for others. All your thoughts bring you a sense of health, calm, and well-being.

You dwell on harmony and balance as you think in a decisive and determined way. You are resolute and certain to achieve the best possible outcome in all that you do. Your view of the world is surrounded by a healthy glow of optimism and self-assuredness. You face your personal obligations by focusing your attention on things you can change for the better. You are attuned to what is best for you, you see the best in the world around you, and you avoid projecting a negative future. You are smart enough to focus only on what you can change and to accept that which you cannot. When you choose what you wish to think about, you have no time left over to worry or to fret.

CHAPTER THREE

Stress, Anxiety, and Depression

Only through experience of trial and suffering can the soul be strengthened, ambition inspired, and success achieved.

—Helen Keller

Let's take a good look at what the terms "stress," "anxiety," and "depression" really mean. As difficult as it is to handle these emotions, they really can be your ally rather than your enemy. In fact, the truth is that stress, anxiety, and yes, even depression, are all integral parts of the healing process in times of challenge and change. With the help of this book, you'll see that these emotions, which you previously judged as bad, are part of the solution of reclaiming your life. We'll use them here to help determine where to place your focus in order to improve areas of your life that need your attention.

WHAT IS STRESS?

If you are alive, you're going to have stress. It's a natural human experience. So while the levels may vary, how you respond is a choice. In fact, stress can be transformed into something positive by using the energy that it generates—the adrenaline rush—in a pro-active way. Therefore, it is extremely important to understand that in difficult and challenging times, your body *will* go through the physical and emotional symptoms of stress, anxiety, and depression. Getting in touch with these emotions and taking control of their side effects are key in learning to manage and reverse stress.

In order to define stress, it's helpful to understand the difference between stress and worry. Simply said, worry is the negative thought process itself, while stress is the physical and emotional reaction to it. This is admittedly a chicken and egg situation since it's difficult to tell which came first. Do you worry yourself into stress, or does your overwhelming stress cause you to worry? While there may be no definitive answer here, for our purposes, let's view stress as a physical experience that, when out of hand, creates anxiety and depression.

In order to define stress clearly and simply, I'd like to turn to Dr. Phillip Fisher, who has worked as the medical director of the Midwest Center for Stress and Anxiety for many years. Dr. Fisher is a medical practitioner with an undergraduate degree in psychology, a partner in one of the busiest family practice offices in the entire Midwest, and a member of the American Academy of Family Practice, the Academy of Medicine, and the Ohio State Medical Association. He is passionate about helping people understand and manage stress as well as related anxiety and depression.

According to Dr. Fisher, "Stress is a physiologic state in the body causing a complex reaction of chemicals that are detrimental to your mental and physical health. Moderate to severe stress often leads to feelings of worry, overwhelming emotions and being out of control, which in turn can create symptoms of anxiety and depression."

He continues, "Part of the reason stress is so frequent and overwhelming for us now is because everything is so instantaneous. You turn on your television, you turn on your computer, and in five minutes (or thirty seconds) you find out eighteen terrible things that happened all around the world and in our country. I just don't think our bodies and brains were designed to cope with that kind of input. We were supposed to be sitting around a campfire, eating berries and looking for food in the woods. That's about as much stress as our bodies were innately given to handle, and we're not even close to that right now."

Instead of being in the moment and living what we might consider a "simpler" existence, we are all running around doing ten things at once, trying to catch our breath. We talk fast, walk fast, and drive fast. We text during dinner and we talk on the phone while we drive. There is no such thing as downtime, something we all need in order to create balance in our lives.

It's time to reevaluate your priorities and your lifestyle. Begin to take time for yourself. When you control your stress, you will see your anxiety and depression symptoms begin to dissipate as well.

Don't just sit around feeling stressed. Get up, get going, and do something creative that will release your energy in a positive way. Make time to walk, run, or go to the gym. Or take time to relax, meditate, listen to music, or take a bath. Above all, be kind to yourself and acknowledge that you're doing the best you can, given what you know right now. With the wisdom, guidance, and tools this book provides, you'll begin to gain mastery over areas of your life that previously felt out of your control.

In order to do this, it is helpful to understand how the brain's functioning affects your mood and even creates the symptoms of stress, anxiety, and depression. In the next few pages, you're going to evaluate your experiences with anxiety and depression. In addition, we'll be looking at the groundbreaking work of Dr. Daniel G. Amen, child and adult psychiatrist, medical director of the Amen Clinic, and best-selling author of *Change Your Brain, Change Your Life.* He is a world-renowned expert in the field of brain scanning to determine brain dysfunction associated with everything from anxiety to weight gain to inappropriate behavior. His latest book is called *Change Your Brain, Change Your Body.*

We'll be referring to Dr. Amen's extensive work on brain function as we look at three brain systems associated with these disorders and their symptoms—the basal ganglia, the deep limbic system, and the prefrontal cortex—to see how they are intimately involved with human behavior. We will also be looking

Day 4

Pro-Active Action

ASSIGNMENT

Are you always in a hurry? Do you push yourself hard? Do you overload your schedule? Ask yourself, "Why am I always running? What's the rush? What's so important?" Your health and peace of mind are more important than anything you're rushing toward. Since we have twenty-four hours in a day, we have to choose the most productive way to use that time so we can flourish rather than stress out. Make a conscious choice to slow down. Walk more slowly, drive more slowly, think more calmly. It's all about making different choices when you feel anxious and stressed. Determine when you function best and replenish when you feel your energy flagging. Try some herbal tea, a short meditation, a healthy snack, or even a power nap.

at natural remedies that can heal these disorders. Just remember throughout this chapter that you should always check with your doctor before taking any supplements.

Let's begin by gaining a better understanding of anxiety and the symptoms associated with it.

DEFINING ANXIETY

Chronically anxious people

- are nervous on the outside while they worry on the inside
- are afraid of everything
- worry about panicking in front of others
- worry about what other people think
- don't feel safe and can't relax
- worry about being out of control
- worry about going crazy
- get anxious about not being in control of a situation
- want answers and quick fixes
- feel that no one understands them
- don't like doctor's and dentist's visits
- worry about their health
- worry about their kids
- often use medication or alcohol to calm down
- don't like to be alone
- are afraid of their anxious feelings
- make excuses for not going places and doing things
- feel bad about their anxiety
- want others to understand their anxiety
- don't understand their own anxiety
- can't turn their minds off
- don't like to feel trapped or closed in
- like to talk about their anxiety
- often repeat themselves

- have a hard time concentrating
- have a short fuse
- get anxious easily
- overreact in stressful situations
- anticipate anxiety and avoid things that might cause it
- are always in a heightened state of alert
- are waiting for bad news, for the other shoe to drop
- are always on edge
- feel like their brain and the world are going 100 miles an hour
- can't sit still and do nothing
- don't sleep well
- often display symptoms of panic episodes such as shortness of breath and rapid heartbeat

Everyone has anxiety because, like stress, it's part of being human. But not everyone struggles with *daily* anxiety. This is unbearable emotional torture that can greatly affect the quality of your life. Here is a dictionary definition of anxiety: *A painful or apprehensive uneasiness of mind usually over an impending and anticipated ill. An abnormal and overwhelming sense of apprehension and fear, marked by physiological signs (sweating, tension, increased pulse), doubt concerning the reality and nature of the threat, and self-doubt of one's capacity to cope with it.*

While anxiety can be debilitating, remember that anxiety is an emotion, which means you can control it. Everyone experiences anxiety to varying degrees, but what you do with it makes all the difference. Will you control it or will you let it control you? Let's look at the two different types of anxiety, external and internal, so you can determine which one (or maybe both) is eating at you.

External anxiety, a symptom of worry, is produced by outside circumstances: a TV show that upsets you, idling in a traffic jam, being late for work, or an argument with your spouse. External situations produce anxiety, a normal human reaction.

Internal anxiety, on the other hand, is generated from within. It begins with a negative thought followed by a chain of additional scary thoughts riding on its coattails. The original thought might be, "What if my husband doesn't like what I just said?" The chain that follows sounds like, "What if he gets so angry, he'll never forgive me? What if he leaves me? What if I end up all alone and I can't take care of myself? What if I go crazy and no one is there to help me? What if I cry until I can't breathe? What if I die?"

Do you see how one upsetting thought creates the next when you're anxious? You feel like a hamster on a wheel, going round and round in endless circles, frustrated and getting nowhere. But you can step off that treadmill at any time. With both internal and external anxiety, it is encouraging to know that you aren't a victim to either. Anxiety doesn't just happen. You worry yourself into it, which means you can also control it. Once you understand the repetitive cycle of anxiety in your life, you are on the way to healing it.

It can be a bit scary to acknowledge your feelings. But the statement *What you resist, persists* addresses this issue. When you deny your feelings and try to suppress your emotions, they don't go away. Rather, they fester and build momentum, becoming more powerful. It's time to observe your feelings and allow them to pass through you, as you gently accept them, confront them, and use them in a positive way.

Your Anxiety Profile

Please read the following statements and write down the appropriate responses from 1 to 4 that represent your level of anxiety during the last two years. The higher the number, the more you can relate to the statement. Add up the numbers to score your evaluation. This is not a diagnostic tool. It is a personal assessment to help you understand how to best help yourself.

1 - RARELY 2 - OCCASIONALLY 3 - SOMETIMES 4 - OFTEN

1. I feel uncomfortable in closed-in places like elevators, airplanes, or large crowds. ____
2. I worry about getting sick or having stomach and bowel problems in public. ____
3. I feel uncomfortable in high places. ____
4. I feel uncomfortable whenever I can't come and go as I please. ____
5. I worry about my health, such as diseases and heart problems. ____
6. I feel anxious and panicky when there is nothing to fear. ____
7. I am uncomfortable speaking or performing in front of others. ____
8. I make excuses for not doing things or going places because of my anxiety. ____
9. I have constant, repetitive, worrisome thoughts that I can't turn off. ____
10. I am uncomfortable going to the doctor, dentist, or hairdresser. ____
11. I dread medical tests, physical exams, and visiting hospitals. ____
12. I anticipate bad things happening to others or to me. ____
13. I worry about doing certain things days before I actually do them. ____
14. I have a hard time falling asleep and staying asleep. ____
15. I feel better in a social situation when I drink alcohol. ____
16. I am concerned about my anger and irritability. ____
17. I worry about losing my mind or becoming mentally ill. ____
18. I get anxious eating in front of others. ____
19. I am uncomfortable driving or riding in cars. ____
20. I worry about other people's opinions of me. ____
21. I often feel restless and wound up. ____

22. I get nervous if I don't feel in control of my surroundings or environment. ____
23. I repeat behaviors such as washing my hands or checking locked doors. ____
24. I am afraid of germs and contamination. ____
25. In certain situations, I feel compelled to run out and get away. ____
26. I feel better when I am with my "safe" person. ____
27. I don't like to be alone. ____
28. I get anxious in shopping malls or stores. ____
29. I prefer to avoid public transportation such as buses, trains, and planes. ____
30. I worry about myself. ____

SCORING
30 – 45: Your life is mildly affected by anxiety. *46 – 85: Your life is moderately affected by anxiety.* *Over 86: Your life is severely affected by anxiety.*

Remember, the anxiety profile is a guide and does not define you or your future. No matter where you fall on the scale, you have the power to effect change.

The Basal Ganglia (anxiety)

According to Dr. Amen, these are the functions of the basal ganglia system:

- integrating feeling and movement
- shifting and smoothing fine motor behavior
- suppressing unwanted motor behaviors
- setting the body's idle speed or anxiety level
- enhancing motivation
- mediating pleasure

Day 5

Pro-Active Action

ASSIGNMENT

Take a break, distract yourself, and breathe. Remove yourself from the pressure and distractions that may be causing anxious or stressful episodes. Take some personal time–ten minutes to an hour or more. Focus on something else, like the people around you or music on the radio–just be in the moment. Now practice "diaphragmatic paced breathing," explained below, to distract yourself from your anxious thoughts, calm yourself down, and prevent a possible panic attack.

Here is how to do it: Place your hand underneath your breasts on your diaphragm, just above your abdomen. Then deliberately slow your breathing to ten to twelve breaths per minute. Inhale through your mouth, count to five, and exhale through your nose. Spell the word "r-e-l-a-x" to yourself each time you breathe out. Watch your hand move up and down with each breath. Intense anxiety can lead to hyperventilation, resulting in symptoms like dizziness, faintness, bewilderment, confusion, and shortness of breath. Slowing your breath at the onset of stress and worry while you breathe from your diaphragm, instead of your throat, will help prevent anxious episodes.

Surrounding the deep limbic system, the basal ganglia are a large set of structures near the center of the brain. They are involved with integrating feelings, thoughts, and movements, while helping to shift and smooth motor behavior. This is why you jump when you're excited, tremble when you're nervous, freeze when you're scared, or get tongue-tied when the boss is chewing you out. When this system is overactive, you are likely to be overwhelmed in stressful situations and become immobile. When this system is underactive, stressful situations will move you to action.

What You Eat May Be Eating You

If your symptoms reflect primarily anxiety issues, you are probably experiencing heightened basal ganglia activity. A balanced diet will help, since hypoglycemic episodes increase anxiety. If your basal ganglia activity is low, you will need a high-protein, low-carbohydrate diet for more energy during the day. Caffeine will raise your anxiety levels. While alcohol decreases anxiety in the short term, withdrawal from alcohol increases anxiety. So avoidance of these two substances is necessary to lessen anxious episodes.

Here's an example of the effect of caffeine on anxiety. In an anxiety group I was facilitating, a woman named Sarah said that her parents were coming the next day for a visit to celebrate Easter. All day Sarah had been struggling with anxiety as she rushed around her house, vacuuming, dusting, and polishing everything in sight. She wanted their visit to be "perfect."

Because it was almost Easter, there was chocolate all over the house and Sarah munched on it while she cleaned. By early evening, she'd gotten so wired on sugar that she was driving her husband crazy, bossing him around, criticizing him for being a slob. She lashed out at the kids, too, yelling at them about picking up the toys in their rooms. It was pretty clear that Sarah was having an anxiety attack, brought on by eating too much chocolate.

It is counterproductive, then, when you are trying to manage anxiety, to start out your day with a tall cup of steaming coffee and a Danish pastry, followed by a cigarette. You'll end up having an anxiety attack, wondering why your stress levels are escalating. As good as it tastes, as nice as the initial lift feels, caffeine triggers an anxiety response in your body that will make you deeply uncomfortable and cause panicky feelings.

- A six-ounce cup of coffee contains 108 milligrams of caffeine.
- A six-ounce cup of tea contains 90 milligrams of caffeine.
- A twelve-ounce glass of cola contains 60 milligrams of caffeine.

- A one-ounce piece of chocolate contains 20 milligrams of caffeine.

Normally 250 milligrams of caffeine is considered excessive and can result in anxiety, nervousness, irritability, diarrhea, irregular heartbeat, inability to concentrate, and an upset stomach. Caffeine elevates cholesterol in the blood and flushes water from your body, causing lethargy and muscle discomfort. Caffeine tolerance differs from person to person, so read the labels and understand what you are putting in your body.

Refined sugar, another offender in anxious people, causes blood sugar fluctuations that affect your anxiety levels. When your sugar level drops too low, your body produces too much insulin, which causes shaking and trembling due to adrenaline release. Refined sugar and white flour deplete vitamin B from your system, causing anxiety and stress.

Here's what you can do to reduce your anxiety levels:

- Minimize sweets and sugars in your diet.
- Eat raw fruits and vegetables.
- Eat raw bran for bowel regulation.
- Cut out fatty foods such as hot dogs, sausages, bakery goods, butter, and cheese.
- Eat fish and lean chicken with the fatty skin removed.
- Avoid caffeine in coffee, tea, soda, and other items.
- Cut your alcohol consumption.
- Try kava extract and valerian root, which have a calming effect on the basal ganglia. B vitamins, particularly vitamin B6, are also helpful. Some people find the scents of essential oils of chamomile and lavender soothing. ***Always check with your doctor before taking any supplement.***
- Practice slow-paced breathing.
- Distract yourself from your anxiety with music or conversation.

- Give your anxiety time to dissipate. Don't overreact to it.
- Use positive, calming words to talk yourself through it. (More in Chapter Ten.)

WHERE DOES DEPRESSION FIT IN?

Depressed people have episodes of

- moodiness, irritability, and mood swings
- increased negative thinking and decreased motivation
- appetite and sleep problems
- decreased sexual responsiveness
- social isolation and problems with bonding
- fear of death
- sadness, negativity
- low energy
- decreased interest in others
- excessive guilt
- feelings of hopelessness, helplessness, powerlessness about the future
- dissatisfaction, boredom, and crying
- lowered interest in things usually considered fun
- low self-esteem
- conflict avoidance and conflict seeking
- disorganization, starting projects but failing to finish them
- headaches, nausea, abdominal pain
- muscle tension, soreness
- low or excessive motivation
- forgetfulness and poor concentration
- a tendency to predict the worse
- anger and aggression
- fear of doing something crazy
- excessive fear of being judged or scrutinized
- shyness, timidity, low threshold of embarrassment

- short attention span, being easily distracted
- lack of clear goals, lack of forward thinking
- lack of perseverance
- chronic lateness, procrastination, poor time management and planning skills
- inability to feel emotions
- short-term memory problems
- poor judgment skills
- feeling "I will make a mistake because I'm not good enough"
- feeling "it's all my fault, I'm weak and pathetic"
- vulnerability and feelings of inadequacy
- feeling like a victim
- excessive daydreaming, lethargy, holding on to past hurts
- oppositional behavior, argumentativeness, uncooperativeness
- addictions to food, drugs, alcohol, shopping, gambling, sex, TV
- black-and-white thinking
- feeling inferior and unwanted
- feeling that nobody respects or listens to them
- feeling unworthy
- feeling blamed or blaming others
- takings things personally

The Oxford Dictionary defines depression as a *pathological state of extreme dejection or melancholy, characterized by a mood of hopelessness and feelings of inadequacy, often with physical symptoms. A reduction in vitality, vigor, and spirits.*

For many people, depression is biochemical. But as with stress and anxiety, certain coping skills can help and may even eliminate your symptoms. Anyone going through challenge and change feels some depression that will pass in time. But if you're having suicidal thoughts, call a doctor immediately. In some cases, medications can be a temporary or long-term solution for depression. Discuss this with your doctor so you can make a decision based on an accurate diagnosis and educated judgment. Many people who are on medication can still benefit from this book.

Depression Profile and Assessment

The following depression evaluation is not a diagnostic tool. Rather, it is a self-evaluation assessment that will provide information about your possible symptoms of depression and how they affect your life. If you are challenged with moderate to severe depression, please talk with your doctor or therapist.

1 – RARELY 2 – OCCASIONALLY 3 – SOMETIMES 4 – OFTEN 5 – ALWAYS

1. I feel tired all the time. ____
2. I don't have any energy. ____
3. I am not excited about my life in the way I used to be. ____
4. I am emotional and cry easily. ____
5. I feel down for no apparent reason. ____
6. I overreact to things emotionally. ____
7. I don't want to eat or I eat too much. ____
8. I am irritable. ____
9. Everything seems to require too much effort. ____
10. I feel lonely. ____
11. I feel like I want to sleep all the time. ____
12. I feel tired when I get up in the morning. ____

SCORING
12 – 19: not a problem *20 – 30: mild depression* *31 – 45: moderate depression* *46 – 60: severe depression*

Mild Depression: You sometimes feel tired or down for no definable reason. You may have a hard time getting motivated to do things. Sleeping may be a problem at times. You may feel sad or overly sensitive about things. Perhaps you cry a little more easily than you used to. Possibly you're eating too much or too little. You may have less energy and enthusiasm. These are all signs of mild depression, which everyone experiences at one time or another. If they continue, get worse, or affect the quality of your life on an ongoing basis, it's time to take action. You don't have to accept this feeling.

Moderate depression: You feel sad and melancholy at times and you can't pinpoint a reason. You have low energy and it may take all your effort to get excited about anything. The simplest things, such as getting ready to go out or sexual activity, are too much effort. You cry easily, you are emotionally sensitive, and you feel the pain of the world. You have a hard time sleeping, either falling asleep or staying asleep, or you're sleeping too much. You may not be eating or you may be overeating. You get irritable and impatient. You feel bad about yourself and your life at times, and you feel that there aren't any answers.

Severe depression: You feel down and emotionally drained most of the time. You feel sad, worried, and tired. You don't have much energy; the effort it takes to do things, such as socialize or make love to your partner, doesn't seem worth the pleasure. You feel as if a dark cloud is hanging over your life. Nothing is working and you aren't sure why not. You cry often and easily. You find it hard to eat or you overeat. You have a difficult time sleeping or you sleep all the time as a temporary escape. You feel like a drain on others, like you bring them down. You feel that no one understands that your life is difficult.

> **Day 6**
>
> **Pro-Active Action**
>
> ASSIGNMENT
>
> Decompose your depression. Make a conscious decision to exercise every day. A walk outside by yourself or with a friend can work wonders for depression and anxiety. Join a gym, get a dog, or hire a trainer, but get up and get going now. Start today. Make exercise as natural a part of your routine as taking a shower or brushing your teeth. It may take a few weeks to become natural, but you'll soon see how much a walk or some exercise can improve your mental state, especially depression. (We'll talk more about the importance of exercise to your overall well-being in Chapter 9.)

The Deep Limbic System (depression)

In his best-selling book *Change Your Brain, Change Your Life,* Dr. Amen suggests that the deep limbic system is the bonding and mood control center, located at the center of the brain. The various functions of this system are

- setting the emotional tone of the mind
- filtering external events
- tagging events as internally important
- modulating motivation
- controlling appetite and sleep cycles
- promoting bonding
- directly processing the sense of smell
- modulating libido

This brain system gives you the capacity to solve problems, plan, organize, and think rationally. It sets your emotional tone, so when the deep limbic system is less active, you feel positive and hopeful. When it gets overactive and heated up, negativity can take over. You experience moodiness, isolation, irritability, depression, negative thinking and perception of events, decreased motivation, appetite and sleep problems, and decreased or increased sexual appetite. But there are solutions for all of it.

During the past decade, there has been significant research done on food, nutrients, and depression. The overwhelming tendency to call "fat" a culprit is not accurate in every case because our deep limbic system needs a certain amount of fat in order to operate properly. It is the *kind* of fat that makes the difference, like that in omega-3 fatty acids, which are prevalent in fish.

Proteins, essential for the deep limbic system, are the building blocks of brain neurotransmitters, such as dopamine, serotonin, and norepinephrine, all implicated in depression and mood disorders. Too much protein restricts the amount of actual "brain proteins" that cross into the brain, while too little leaves you with a brain protein deficit. The richest sources for protein are lean fish, cheese, beans, and nuts.

To enhance serotonin levels (responsible for controlling worrying, moodiness, emotional rigidity, and irritability), eat balanced meals with complex carbohydrate snacks such as whole wheat crackers and bread. Exercise is a tremendous help, as is the amino acid l-tryptophan, naturally occurring in milk, meat, and eggs. It has no side effects and will help insomnia, aggression, and bad moods.

Low *norepinephrine* and *dopamine* levels are often associated with depression, lethargy, trouble focusing, negativity, and mental fuzziness. To enhance these levels, Dr. Amen suggests protein snacks like meat, eggs, or cheese, while avoiding simple carbohydrates like bread, pasta, cakes, and candy. He recommends amino acids such as tyrosine for energy focus and impulse control, and *dl-phenylalanine* for moodiness and irritability.

Here's what you can do to minimize your depression levels:

- Exercise regularly.
- Avoid caffeine and alcohol.
- Avoid sugar and other stimulants.
- Get plenty of sleep.
- Eat more fruits and veggies.

- Eat more meat, eggs, and cheese.
- Avoid bread, pasta, and desserts.
- Surround yourself with positive people.

During times of depression, a simple statement like *This too shall pass* can help a lot. It helped me get through times when I felt a cloud of depression hanging over me for weeks or months at a time. I reminded myself that I had felt these overwhelming negative feelings before, but they passed and opened into feelings of joy. This is the ebb and flow of life.

While you may feel embarrassed and uncomfortable admitting to your problems with depression, you are not alone. Just remember that in many cases, elements of depression can act as sources for creativity. Media mogul Ted Turner has battled bipolar disorder (severe mood swings from elation to depression) all his life and is a good example of someone who achieved great success despite his depression.

Ted Turner

Born in Cincinnati, Ohio, in 1938, Ted Turner was a pioneer in the field of cable television, establishing the first satellite superstation and the first all-news network. But his success did not come easy. In fact, his childhood was deeply troubled, as his father was harsh and domineering.

A successful businessman in his own right, Robert Turner, Ted's dad, abused his son with severe, random beatings with coat hangers and straps. It was unfortunate that Ted suffered from bipolar disorder, previously known as manic-depression, because as much as he wanted to please his father, Ted had problems with concentration and terrible mood swings. He was sent to military school and had designs on a naval career, but instead, to please his father, he enrolled at Brown University, from which he was quickly expelled for entertaining a woman in his dormitory room.

In 1963, Robert Turner made Ted a branch manager at Turner Advertising's office in Macon, Georgia. When his skills in sales more than doubled the office's revenue in a year, Ted was promoted to assistant manager of the Atlanta branch. On March 5, 1963, Ted's dad, seemingly in good spirits, had his breakfast, strolled into the bathroom, and shot himself in the head. Ted was twenty-four and there was no time to mourn as he took over and saved the family's wealth-producing billboard business, growing it massively, despite his loss and his illness. When his famous marriage to Jane Fonda dissolved in 2001, Turner reported that he had contemplated suicide like his father, but he decided against it.

While working to manage his bipolar disorder, Turner also managed to create CNN, the first twenty-four-hour news cable station. He is the largest private landowner in America (he owns about 2 million acres) and has the largest commercial herds of bison (about 32,000 head) spread across his various ranches. But rather than touting himself as one of the richest individuals in the world, Ted donates large amounts of his wealth to worthwhile causes, including a $1 billion commitment to the United Nations. While his choices prevented him from being part of *Forbes Magazine*'s top ten wealthiest people, leaving a lasting legacy is more important to him. ❧

Imagine what might have happened to Turner if he had used his depression as an excuse for not performing. He could have ended up unsuccessful and feeling victimized. But his illness presented him with an opportunity to take control of himself and find the best within him to counteract his difficulties. Like Ted Turner, the people below have used their anxiety and depression as motivation to tap into a form of expression in their work, to get healthier, and to appreciate and focus on the good times:

Buzz Aldrin: Astronaut who walked on the moon. Hospitalized for depression that began shortly after his space odyssey.

Drew Barrymore: Successful actor with a history of depression who was hospitalized after a suicide attempt.

Lorraine Bracco: Known for her role on *The Sopranos.* Overcame depression through antidepressants and talk therapy. No longer on medication, but still finds talk therapy helpful.

Terry Bradshaw: Football quarterback who had panic attacks after games. Diagnosed with depression in the late 1990s.

Jim Carrey: A-list movie star with great wealth who spoke on *60 Minutes* about his history of depression.

Ty Cobb: Professional baseball player who was hospitalized for depression during his first season with the Detroit Tigers.

Ellen DeGeneres: Comedian, actor, and talk show host who suffered depression for a full year after her sitcom was canceled.

Princess Diana: Suffered from postpartum depression after her elder son was born. Also depressed because of marital problems.

William Faulkner: Nobel Laureate in Literature who struggled with depression and alcoholism.

Tipper Gore: Wife of Vice President Al Gore who suffered depression after her son's near-fatal accident. Officially diagnosed with clinical depression two months later; now fully recovered due to medication and therapy.

Billy Joel: Musician and songwriter who admitted himself to a hospital when he tried to end his life in the 1970s.

Elton John: British pop star who fell into depression twice, once in 1999 when he was battling drug abuse and later at the death of two of his best friends, Princess Diana and Gianni Versace.

John Keats: Nineteenth-century romantic poet and writer who had periods of severe depression.

Abraham Lincoln: Sixteenth U.S. president whose first major depression occurred when he was in his twenties. Struggled with this problem for the rest of his life.

Greg Louganis: Olympic diving champion who first experienced depression at age twelve and attempted suicide twice.

Brooke Shields: Model and actor who suffered from postpartum depression after the birth of her son.

Rod Steiger: Award-winning actor who became depressed following a triple heart bypass.

Sting: Award-winning rock star and songwriter who fell into a two-year depression that began when he was writing his memoir.

Mike Wallace: Journalist and TV news correspondent who overcame severe depressive episodes through therapy and medication.

The message here is that these people, in their struggle to maintain a healthy emotional state during times of challenge, found success in spite and because of their depression.

The Prefrontal Cortex (attention, ADHD, focus, clarity of thinking)

Understanding your brain, taking care of it, and nurturing it are extremely useful in maintaining healthy emotions. Dr. Amen explains the importance of maintaining a healthy brain, not just to manage your negative emotions, but also to improve your thinking and functioning. Only then can you operate at peak performance, think more clearly, have a stronger memory, make better decisions, feel mentally alert, and control impulsive behaviors. All this brain activity takes place in the prefrontal cortex. According to Dr. Amen, the prefrontal cortex (pfc) is the most evolved part of the brain.

Occupying the front third of the brain just beneath the forehead, this cortex is divided into three sections: the lateral dorsal section on the outside surface of the pfc, the inferior orbital section on the front undersurface of the brain, and the *cingulate gyrus,* which runs through the middle of the frontal lobe.

Here are the functions of the pfc:

- Attention span
- Perseverance
- Judgment
- Impulse control
- Organization
- Self-monitoring, supervision
- Problem-solving
- Creative thinking
- Learning from experience
- Ability to feel and express emotions
- Interaction with the limbic system
- Empathy

This part of the brain watches, supervises, guides, directs, and focuses behavior. Our "executive" function, the pfc supervises governing abilities like time management, judgment, impulse control, planning, organization, and critical thinking. It influences us to think clearly, plan ahead, use our time wisely, and communicate with others—behaviors necessary if we wish to be goal-directed, socially responsible, and effective. Good pfc function doesn't mean you won't make mistakes, but it *does* mean that you won't repeat them. This brain function helps you learn from the past and apply those lessons to the future.

In order to balance the pfc, Dr. Amen recommends a high-protein, low-carbohydrate diet, relatively low in fat. Get your protein from lean meats, eggs, low-fat cheeses, nuts, and legumes, mixed with a healthy portion of vegetables.

An ideal breakfast: an omelet with low-fat cheese and lean chicken

An ideal lunch: tuna, chicken, or fresh fish with mixed vegetables

For dinner: more carbohydrates with lean meat and vegetables

Avoid simple sugars in cakes, candy, ice cream, and pastries. Try a combination of tyrosine, grape seed, pine bark, and gingko biloba. Always check with your doctor before taking these or any other supplements.

Stress, anxiety, and depression don't have to be a life sentence or an excuse for nonproductive living. Just remember that these common emotional challenges are just that—common. Many people struggle with these issues at various times in their lives, but it doesn't keep them from thriving. In fact, some people thrive *because* of the creative energy resulting from their anxiety, stress, or depression. The key is to understand yourself, how you function, and how you can manage negative emotions in a healthy way. No more excuses. It's time to live life fully.

Re-Active to Pro-Active Attitude Adjustments

1. **RE-ACTIVE:** I allow the negative, re-active energy of stress to deplete my motivation, drain my energy, lower my self-esteem, and create chaos in my life.
   PRO-ACTIVE: I am using the positive, pro-active energy of stress to get things done, be more organized, be inspired, and have fun.

2. **RE-ACTIVE:** I let my anxiety create fear, avoidance, and insecurity, causing me to have an over-reactive personality.
   PRO-ACTIVE: I am viewing the energy of anxiety as excitement and anticipation. I expect positive side effects from taking risks and dealing with change and challenge.

3. **RE-ACTIVE:** I allow my depression to color my self-perception, my view of the world, and my life. I wallow in self-pity. I can't stop.
   PRO-ACTIVE: I am giving myself permission to feel depression but I am minimizing how long I spend there. I know it's temporary so I surround myself with positive friends and family, and I do things that are uplifting and motivating.

I am emotionally empowered with positive feelings of courage and strength. I am peaceful and serene, and the negative energies of anxiety, stress, and depression are leaving my body. I am capable; I have great expertise and a lot of know-how. I am secure that I can dissolve all obstacles as I leave fear and anxiety in the past. I know what is in my power to change and I also know what I cannot change. I understand that anxiety, stress, and depression are reactions that I choose. I conscientiously choose a more powerful way of thinking and responding. I am working toward becoming an under-reactor.

I embrace life to the fullest with an optimistic attitude. I have the power to let go of stress, anxiety, and depression as I connect to that deeper wisdom that lies within for guidance. I refuse to allow fear and anxiety to control my future. As I release them, I am filled with energy and vitality. I have the ability to handle all of life's challenges. I see them as opportunities to develop my personal power and abilities. I choose to be less affected and more effective in dealing with stress, anxiety, and depression.

I fill my mind with positive thoughts as I honor myself for the unique gifts, talents, and skills that I possess. I trust in my ability to stay strong and to be resourceful in any and all situations. I love, trust, and believe in myself.

CHAPTER FOUR

What Is Your Biggest Fear?

You can conquer almost any fear if you will only make up your mind to do so. For remember, fear doesn't exist anywhere except in the mind.

—Dale Carnegie

From the deck upstairs, I could hear him crying, sobbing really. It was early evening, and my son, Sammy, six years old at the time, was playing in his sandbox down the hill.

"Don't run down there," my husband David warned. "The doctor said if you do, he'll manipulate you with the same tactics over and over. You can't go running every time you hear him cry." But I was his mother and I knew that this cry was different. It was heartbreaking and, in some eerie way, familiar to me, as if I had cried this way myself, many times.

I wandered down the steps toward the sandbox. "Sammy, what's wrong?" I said, observing my little boy sitting Indian-style in his sandbox with his tear-drenched face dropped into his dirty little hands.

"Mommy, I just want to sit here and play," he sobbed, "and not be afraid."

"Afraid? What are you afraid of?" I asked, wiping his face with my sleeve.

"I'm afraid that hands will come out of the bushes. I'm afraid of monsters and witches. I heard a noise over there." He pointed to a tree whose leaves were blowing gently in the wind. I brushed my hand through his soft, wind-blown hair. He looked up at me and again he pleaded, "Mommy, I just want to sit here and play and not be afraid."

In that moment I understood his fear, his overwhelming obsession to look over his shoulder because something was "out there," something that was going to get him. I understood because I had spent a good part of my own life living in fear: afraid of death and dying; afraid of failure and success; afraid of relationships, commitments, people's opinions, not being good enough, and the list goes on.

"It's okay, Sammy," I said in my most soothing "mommy" voice. "You just relax and play and I'll stay here with you. You're safe and nothing is going to hurt you."

As I sat watching him, I thought how ironic it was that for most of my life, I had wanted exactly what he wanted. I just wanted to live my life and not be afraid. I wanted to stop worrying, stop living in fear of what tomorrow would bring. I wanted to stop obsessing about everything from illness to embarrassment.

Sometimes it had seemed that my mind was spinning in endless circles, imagining every worst-case scenario. I worried about disease, dysfunction, and disaster. If the situation didn't kill me, the worry surely would. Would I catch what my friend had? Would my father's alcoholism ruin my life? Would the world come to an end? I was afraid that danger lurked just around the next corner, and I couldn't relax and play. My fears clouded everything. They kept me from doing things I wanted to do, and even when I did them, fear was always lurking in the back of my mind.

I watched Sammy let go and lose himself in the moment, soothing himself with gentle humming sounds. I thought about the parallels between this moment and my life. Sammy's fears were unrealistic, but then, so were most of mine. He needed to learn to trust his surroundings, comfort himself, and stay in the moment. And so did I.

How many hours, days, and weeks had I wasted in my life, how many vacations or nights out had I destroyed worrying about something that never came to be? How many wonderful opportunities had I let pass because I was too exhausted from fear and the insecurity that accompanied it to go after them?

It was interesting to watch Sammy relax and trust that I would do the "watching out." I would look over his shoulder. He handed all that fear to me to hold, and now he could enjoy the present moment, fully and completely.

Who can do this for me, I thought? *Who can make me feel safe and protected? Who can reassure me, tell me that nothing will hurt me, and help me put my worries and fears into a healthy perspective?* I can, and I have . . . and I will. And so can you. The information in this book helped me find the solution to my overwhelming fears and I guarantee it will help you, too.

It seems that no matter how hard we try to overcome fear, everyone is afraid of something. Life is a fabulous adventure, but from the most powerful people in the world to those who work quietly and privately in their communities, we all are afraid of something and we suffer from our programmed responses to it.

THE FEAR RESPONSE

Fear is arguably the most primal emotion of all because its basic purpose is to alert you to danger. Maybe you've heard about the familiar "fight-or-flight" response that is programmed into your physiology. I'm talking about how fear causes you to shoot adrenaline to stay and fight for your life or take off swiftly in order to save yourself.

Imagine you just pulled up in front of your home in the early evening and you're carrying a bag of groceries into the house, balancing your purse and your keys. Suddenly, someone grabs you from behind. Without thinking, your automatic fight-or-flight response kicks in. With no conscious message from you, the brain alerts the body that danger is present. In an instant, your heart starts pumping faster, and your blood shoots oxygen and adrenaline throughout your body.

In dangerous situations like this, the adrenaline rushes blood to the large muscle groups—the shoulders, arms, and legs—that are needed for fighting. As blood travels from the stomach into other areas, you may feel nauseated and cramping may set in. As the fear response continues, your feet and toes go numb as the body takes blood from these areas and moves it into the large muscle groups. The body is programmed to know that the less blood you have in these large muscle group areas, the less blood you can lose. Since adrenaline inhibits feelings of pain, you may not feel the worst of it until it's over.

Another part of the fear response is shallow breathing. Think about revving your car in high gear with the brakes on. That's how it feels when adrenaline shoots through you. As you look to release the energy caused by adrenaline, instead of moving around, it is common to just sit and stew, which further stresses the body.

At this point, you are on high alert, you begin to actively look for danger, and the more bewildered you feel, the less focused you become. You will most likely end up exhausted and depressed. Your body *will* restabilize, but it takes time and you must let go of the fearful thoughts in order to return to a place of calm. The worst part is that you often go through this response for no reason, because most of your fears are imagined.

Finally, the fear response can damage your quality of life. It stops you from having pleasure, it warns you to avoid risks, and it coaxes you to run in the opposite direction rather than try something new. But if you think you're the only one who is afraid, I'm here to tell you that the most powerful people in the world have very big fears:

- I worked with an entrepreneur who graced the cover of many a magazine who regularly gave lectures on how to run a successful business. But he was deathly afraid of public speaking!
- I worked with a very well-known rock star who wouldn't fly in his own Lear jet for fear of having a heart attack on the plane with no one to save him.
- I worked with a gold cup soccer player who was terrified of dying of a heart attack during every game he played.
- I worked with a brilliant New York stockbroker who constantly feared she was going to lose her mind.
- I worked with a corporate marketing genius who was laid off and lives in constant fear of never landing another job and losing everything he worked so hard to acquire.
- I worked with a well-known sports medicine physician who was having panic attacks but wouldn't take the prescription medications he prescribed to his own patients.
- I worked with one of the top talent agents in the world who dealt with some of the most challenging celebrity clients—yet he was afraid to ride in an elevator.

As you can see from the examples above, fears come in a variety of different forms and levels of severity. So instead of judging yourself as inferior to people out there who *appear* to be fearless, understand that fear is a normal emotion shared by almost everyone. You just can't always see it in someone else. Up until now, the only thing that sets you apart from these so-called courageous and successful individuals is that they've been able to push beyond their fears and strive toward their goals. So don't despair.

IS YOUR FEAR RATIONAL OR IRRATIONAL?

We are all afraid of something, so you need to get to the source of your specific fear. Ask yourself, what is my core issue here? What is at the base of my fears? Only then can you learn to control your fear and eventually use it for motivation.

There are two different types of fears that will determine your actual danger level in any situation.

- A **rational fear** operates from reason. It is logical, which creates the basis that will eventually lead to right action.
- The second kind of fear, **irrational fear,** defies reason and is therefore illogical. Although irrational fears feel real and dangerous, they are not based in reality and therefore have a slim chance of ever occurring.

A good example of an irrational fear is the very common fear of flying. People need to understand, however, that the perceived danger of flying isn't valid. The truth is that commercial flights are one of the safest travel methods available. While the results of a plane crash can be devastating, you are far more likely to die in other ways:

- You are twice as likely to die from a bee sting.
- You are 19 times more likely to die in a car.
- You are 110 times more likely to die on a bicycle.
- Your chances of dying in a tornado is 1 in 150,000.
- Your chance of dying on a commercial plane is 1 in 10 million.

When you determine that your fear is irrational, the solution is to block and eliminate the fear. You need to recognize it for what it is and take the appropriate action to get it under control. The following story is a great example of someone who refused to let fear define or determine the course of her life.

Liz Murray

LIZ AND HER SISTER WERE RAISED IN A FILTHY APARTMENT in the Bronx by their AIDS-infected, drug-addicted parents. Liz lived in a constant state of fear and anxiety, mostly afraid that her parents would die and abandon her. At a very young age, she got a job bagging groceries and she fed the family with food she bought with her modest salary, but they ate on the same table where her parents regularly snorted lines of cocaine.

When Liz was sixteen, her worst fears were realized when her mother died. At this point she couldn't envision a better future for herself than her parents had, and when her father moved into a homeless shelter, Liz and her sister were homeless, too. But even though she rarely attended school and slept on park benches, in subways, or on a friend's couch, she was determine to change her life and overcome her fears. When a previous neighbor gave her a free set of encyclopedias retrieved from the trash, Liz pored over them, knowing she could make something of herself.

Inflamed with a desire to study and learn, Murray found an alternative high school where she got help making up what she had missed. In a video produced by Human Relations Media, she recalls,

"I realized my time was limited. I knew that if I kept going like I was, I'd end up wasting my life. I needed to go to school because I had all this potential inside of me. How would I ever become anything?"

Liz continued to study and the miracle happened when, at twenty years old, she was accepted into Harvard University on a *New York Times* scholarship for needy students. She matriculated in the fall semester of 2000, no longer a fearful, homeless, victimized young woman but one who had learned to overcome fear and anxiety in order to create a better and rewarding life.

Today, Liz is finishing her degree while she travels the country, inspiring high school kids as well as middle-aged managers of large corporations. She was one of the first people to receive Oprah Winfrey's "Chutzpah Award"; her inspirational story was captured in Lifetime Television's Emmy-nominated original movie *Homeless to Harvard.* When she speaks to groups about overcoming fear, she encourages them to stop focusing on fear and anxiety and, instead, to focus on making things happen. She says, "Don't look at the people around you who are doing things and think they're made of something more than you or are less fearful than you. Don't get psyched out by anyone, because they're not made of anything different than you are. You just need to believe that something better is waiting for you."

USING FEAR AS A MOTIVATOR

Liz Murray used her fear to motivate herself toward a better life. The following seven categories of fear define an operating base for many of our fears, as we embrace the possibility of using them in a creative and positive way:

Fear of loss of control. Fear of loss of control is the second most common fear in my seminar audiences. The first is public speaking, with fear of death coming in third. That means people would rather die than feel out of control! This fear works in a chain—you lose your job, which creates financial instability, which creates a fear of losing control of your life. The perception of loss of control can create overwhelming anxiety. How ironic that real control only comes when you relinquish the need for it!

No one can control which events will occur, but you can control how you react to them. If losing control is your biggest fear, give the reins to somebody else for a change. Delegate. Then sit back and relax. Let someone else pick the movie or the restaurant. Let someone else run the meeting while you practice being less affected and more effective in the midst of what you may consider a less than perfect situation. The idea is to "under-react" when things feel out of control.

FEAR OF BEING ALONE. I think most people fear being alone. I call this the "Who Will Be There for Me?" syndrome. What if you get sick? What if you can't get around in your later years? Who will be there to help you, sit with you, take care of you? This fear is based on a misperception of what "alone" really means. The word has come to suggest loneliness, emptiness, sadness, and lack of fulfillment.

But when you take a good look at life, you'll see that most of us are alone a great deal and we handle it. When we're challenged to move forward by ourselves in spite of our fears, we ultimately grow in a positive way. Then we can shift our perception from fear of being alone to a state of inner reflection, strength, and self-reliance. Use your fear of being alone as motivation to build and appreciate your independence. We will all be alone at some time in life, so why not get comfortable with it? Use your alone time to practice being enough for yourself and your own best emotional support.

FEAR OF ILLNESS AND DEATH. This is another name for "fear of the unknown." Do you want to be so afraid of getting sick and dying that you don't allow yourself to really live? I suggest using your fear of death as a motivator to stay healthy.

I find it ironic that many people who suffer from fear of illness and death are excessive in their lifestyles. Many of them smoke cigarettes, drink too much alcohol, ingest too much caffeine, and don't exercise. Do they avoid physical checkups because they fear that the doctor will find they have a serious medical problem? Or do they fear *not* finding a problem and still feeling poorly? The point is that if you *do* have a medical condition, you can do something about it. If you don't, you can relax. Either way, you can use your fear as motivation to live a fuller life.

Fear of embarrassment: You may feel embarrassed when you make a mistake or fail at something, but you don't have to. The only way to combat embarrassment is to cultivate a thicker skin, a sense that it doesn't matter what others think about you. If you have low self-confidence, this will be a challenge, but try embracing the fact that you are *not* the center of the universe. Other people are so busy thinking about themselves, they really don't spend much time thinking about you. So if you do something silly or unusual, you're the only one who keeps thinking about it for more than a minute.

Simple embarrassment has no deep purpose, unless it is a form of shame for a wrongdoing. If you acted rudely or offensively or told lies, the ensuing embarrassment can motivate you to define your boundaries of integrity. I urge you never to allow fear of embarrassment to stop you from taking a risk. If this fear is holding you back, go make a public fool of yourself. Go out on a limb, act crazy, and that will probably make you a more interesting person. Whatever the outcome, it will be obvious how little other people's opinions matter in the long run.

Fear of financial destitution. Everyone fears financial loss, but men are hit hardest since they generally see themselves as the provider, the responsible party for the family's financial security.

But both men and women associate financial destitution with personal security, self-worth, and self-esteem.

If this is your fear, begin studying, budgeting, and investing to gain a sense of personal empowerment. Perhaps you'll need to take a risk to move yourself to the next level of empowerment. Try using your fear of financial loss as motivation to take action instead of constantly fretting about money. This attitudinal change can bring new energy and creativity into your life, which will open you to opportunity, to keeping an open mind, and to staying positive.

Fear of criticism. When someone offers you constructive criticism, it can be a gift, a way to gain valuable personal insight. It all depends on how you look at it. When someone criticizes me, I either ignore the criticism if I deem it useless, or if it has merit, I use it to make a positive change. What do you do?

When people criticize you, try to pretend they're talking to someone else. If you can listen without getting defensive, you'll be able to see the bigger picture. Then you can determine if the criticism is valuable without your emotional response clouding your thinking. This is called being an objective listener. Once you've analyzed the critique in an unemotional way, you can take the advice or discard it, depending on your honest evaluation of the situation. The trick is to learn to view criticism not as a cruel judgment but as an opportunity for growth.

Fear of losing what you have. There is no better way to lay waste to a successful life than to spend all your time being afraid of losing what you have. Use your fear of loss to become grateful—for your health, your family, your home, and whatever else you value. The fear of loss goes back to the need for control, whether of your material possessions, your lifestyle, or a relationship.

Start handling this fear by securing what you have in the best way you know how. Then forget about it and move on because no one can predict the future. No one knows what you'll lose or gain, so why not turn your fear of loss into a healthy appreciation of what you have right now? When you worry about loss, you're living in the past and the future. When you give yourself permission to enjoy what you have, you're living in the present and you remember that possessions are simply "things." Consider this—what good is a great life if you spend all your time afraid you're going to lose it?

WHAT IS YOUR BIGGEST FEAR?

Here is a cross-section of the most common responses when groups of people across America were asked about their biggest fears:

- Being alone
- Losing control
- Flying
- Enclosed places
- Abandonment
- Death and dying
- Becoming like my mother
- Never finding my soul mate
- Losing the people closest to me
- Becoming mentally incapacitated
- Failure
- Heights
- Spiders
- Becoming sick

FEAR AND THE BRAIN

According to Dr. Daniel Amen, fear response function is located in the basal ganglia, a set of large structures toward the center of the brain that surround the deep limbic system. Too much input can cause this system to go on overload, causing paralysis.

He cites an example of one of his clients who was burned in a fire following a motorcycle accident, which the man survived. In his book *Change Your Brain, Change Your Life,* Dr. Amen says, "As he lay on the ground, people stood nearby, frozen with fear, unable to move to help him. For years, he was confounded by their actions, wondering why no one had moved to help him. 'Didn't they care? Was I not worth trying to help?' he wondered. For years, this man lived with both the physical pain from the accident and the emotional pain of feeling that others hadn't cared enough to jump in and help. He was relieved to gain a new interpretation of the situation: The intensity of emotion caused by the fiery accident had overwhelmed the onlookers' basal ganglia, and they became unable to move, even though most of them probably wanted to help."

While we all feel fear from time to time, people who are constantly in fear can assume they have an imbalance in the basal ganglia section of the brain. If you have an ongoing or intrusive issue with fear, refer back to Chapter Three and follow the suggestions for healing the basal ganglia area of the brain.

Day 7

Pro-Active Action

ASSIGNMENT

Reward yourself for overcoming fear. Choose a fear you want to overcome and give yourself a planned reward for doing it. For example, if you're afraid to fly, book a trip to a wonderful place. If you're afraid of becoming sick or taking a medical test, once you get that physical or have that test, give yourself a spa day to celebrate. If you're afraid to make a date, meet at a special bar or restaurant, one that you've always wanted to try. Choose a fear, think of a reward that would motivate you to move toward that fear, and give it to yourself after you have attempted and conquered that fear.

SECONDARY GAINS

How often have you used your fear as a reason for not doing something? I call this concept "secondary gains." For example, *I can't take the new job because what if I get anxious? What if I fail the audition and make a fool of myself?* Now you're off the hook because, in your mind, you've given yourself an out.

These thoughts that produce secondary gains, although painful, are at least familiar. Taking risks and facing possible failure are unfamiliar actions, so anxiety becomes an avoidance mechanism. It is a real breakthrough, then, when you begin to see how you use your fear to ensure failure.

Take a look at the following list of secondary gains (negative benefits) you may be getting from holding on to fear. Then take a look at the real, positive benefits you can achieve by facing that fear and moving beyond it:

Avoiding pain. We all want to eliminate pain from our lives, but sometimes a pain-inducing action is the only way to get back on the right track. You may need to end a negative relationship or quit a dead-end job, which can be painful. But the stress of being where you don't belong will be more painful in the long run. Be aware that *not* taking action can cause you more suffering than doing something about the situation. *Feel the fear and do it anyway.* Once you've made the decision to face the pain, it won't be as bad as you thought. The anticipation is always worse, and you'll find strength in knowing you can face pain when it comes around again. In addition, you'll be making conscious instead of fear-based decisions.

Avoiding confrontation. People pleasers, those with low self-esteem, are uncomfortable with confrontation. If this describes you, you want to be liked by everyone. You want to be seen as good, kind, nice, and in control at all times. But successful people don't generally fall into the categories of "good, kind, and nice." Being assertive and standing up for yourself will not win you any popularity contests, but it will help you avoid fear and frustration and you'll win respect from yourself and others. It may be difficult at first, but the more you practice being assertive, the more you'll stop running away and the stronger you'll become. No longer will you feel like a victim, because you won't allow yourself to be one.

Avoiding failure: I've failed so many times in my life, I've lost count. But I know that failing and being a loser are completely different. Most successful people have taken great risks and, as a result, have failed over and over again. If you refuse to take risks or confront failure, you are allowing fear to control your life. If you haven't failed much in life, you haven't risked much. It's like flying—the more you do it, the less it scares you, and just imagine the places you can go when you give yourself permission to fly—or to fail. Take risks, make changes, and expect failure. Then it won't surprise you. But your success will!

Avoiding change. While change is hard for most of us, without it, we get stuck in a comfort zone that quickly becomes a discomfort zone. However, you can learn to thrive on the change and the chaos that discomfort creates. Change and the vulnerability that follows in its wake are perfect opportunities to practice letting go and facing change with a positive attitude. Change can be growth-oriented and fulfilling, so the goal is to find your way through that wall of fear and revel in the rewards. The next time you are faced with change, see it as an opportunity for something new and exciting to happen in your life. Begin embracing it immediately. Change your attitude about it and watch what happens.

Avoiding hard work. With more responsibility comes more work and you may fear the level of effort that may be required of you. If your subconscious mind doesn't want to work harder and give up more of your time, your fear may start making decisions *for* you. When you evaluate what you really want and base your decisions on a solid and clear self-evaluation, you'll be making the decisions instead of your fear. If you don't want to work hard, that's okay, but don't reach for a dream that demands it. Be honest with yourself and reevaluate your long-term goals. Most importantly, accept yourself for who you are.

Avoiding anxiety. Fear can stop you from engaging in whatever brings up your anxiety, such as flying, public speaking, or saying yes to a date. But while avoidance may alleviate immediate anxiety, it will also cause it to quickly escalate. When you try to avoid anxiety, you feel bad about yourself because your fears are running the show. Your goal is not to avoid anxiety and situations that could cause it. Rather, your goal is to face it and control it. When you feel the anxiety and deal with it, you are living life to its fullest.

IT'S TIME TO FLY

Fear is a powerful emotion that can work for you as it has worked for me, but, of course, you have to work it. When I was having my worst fear symptoms, I got so sick and tired of my debilitating feelings and self-imposed limitations, I decided to do something about it. Using the skills in this book, I pushed through my wall of anxiety and I turned my fear into motivation and determination. I just knew that I could accomplish great things if I stepped out of my comfort zone—and I was right. I discovered that the solution was not to waste my precious energy fighting my fears, denying their existence, or letting them dictate my life. Instead, I used the force of this very strong emotion to propel me toward my dreams and goals.

As I mentioned above, I know the truth in the saying *Feel the fear and do it anyway.* I'm a big believer in that philosophy. Fear is a horribly consuming emotion—but only if you allow it to be. Whatever you fear the most and for the longest period of time is necessary to overcome, since that kind of fear is negatively affecting your life. You need to be honest with yourself, utilize your newfound skills, and let go of the old you. Once you tap into this new pro-active method of thinking and reacting, you'll find that you can fly—in more ways than you ever imagined!

The following piece, written by Marianne Williamson, best-selling author and lecturer, describes using fear to create opportunity.

OUR DEEPEST FEAR

from *A Return to Love:*
Reflections on the Principles of A Course in Miracles

> Our deepest fear is not that we are inadequate. Our deepest fear is that we are powerful beyond measure. It is our light, not our darkness that most frightens us. We ask ourselves, Who am I to be brilliant, gorgeous, talented, fabulous? Actually, who are you *not* to be? You are a child of God. Your playing small does not serve the world. There is nothing enlightened about shrinking so that other people won't feel insecure around you. We are all meant to shine, as children do. We were born to make manifest the glory of God that is within us. It's not just in some of us; it's in everyone. And as we let our own light shine, we unconsciously give other people permission to do the same. As we are liberated from our own fear, our presence automatically liberates others.

Re-Active to Pro-Active Attitude Adjustments

1. **RE-ACTIVE:** I allow my fears to consume and control me and determine how I am going to live my life.
   PRO-ACTIVE: Although I still feel the fear, I am stepping through and beyond these feelings and living my life to its fullest unlimited potential and possibility.

2. **RE-ACTIVE:** I have bought into the belief that my fears will protect me and keep me safe in my controlled, predictable, safe world.
   PRO-ACTIVE: I am going beyond my self-imposed limitations and living a life of courage and adventure, exploring the new horizons and possibilities that await me.

3. **RE-ACTIVE:** I ignore, suppress, deny, and run away from my fears.
   PRO-ACTIVE: I see my fears as benevolent guides and signposts that inform and direct me to areas of my life that need to be healed and integrated, so I can move forward and courageously lead the life of my dreams.

You are in control of yourself and your fears. You have chosen to free yourself of all destructive fears and doubts. You know you can master your fears, no matter what they are. You are learning to trust the process of life. You are releasing your need to control things that cannot be controlled. You are safe and protected from anything that stops you from fulfilling your mission. You know that your fears come from lack of knowledge and trust.

Discovering and challenging your fears boosts your energy rather than drains you. You relax in the knowledge that you can handle whatever life sends your way. You take full responsibility for your life. You let go and trust that life is happening exactly as it was meant to. Now you simply allow your life to unfold.

You are powerful and loving, and you know that you have nothing to fear. When you feel afraid, you focus on your strengths. Each day, you courageously expand your comfort zone by inviting in new kinds of risk. You find value in challenging your fears, no matter how difficult it is. You choose to dissipate the vagueness of fear by focusing on a world of infinite beauty and joy.

CHAPTER FIVE

Success Sabotage Syndromes

Self-sabotage is when we say we want something and then go about making sure it doesn't happen.

—ALYCE P. CORNYN-SELBY, author and lecturer

IF ONLY TERESA, A SEVENTEEN-YEAR-OLD GIRL IN MY COMMUNITY, understood that the above affirmations were about her. A very talented ballet dancer, Teresa performed most of the leading roles in our local ballet troupe and everyone noticed her. She gave off a glow, it was obvious how much she loved to dance, and she stood out as a talented young woman with a great deal of promise for her future.

I ran into her at Starbuck's the other day and I complimented her on her latest performance. "So where will you be studying ballet when you graduate from high school?" I asked her. I imagined she was poring over catalogs from various colleges with excellent dance programs. She was so good, maybe she could even get a scholarship.

But she looked away from me and said with her smile fading, "Oh, I'm not majoring in dance. That won't be my career. I think I'll probably be an interior decorator."

"But you love ballet," I protested, "and you're so good at it. Won't you miss it terribly?"

Teresa proceeded to systematically lay out a well-practiced array of reasons why she knew she would never make it as a ballerina. I felt sad as she talked. I couldn't help but feel that someone had programmed these obstacles into her malleable young mind, encouraging her to sabotage her dreams. I tried to reinforce how talented she was, but Teresa was clear that ballet was not in her future. She was demonstrating a pattern of success sabotage thinking.

DENYING SUCCESS, DENYING OUR DREAMS

Teresa's story, sad but true, is not uncommon. Teresa had fallen into a success sabotage syndrome and she had no idea that she was limiting her future. As we parted company, I decided that if I could teach my children one important lesson in life it would be this: Go after your dreams. Whatever you want to do or be, you can do it and become it. It has very little to do with intelligence and talent, although those things certainly help. But the truth is that you can achieve your dreams only when you know what you want, believe you can get it, and go after it with everything in you.

People often deny their dreams because they fear the responsibility that comes with achievement. They feel inadequate, as Teresa did, for no good reason. They are simply afraid that if they are put to the test of really having to perform, they will fall way below anyone's expectations, particularly their own. They may consider themselves failures simply because they come from a family of failures and underachievers. Failure helps them feel like they fit into the family history. But if this is you, wouldn't you rather rewrite that history? Don't be deterred, because nothing about you is set in stone.

Many people who defy success by sabotaging opportunities, even when they appear within their grasp, have myriad reasons and excuses for their actions. But those reasons are as vague and unclear to themselves as they are to others. I've met many people who chose not to go after their dreams because they felt that doing so would be potentially harmful in some area of their lives. But these are not conscious decisions. Rather, they are subconscious reactions, making it very hard to recognize the behavioral patterns.

I recognized this behavior in my own life a few years ago when I ran across some notes I had written about a dream I had. It revealed a great deal to me about my career choices over the last several years.

Last night I dreamed I had a flying machine strapped to my back. It wrapped around to the front of my body, silver tubes that pointed upward, and the hand controls were on a center unit at my fingertips. There were lots of buttons to push and I controlled everything—the speed, the height, the direction I wanted to go. Even the length of my flight was at my command.

When I wanted to fly, I stood up, I ran really fast, I pushed the right buttons, and up I went—over the treetops, into the sky, and then into the unknown to places that were unreachable for most people. I stayed at about thirty feet elevation because I knew it was fairly safe there and I would still be okay if I fell. By the way, I did fall a few times, straight down, but I just stood up, took a deep breath, started running fast, pressed the buttons, and up I would go again.

It was such an incredible feeling soaring toward the sky. A crowd ran after me, looking up and yelling different things, and I noticed two different types of people. One type wanted my machine so they could do what I was doing and feel what I was feeling. But the other type grabbed at my feet, trying to pull me down. They kept screaming at me that I was foolish and I was doing a dangerous thing that I would regret.

I just kept going up and up. It felt wonderful because I was flying high enough to feel the thrill but low enough to feel safe if I fell. I remember saying to the people who thought I was foolish, "If you could try this and feel what I'm feeling, then you'd know why I do it. It is such an incredible feeling."

This dream reminded me that without really defining them, I'd made my career and life choices on a subconscious level, based on what I thought was best for my family. I've actually spent most of my life reaching for the sky and the stars. But now I realize that there is a price to pay for glory; to gain that type of success and to reach heights so intense, you have to run fast and constantly push buttons to stay there. I don't think I grasped this when I first began my journey. I was following my dreams and I thought I could do it all, have it all, and balance it all.

Then I became a mother to two beautiful children and I was forced to base my choices not only on what worked for me, but also on what worked for my family and my marriage. I couldn't throw caution to the wind and fly hundreds of feet off the ground and still be there for a son struggling with Tourette's syndrome. I couldn't be preoccupied with pushing the buttons and still be there for my confused teenage daughter. I had to stay grounded, although sometimes I resented it. I had to accept the fact that I would not be landing on Mars and reveling in fame and glory—if I wanted to keep my life in balance. When I really looked at my life, it seemed like I was involved in self-sabotage because I needed to stay grounded so I gave up my lofty ideas. But the truth was that going for the glory would have resulted in self-sabotage because of how much attention I would have needed to withhold from my family. Flying at an exciting yet safe level was my attempt to prevent self-sabotage, because having a healthy, happy family turned out to be more important than anything.

Because success is associated with achieving our dreams, let's look at various reasons why our dreams don't become our reality. In my case, the above dream showed me that I stayed at a safe height in my career so that if I fell, it wouldn't hurt me or my family. As I moved closer to my lifelong dream of becoming extremely successful, I saw that the type of success I sought would make me less available to the people who needed me. I made subconscious choices *not* to go after certain things that beckoned to me, because the price was too high for my family to pay at the time. Today I consider that a wise decision.

It's all about finding the balance for your personal needs so you can have healthy, clear dreams, work toward achieving them, and still live in the moment and appreciate the now to the fullest. In this balanced scenario, success isn't something you strive for. It's something you acknowledge in your daily experience. The solution to achieving this level of success is within your grasp and available to you right now.

WHAT IS SUCCESS?

Today, we think of success as a level of achievement in which people have everything they want at their fingertips. But in my understanding, success is not about how much money you make or how powerful a position you may hold in your company.

I define successful living as having loving relationships, good friends, good health, and a comfortable, stable financial base. It's all about feeling healthy and content with who you are, where you are, and how you spend your time. It's about knowing that you have a sense of purpose and you're working toward fulfilling your passions in this life. In fact, the wealthiest people may be miserable a great deal of the time because they've lost sight of their dreams and desires; they've sold out, which is the same thing as self-sabotage.

Have you ever wondered where the word "sabotage" comes from? Its origin is the Dutch word *sabot,* meaning a wooden shoe. It seems that there was once a strike against the Dutch shoe manufacturers for treating their workers poorly. In an act of defiance, the workers threw their wooden shoes into the machinery gears and broke them. Hence the word "sabotage" came to mean "an underhanded effort to do harm to a successful endeavor."

We are all full of ideas, dreams, desires, and feelings. The mind is a powerful tool that offers us incredible information if we pay attention. But many of us in our fifties and sixties are realizing that we forgot an important step along our path to success—we forgot to define our goals. That means we forgot to figure out what makes us happy in life. Too bad they didn't teach "success" along with math and English in school. Imagine where you'd be right now if you had a clear vision by the time you reached your late teens of exactly what you wanted. What if you had created a clear plan of action?

You might be thinking, "Who knows what they want at seventeen?" It's a fair question, but the truth is that many people don't know what they want at forty or fifty. Frustration and dissatisfaction occur at any age, so it's important to define success for yourself.

WHAT IS SELF-SABOTAGE?

The dictionary defines sabotage as *an act or process tending to hamper or hurt; deliberate subversion.* Adding the prefix "self-" suggests a turning inward of this behavior. In other words, we are doing harm to ourselves, not to someone else. So why on earth would we sabotage ourselves?

Edward A. Selby, a National Institute of Mental Health Predoctoral Research Fellow and PhD candidate in clinical psychology at Florida State University, says that people hate it when they sabotage themselves. So why don't they just stop? Are they weak or do they lack self-control? The problem is, Selby states, that there are a number of positive contributing factors that play a role in these behaviors. Smoking is a perfect example.

Selby says that most people know that smoking is bad for their health. They know the social stigma involved, the bad smells and the gross factor, but at the same time, smoking makes them feel good. When they smoke, they get a nice little buzz that can dissolve the stress of daily life. Smoking is also considered a social event, as people discuss politics and relationships over a cup of coffee and a cigarette. When you consider these benefits, continuing to smoke makes sense in a convoluted sort of way.

Professional counselor Ken Fields agrees that self-sabotaging behavior can serve a positive need. He introduces the concept of "approach avoidance," which means that the closer you get to your goal, the more you try to avoid reaching it. Perhaps reaching that goal will mean an end to the need for other goals. Or maybe family and friends will be envious of your success, so sabotaging will ensure that you remain in their good graces. Therefore, the goal of that form of self-sabotage would be maintaining friendly relations and avoiding unpleasant feelings in others.

Fields likens self-sabotage to the flu or a seasonal cold, as the body attempts to purify and heal itself of foreign elements. But the mind is trying to meet a psychological and emotional need. Fields suggests that if you think you're engaging in self-sabotaging behaviors, consider the underlying needs that are striving to be met.

HOW I DID IT

There are endless ways to achieve your goals and become successful. You're never too old and it's never too late. In my case, my definition of success has changed over the years. In my twenties, I have to admit that I saw success as becoming a famous singer and entertainer, having a tall, dark, handsome husband, living in a tropical paradise, and traveling the world.

At first I came up with a ton of excuses as to why I didn't achieve my idea of success, however unrealistic it was. But when I finally reevaluated my definition of success, I realized that I really wanted a loving, supportive partner, children, a career that would allow me to make a difference in the world, and an opportunity to express the entertainer part of me. And, of course, I wanted to stop sabotaging success in my life, in any form that it came.

Today, I define success as good health for myself and my family, time to spend with them, peace in my heart, contentment with my career and my life, time to have fun, helping people empower themselves, and writing inspirational books. I am no longer sabotaging my success. Rather I have redefined it and I feel successful most of the time, no matter what is happening or how much money I make or don't make.

In order to understand why you sabotage your success, let's acknowledge that we all live in a highly competitive, uncertain world. If you want to survive and thrive, you must know what you want and find a way to optimize your dreams, take risks, and go after what you want. Part of the solution is to recognize that it's all about attitude and how you overcome your own self-sabotage syndromes. Here's how it happened for me:

I started my business, the Midwest Center for Stress and Anxiety, in my bedroom in our old farmhouse, with an ancient Apple II computer that my husband bought for me. I recorded our first tapes in the living room, discussing recovery with people who were struggling with anxiety and depression. Boy, those were great times! I was pregnant with my daughter, Brittany; life was simple; I was doing group therapy sessions with Dr. Phillip Fisher and it seemed that divine direction was keeping me going. At that time, I trusted the universe as I directed my passion and energy into my work and my personal life. I was right where I was supposed to be, creating our outpatient group program, Attacking Anxiety and Depression; shooting my own infomercial; and, finally, picking up the phone and getting myself on Oprah. That's right. I got myself on *The Oprah Winfrey Show* while I conducted and sold stress seminars to corporations—when I'd never done a stress seminar in my life!

Then I started writing my first book. I was inspired with ideas about turning panic into power, about utilizing fear of failure to help make dreams come true, and about using those same skills to turn a negative past into a positive future. I was passionate about turning this inner, creative worry energy outward—to make my life more successful on every level. I had no book proposal to submit to a publisher; I didn't even have an outline—only a really good idea.

Do you believe in synchronicity? I do now, since my husband, David, met a literary agent, Margret McBride, at a conference while I was still formulating my book idea. They hit it off and when I met Margret a day or so later, we reveled in the energy, the excitement, and our shared passion about the possibilities. We were both convinced that I had a great idea. Both Margret and I felt that the book was destined to happen, so she set up a couple of meetings with some top editors in New York. Remember, we had no outline or book proposal. We didn't follow the rules, but then I like to follow my gut and my passion.

One of the editors I met was a woman named Diane Reverand from HarperCollins Publishing, and she understood exactly what I was talking about. I had the advantage of a successful infomercial that was already on the air, I'd appeared on Oprah several times, and I was giving lectures across the country. Diane decided to take a chance with me after I showed up, did the dance, and demonstrated my confidence and belief in myself. We sold that book, *From Panic to Power,* for close to a million-dollar advance, unheard of at the time since I was basically an unknown who had never written a book. All this sounds pretty exciting and must be the end of the story. Right? Wrong.

As thrilling as it was, I was also terrified. They were giving a huge advance to me, little Cindy Redick, from Findlay, Ohio, the girl from the dead-end street with an alcoholic father. It seemed like a fairy tale ending, but it wasn't. In fact, the stress and pressure were only beginning, because once the deal was done, I was expected to perform.

The what-ifs came spilling out. What if I couldn't do it? What if I didn't have a whole book in me? What if I couldn't write? What if it wasn't fabulous? What if it didn't sell? What if, what if, what if. Do you know what that is? It's self-sabotage. Despite my good fortune and all my previous hard work, I felt the need to sabotage the moment instead of savoring it.

Gratefully, I didn't get in my own way too much. After I submitted my first three chapters, Diane Reverand called me. I picked up the phone expecting her to hate the material and realize what a huge mistake she had made. *Would I have to pay back all the money?* I wondered. But she said, "Lucinda, this is fabulous. This is exactly what we're looking for. I love it!" What an affirmation of who I was, of what I was capable of, and where I could go in my life! No matter that I wasn't an English major. I had passion and I was willing to put myself out there, take a risk, and do the work.

Think about this story whenever you feel insecure about your ability to perform or when you fear you can't live up to someone else's expectations. We all have talents and special gifts. We all have a star inside of us, just waiting to emerge. Yours may show up in the form of being a great parent or maybe you'll be a performer, a teacher, or even write your own book someday. Just be creative, open your eyes, and ask yourself: What am I passionate about? What do I absolutely love to do?

The answers will come, but most likely you'll have to step out of your comfort zone, once they do. You have to be willing to step through the insecurity and the wall of anticipatory anxiety that we all know so well, in order to get to the other side. There are endless opportunities out there, but you have to stretch yourself and try something new. You have to get informed, stay motivated, and surround yourself with creative and supportive people. It's all about hope, new ideas, and, most important of all, believing that you are worthy of success.

Day 8

Pro-Active Action

ASSIGNMENT

In order to get in touch with your tendency to sabotage yourself, divide a piece of paper into two columns. In the left-hand column, list the healthy habits you would like to engage in, such as exercising, building better relationships, improving your health, cleaning up your diet, financial strategizing, spending more time with your children. Think about times in your life when you tried to implement them. In the right-hand column, write down the action or thought that stopped you. These are the self-sabotage behaviors you need to recognize and eliminate so you can reach your goals and dreams.

Do not judge yourself or use this evidence to fuel your sabotage tendencies. Instead, why not feel excited that you have uncovered a part of the problem that has held you back in the past? To be informed is to be well armed. The solution is to forge ahead, armed with a newfound awareness of the specific self-sabotaging behaviors that have previously blocked your path to success.

SUCCESSFUL IMPERFECTION

Do you want your children to develop healthy self-esteem and to feel capable at an early age of achieving their dreams and goals? Do you want them to believe in themselves unconditionally and know that their options are varied and infinite? As your kids enter adulthood, do you want them to figure out what they are passionate about and focus on making that passion their future reality—in spite of competition, insecurities, and fears? If you want these things, you'll need to adopt an attitude of "successful imperfection" that Dr. Robert Leahy, clinical professor in psychiatry at Weill Medical College of Cornell University, describes in his book *The Worry Cure.*

Although the term "successful imperfection" sounds like a contradiction in terms, it really isn't. It refers to carrying out actions that will not have a perfect outcome, no matter how hard you work at it. But they have great value, nonetheless. It's about moving forward with baby steps, imperfect steps, in the right direction. In other words, you can't lose fifty pounds in one week just because you want to. But you can take a baby step toward that goal by losing two pounds, and then two more the next week. Each pound of weight loss is imperfect in relation to your final goal, but if you look at it in increments, each pound you lose is perfect because you are out there exercising and moving in a good direction. You're making a commitment and sticking to it.

Dr. Leahy asks us to notice what we get from perfectionism. Have you ever thought to yourself, *What's the use of exercising today? I still won't be able to fit into that dress for the party tomorrow.* But we are not looking for perfection, he says. We're looking for progress, which involves becoming successful at being actively imperfect each and every day. You commit to a certain behavior, knowing that you will embark on a chain of imperfect actions, until one day you reach your goal. When is not the issue. Doing something, anything, right now, is a pro-active effort.

I want my children to know the value of taking imperfect steps toward success. I want them to believe beyond a doubt that they can have whatever they want if they just keep going and believe in themselves. As they move imperfectly toward success, I want to instill in my children the concept of never giving up and not letting the outside world manipulate them into second-guessing themselves.

I want them to know that anything is possible as they learn the importance of balance, happiness, and making choices in life. And finally, I want them to pay attention to their dreams because dreams are a very important part of our identity and a great tool in defining who we are and what we want for ourselves—even if it takes some successful imperfection to get there.

SUCCESS SABOTAGE SYNDROMES

Why do our dreams often elude us? Why does getting what we want seem so complicated? Let's look at some of the ways that we sabotage our dreams.

Lack of Clarity

Many people go through their entire lives never knowing what they want, what kind of lifestyle appeals to them, or what type of career would pay the bills and make them happy. As a result, they make bad choices and toil much too hard over work they don't like. This kind of person ends up feeling unfulfilled and empty.

Did you have positive role models when you were growing up? Did your parents live their dreams, or did they just do what it took to pay the bills and keep food on the table? My father dreamed of being a famous musician. Music meant a great deal to him, but he lacked the confidence and clarity to follow through. My mother was a writer and an artist, but she gave up her dreams and worked in a factory as a secretary for thirty years. What happened to their dreams?

Their fear left them bereft of a clear direction. My father dealt with his frustration by picking up the bottle, and my mother became unhappy and victimized by him. If you had negative role models, it is all the more crucial that you clarify your goals and create a plan of action to achieve your dreams. Your family's legacy does not have to be your destiny.

Lack of Motivation

Motivation comes from desires and needs: a desire for more, a longing for a better life, envy of someone else, a need for control, a desire for change, a desire for self-improvement, or a need for more security. Even the fear of being alone or ending up like a bag lady can be a powerful source of motivation. It really doesn't matter what motivates you. It only matters that you don't sit around, doing nothing and wondering where your dreams went.

Each of us has to figure out what motivates us, and then we have to do it. I never used to go to the gym, for example, because I thought I didn't have to. I took walks, tried to eat right, and I felt that was enough—until I met Alyssa at a business meeting. I immediately noticed this beautifully feminine and physically fit woman, who had great posture and glowing energy. When she took off her jacket, she revealed beautifully toned arms and shoulders and I envied her. I wanted to look and feel as good as she did. At first I made excuses like, *Oh, she's younger than I am. That's why she looks so much better than I do. I'm too old.* But when I got to know Alyssa, I found out that she was actually older than I was (ouch!). *Wow,* I thought, *I want to look that healthy and feel that wonderful. How can I do that?* I joined the gym and it took me about six weeks to get into a steady habit of working out and drinking lots of water. Within three months I looked and felt better than I had in years. Instead of giving up on myself, sabotaging my life, and becoming bitter toward Alyssa, I used my envy as motivation. Today, exercise has become a very important part of my life and has helped me get healthier and feel better about myself.

The Fraud Syndrome

What if people find out I'm not who they think I am? What if I'm actually a fraud? Am I a hypocrite?

If you ask yourself these questions, you have fallen prey to the fraud syndrome, based in insecurity and fear of failure. Each time I step into a new role, whether it's self-help expert, talk show host, or writer, I am barraged with internal questions: What experience do I have? Do I have a PhD in psychology? Was I an English major? Have I hosted talk shows before? No, no, and NO. But I realize now that many successful people don't have advanced academic degrees and didn't major in the career in which they now excel. Like me, they became experts in their fields by taking risks, making mistakes, and learning from their experiences. For example:

- Martha Stewart and Rachael Ray didn't go to culinary school.
- Dr. Laura Schlessinger, radio host, isn't an accredited psychologist.
- Tom Hanks didn't go to film school.
- Tom Cruise didn't finish high school and was never a theater major.
- Tony Robbins, a world-recognized motivator, didn't go to college.

There are far too many of us who worry about being "found out." Maybe you fear you aren't as strong, smart, confident, or qualified as other people think you are. Just do the best you can and stop worrying about being a fraud or a hypocrite. We all feel like that sometimes because we want to be perfect. But perfection is an impossible, unachievable goal. Let's just get real and get happy.

Fear of Responsibility

Let's be honest. Some of us are lazy at heart. We don't want to work hard and take on a lot of responsibility. But your dream might not require as much responsibility as you think. You may be blowing it out of proportion in order to sabotage your success before you even start. If you don't want to work long, hard hours, choose a dream that is more realistic, less demanding, and requires only the amount of responsibility you're willing to take on. If you want to do less, be okay with that.

But if responsibility doesn't scare you, keep moving toward that goal, because nothing wonderful comes without hard work and the accompanying responsibility. When I'm doing something I love, I get so involved that I sometimes have to stop myself from overworking. As much as responsibility challenges me, I find people who share my goals and are willing to share some of the responsibility. That's the way the universe works.

Fear of Failure

We've all tried things that didn't work, even though we poured our hearts into it. I know how it feels to fail, but the more we experience failure, the easier we will accept it as a part of life. If you told me, "I really haven't experienced much failure in my life," I'd say, "Then you must not push yourself very often or take many risks."

I used to believe that if I did all the right things and didn't give up, I'd eventually get what I wanted. But for many different reasons, that's not always the case. Maybe the years of your trying to do something that never came to pass taught you exactly what you needed to know for next time. You may not have realized your original goal, but you didn't fail either. You just learned something you weren't expecting to learn. If you go for your dream with integrity and fortitude, even if it doesn't come to pass, you'll feel good about what you learned along the way. Who knows where you'll end up next? You may be guided around the original goal to something far more fulfilling than you ever dreamed possible.

In Debbie Ford's book *The Shadow Effect,* which she co-wrote with Deepak Chopra and Marianne Williamson, she says, "The people we blame offer a perfect excuse for a self-sabotage. We are unconsciously punishing them when we say, either verbally or nonverbally, 'Look, I really am a failure, you really did hurt me.' The bottom line here is that failing is as natural to human beings as making a mistake. And the more willing you are to take risks and really put yourself out there, you will become more resilient, less sensitive, and more appreciative of real success when it does come along."

Fear of Success

This is a hard concept to grasp—that people fear success. How can that be? But the real fear here is feeling *undeserving* of success. Secretly, people feel that success won't last, which comes from negative belief systems they've carried for a lifetime. They fear if they actually attain success, it might change their lives and affect their relationships—which it will, but in a positive way rather than a negative one.

The perfect antidote to fear of success in one area is becoming successful in a different area. Once you feel empowered and strong, you will be inspired to do more and risk more. Be a winner. Give yourself permission to have success, money, nice things, good friends, and a healthy body and mind. You deserve it and you may be surprised to discover that good things *do* last if you nurture them.

Life Changes

Change is one of the few things we can count on in this life. You can be absolutely sure that your life *will* change, often when you least expect it and in some ways that you may not like. But you can also be sure that with those inevitable life changes come opportunities.

I know several people who were forced out of their jobs, only to become successful entrepreneurs after going into business for themselves. Mothers who wanted out of the system have become successful business owners and now they have more time for their kids. You just never know where life changes will lead you, so look for opportunities and don't let fear stop you. Stay focused and trust that all paths lead straight to your dream.

The "I'll Be Happy When . . ." Syndrome

Many people get caught up in thinking that until they reach their goals and achieve their dreams, they simply cannot be happy. But why not? Why can't they enjoy the process along the way? If they don't, it becomes almost impossible to reach their goals because they are never satisfied. They get so used to being dissatisfied that whatever they end up doing will never be good enough.

The key to overcoming this syndrome is to set goals, strive for them, and remain happy and engaged in your present life. Don't delay your happiness. Calmly tell yourself, "I eventually want to achieve this. In the meantime I can be happy and enjoy my life the way it is now because *now* is all there is." Then the journey will be a pleasant one, the energy surrounding you will be positive, and you will draw good things and people into your life. No matter what happens, you'll keep going because your foundation is a satisfaction and self-acceptance that no setback can touch or destroy. If you believe you can't be happy until you achieve something specific, you'll be likely to give up and walk away. But when you choose to feel happy just because you are you, you will experience added stamina and patience.

Envy and Jealousy

Envy and jealousy can wreak havoc on your dreams. When you see others living their dream in a grand style, you may feel jealous that they got there first or did a better job than you did. But envy can be extremely destructive. Why not use envy and jealousy to motivate you to keep going? When you see someone doing something you admire, emulate them, learn from them, like I did with Alyssa, and use their success as motivation to move closer to your own goal.

When our infomercial "Attacking Anxiety" had been out for a few years, a woman named Susan Powter exploded onto the scene with a diet infomercial that became hugely successful in a matter of months. People in my business, including my partners, asked me why her show was so big and why ours wasn't doing the same kind of sales numbers. While ours was steadily doing well and we were certainly helping people recover from anxiety and depression, we still felt awe and admiration (and a little envy and jealousy) at how well her show was doing. Then I heard she'd written a book based on her infomercial appeal.

Well, if she can do that, I thought to myself, *maybe I can too.* On the heels of her book's success, and probably to some degree as a result of hers, I came up with a wonderful concept for a book and, after a lot of work and many meetings, I too got a great book deal. As a result I wrote my first book, *From Panic to Power.* It became one of the best-selling books about anxiety ever published, and my infomercial is still on the air. Instead of getting caught up in feelings of jealousy and insecurity, I used these feelings as motivation to reach even further, and make a new dream, a dream of writing a book, my reality. That book is still being sold around the world today, and I get thousands of letters from people explaining how that one book has changed their lives.

WHAT TYPE OF SELF-SABOTAGER ARE YOU?

Elizabeth Scott, in About.com's Guide to Stress Management, counsels and coaches people on effective stress management and healthy living strategies. She lists several different types of sabotage in which people engage, continuously escalating their mental and emotional stress, without being aware that they are doing it.

"Type A" personality. These people rush through the world and their lives, feeling frantic, hostile, and re-active. If this is you, you typically bring unnecessary emotional stress into your life with aggression. In such a state, you miss the simplest solutions to problems because your fast pace undermines your ability to pay close attention to detail, which can cause larger problems. Type A people generally undergo health problems somewhere down the line.

Negative self-talk. When the enemy is inside your head, the pattern of negative self-talk, formed during childhood, can color your experience like a dark cloud blocking your vision. If this is you, you tend to see negativity where none exists. You tend to interpret potentially positive outcomes as negative and worthless; you project a self-fulfilling prophecy that your life is more than you can handle. Just remember that it's never too late to reverse this thought process. When you surround yourself with positive people who put out positive energy, you will experience much less stress and negativity in your daily life.

Poor conflict resolution skills. Part of being human and communicating with others is facing conflict. But you can decide how to approach that conflict. Will you act aggressively and send the other person into a defense mode? Or will you be assertive and work with others? The way you handle conflict can strengthen your relationships or cause you additional emotional stress. Many people who act aggressively are not fully aware that they are doing so.

Pessimism. Pessimists see situations as worse than they really are. But this state of mind is more than just seeing the glass half-empty. Rather, it's a specific worldview that undermines your belief in yourself, damages your health, and acts like a magnet for negative consequences. Because the traits of optimists and pessimists are specific and slightly elusive, many people with pessimistic tendencies view themselves as optimists. But if you pass up opportunities, overlook solutions, and cause yourself mental stress, you are acting like a pessimist.

Taking on too much. You may often take on more than you can handle because you're a type A personality, you don't know how to say no to other people's demands on your time, or you're uncomfortable doing nothing and feel a need to always stay busy. You may live in a state of chronic stress, habitually taking on more than you can cope with. Try easing up on your schedule, giving yourself some free time, and letting go of the idea that if you're not overburdened, you're not really living.

Day 9

Pro-Active Action

ASSIGNMENT

It's time to sabotage your sabotage syndromes. Here are two steps you can take to overcome the sabotage syndromes you created for yourself:

- Do an honest evaluation of the sabotage syndromes you are using now or have used in the past. Write them in your journal and begin to recognize your own negative dialogue with yourself.
- Make a strong commitment to start the work of eliminating these syndromes from your list of bad habit behaviors.

Re-Active to Pro-Active Attitude Adjustments

1. RE-ACTIVE: I allow my fear of failure to inhibit me from taking any action steps toward accomplishing my goals.

   PRO-ACTIVE: I am viewing my so-called failures as learning opportunities that have given me valuable feedback and information. I put them to good use in helping me to achieve my future dreams and desires.

2. RE-ACTIVE: I tell myself that I'm not good enough or talented enough or deserving enough to achieve any level of success in life.

   PRO-ACTIVE: I remind myself that I am just as deserving, valuable, and worthy as anyone else on the planet and that I possess my own unique set of skills, talents, and gifts.

3. **RE-ACTIVE:** I criticize and berate myself for not being or doing something perfectly, which leads to procrastination and stagnation.

   PRO-ACTIVE: I recognize that perfectionism is an unhealthy expectation I put on myself that gets in the way of living a rich, satisfying, and rewarding life. I remind myself that I am an "imperfectly perfect work in progress" and that I am good enough.

You are amazing. You're bright and strong and confident. You're full of potential. There are so many wonderful opportunities for someone just like you. You're beautiful. You're exceptional in so many ways. You're an incredible work of art—your face, your sparkly eyes; everything about you is embraceable. People enjoy being around you and you draw them to you. You're good company. You light up a room. You're very special.

Time spent with you is a memorable experience. You make the world a better place. You make the word "love" easy to understand. You radiate good energy. You're capable of great things and full of spirit. You're a breath of fresh air, a beautiful flower opening to the warmth of the sun. You make me want to dance and laugh and play. I know I'm safe with you, because everyone is. You're a good soul. You're alive and you live your life with gusto. You're valuable, worthy, and unique.

CHAPTER SIX

Challenge & Change

What is important is to keep learning,
to enjoy challenge, and to tolerate ambiguity.
In the end there are no certain answers.

—Martin Horner

In spite of all my hard work and a fair amount of success, my life has had its challenges and stressors throughout the years. We lost my sister and my sister-in-law to cancer; we lost my brother and my father; and my son was diagnosed with Tourette's syndrome at six years old. My life has been a bumpy ride, but I can remember a time in my forties when it felt relatively stable. We bought a beautiful house, we took family vacations, we had nice cars, we put our daughter through college, we had good Christmases, our son was getting the help he needed, and we thought our 401(k)s were secure. Life felt predictable.

Then came the year of what I call "no crystal ball": a very hard time that was unpredictable and extremely challenging for my family. My son became sick with daily, repeated, unexplainable vomiting. He couldn't attend school for months, we had to homeschool him since he was nauseous all the time, and he had to give up his favorite sport, water polo. Next, my brother had an unexpected seizure and, after suffering horribly for over two months, passed away. My daughter Brittany, who had graduated from college and was about to start a new, exciting career in New York, decided to put her life on hold and flew back home to help us. In a matter of a few months, our stable, secure, predictable life had been turned upside down. I felt like I'd aged ten years and, just when I needed to take especially good care of myself, I was too overwhelmed and exhausted to do much of anything. In short, we were surrounded with challenge, change, and uncertainty.

Then our bird flew away.

My son Sammy had asked us for a pet bird a few years back, so we bought him a yellow-headed Amazon parrot we named Jasmine. As is typical with kids and their pets, she soon became "our" pet since I fed her, took care of her, and got very attached to her. One day when I was taking Sammy to yet another doctor's appointment, a friend came by to take Jasmine's cage outside so she could get some fresh air. But our friend wasn't careful. The door to the cage suddenly opened, Jasmine got spooked, and she flew up into a fifty-foot tree at the end of our property.

For days, as we struggled with Sammy's vomiting and doctor's appointments, I felt completely out of control. So while I was depressed, overwhelmed, and worried sick about Sammy, I distracted myself by focusing on the bird that was still languishing in the trees. We even called the local firefighters, but all they could do was stand and scratch their heads. The night before Sammy's next doctor's appointment, I wandered up and down the driveway trying to coax the bird home. I remember thinking, "The sky is falling, and everything's going to take a turn for the worse." Was this a sign of my life to come? Would everything fall apart or fly away?

The next day, however, the doctor gave us great news: He had found nothing seriously wrong with Sammy. I was tremendously relieved and grateful. On our way home, my cell phone rang. "Mom, you'll never believe it!" Brittany practically sang to me. "Jasmine just flew to a tree close to the house. I went upstairs, I opened up all the windows and I called to her and she tried to fly to me twice." This was astonishing because Brittany had never really liked the bird and they had never made a connection. "Mom," she said, "I think she'll come through an upstairs window for you."

Not everyone knows that domestic birds don't like to fly downward. In fact, it's impossible to get them to do so and, believe me, those last few days we had tried. But while we had been trying to get Jasmine to fly down from the tree, Brittany opened an upstairs window. While Sammy and I weren't thinking outside the box, Brittany was.

Sammy and I raced home, grabbed a crust of bread, and headed upstairs. We leaned out of one of the tall windows, holding the crust out and singing and calling to Jasmine. She watched us, swaying back and forth. Would she trust us? Would she trust herself and fly to us, even though she thought she could fall? All of a sudden, she flew through the open window and into my hands. She was back.

In retrospect, I was certain we were going to lose Jasmine forever. But Brittany opened not only the upstairs window, but also other ones that had been closed. I would never have thought of it. *Where are the other windows I'm not seeing in our life right now?* I thought. *They're somewhere; we just have to look for them.* And I did.

There were many, and one of them is this book you're holding in your hands right now. *Lots of people are struggling to find their way these days,* I thought. *I need to create a new product, an easy-to-use solution for people that will help them get their lives back on track.*

People need help more than ever these days since we are all dealing with challenge and change. Ask yourself, "What's my challenge right now? Am I worried about finances or health? Am I sleeping poorly due to anxiety? Am I afraid my boyfriend is going to leave me? Does my life feel totally feel out of control?" Well, take a deep breath because I believe you've got the solution in your hands.

WHO DO YOU BLAME?

When you feel heavily challenged, it's easy to point your finger and find the reasons outside of yourself: "It's the economy. It's the last president. It's the current president. It's my job, my husband, my kids."

It's common practice to look around and justify why you don't have what you want, whether it's money, a relationship, security, support—whatever you lack. It's easy to say, "Of course I'm afraid of change. Just look at my problems. That's why I can't sleep at night. That's why I can't be happy. That's why I'm insecure and overwhelmed."

But remember, when you point your finger outside yourself, there are three fingers pointing back at you—for a reason. YOU are the only one who can change your life and how things affect you. YOU are the only one who can take back control. Rather than blaming others, try turning inward and taking responsibility for your automatic response and learned behavioral problems. Once you realize that YOU are in control of your emotions, you can take back your power.

It all begins with a decision to stand up and fight, to *embrace challenge and change.* You make the decision that you're not going to let it beat you, whatever "it" is, whether it's a relationship issue, a financial issue, a health issue, or a job issue. You've got to say, "I'm willing to fight for what's worth fighting for, and I'm going to do whatever I can to take back my control."

The harder you fall, the higher you bounce.

—HORACE

You have to become a fighter because nobody out there is going to do it for you. Sure, it's a tough world, but it's also a wonderful world full of opportunity. When you're vulnerable, depressed, anxious, tired, or insecure about a change that's coming, it's time to fight harder than ever to embrace the challenge, even if you're scared to death. Believe me, I've been there, I've done it, and I'm still standing. We've all heard the familiar sayings: *Only the strong survive, and When the going gets tough, the tough get going,* and *Whatever doesn't kill you makes you stronger.* Yes, they're trite expressions, but they're also true. In hard times, you find out who you are and what you're made of. And so do your children, your spouse, your boss, and your friends.

How would you like them to see you? When you use the skills in this book, your coworkers and loved ones will see you as someone who stays calm, focused, and responsible. Someone who considers options, stays optimistic, and takes chances. A person who learns from change and bounces back, even under the worst possible conditions.

Besides, what's the alternative? You could fold, give up, and wait for someone to save you. You could drink a few glasses of wine, do some drugs, go on a shopping spree, and spend money you don't have. You could complain and be negative. But you'll just end up more frightened and depressed than you already are.

Times of adversity can be great gifts that carry with them the opportunity to be more responsible for your life and your finances, to make better decisions, to get more involved, and to be more accountable for yourself—all great skills for coping with change. As you get more comfortable with not being in control, your children will learn, by example, a better way to respond during times of challenge and change.

THE FUTURE

Since there is no way to control what is happening in the world, there is no way to predict the future. That gives many people cause for worry, but in this book, we're learning to accept change and challenge and turn them into opportunity. Are you worrying about change so much that it's making you sick? Are you allowing challenge to make you feel insecure? Are you using your stress to justify your misery? Are you allowing your negative emotions to make you angry at your loved ones?

If you answered yes to any of the above questions, it's time to learn to be your own parachute, your own safe place, your own safe person. There are many inspiring stories about people who led difficult lives but went after their dreams in spite of the challenges and actually achieved them. Here are some examples:

- Actor and comedian Jim Carrey dropped out of high school and took a job as a janitor in a factory while he and his entire family lived in a minivan.
- Actor and comedian Adam Sandler spent years scraping by, living from paycheck to paycheck, in order to finance his own movies.
- British author J.K. Rowling, whose *Harry Potter* franchise has made her richer than Queen Elizabeth, was divorced and raising a young daughter on welfare. After writing her first book on cocktail napkins at work, she has risen to fame as her franchises have made her a staggering $1.4 billion.

- Then there was Janice Smith. Never heard of her? That's because she never took a risk or tried to transform her changes into opportunity.

What if the above well-known achievers had decided not to challenge themselves or hope for a better future? We'd never have heard their names or been able to take advantage of their amazing gifts. Of course, we aren't all going to become famous actors or billionaire novelists, but we all need to learn how to turn our personal challenges and changes into opportunity, a task which requires perseverance.

Here is an excerpt from an interview I did with Glen Hiemstra, author and futurist. He routinely gives lectures for highly successful corporations such as Boeing, Microsoft, and Hewlett Packard.

BASSETT: So tell me, Glen, what is a futurist?

HIEMSTRA: A futurist develops the capacity to remember the past and anticipate the future, in order to live more fully in the present. We all do this to some extent, but a futurist takes that more seriously than the average person, as we try to learn from history, to anticipate the future, as well as create images and visions about what is coming.

BASSETT: So you look at the past to determine the future so you can have a better present moment?

HIEMSTRA: That's exactly right. My mentor once told me, "If you don't go far enough back in memory or far enough ahead in hope, your present will be impoverished." That was a really beautiful way of trying to capture our great human capacity to remember in a dream and try to pull those things together so that you can really see where you've come from and what you want to be doing. You see your choices much more clearly. Futurists focus on strategic and long-term planning, both personally and professionally.

BASSETT: When we're in anxious or challenging times because of global situations like the economy or a health issue, why do we look toward the future with a load of "what-if" thinking?

HIEMSTRA: Partly because you tend to conjure up all kinds of emergencies and scary scenarios, and you want to avoid thinking. Ultimately, it all comes down to choices. There are a few known things in life that we can't avoid—death and taxes are two of them. But we also can't avoid challenge and change. We have to make choices in this life. And if you do nothing, that's a choice, too.

BASSETT: The wonderful thing is that with challenge and change come a ton of opportunities. Many opportunities in my life came from situations where I was challenged and I was forced to change. It opened a door and created an opportunity that I never dreamed possible. That took me to a whole new level of living a full life.

HIEMSTRA: When people are confronted with change that sort of comes at them, their usual response is to circle the wagons and try to hunker down a little bit, but that's not necessarily the best strategy. You have to try to open up the windows and come up with some alternatives for yourself.

BASSETT: What is the single most important element that makes you feel as if you have a sense of control over your future and your security?

HIEMSTRA: Knowing what matters most to you, and trying to get some sense of what that is. Some people are very, very strategic in how they're going to do that. I dream about winning the lottery but it's not like I'll ever take the sequence of steps that will ensure that happens—because a moment that's more important to me is going to get in the way. If you understand that core value, then you make choices about the stuff that you can control.

> To me the key is to recognize that challenge and change create growth opportunities, and there are always open windows. You're an example for your children, you're an example for your friends, you're an example for your coworkers. And what are they going to see in you when you're put to the test? I've certainly been through challenges in my own life, and I have used those challenges to create opportunities for something new and exciting in life. And that's what's worked for me because what choice do we have?

Let's take a look at a man who embraced change as creator and spokesman of a powerful franchise with a logo we all recognize today: "Finger-lickin' good."

COLONEL SANDERS

HARLAND SANDERS, LATER KNOWN AS COLONEL SANDERS, was the founder of Kentucky Fried Chicken (KFC), one of the largest fast-food chains in existence. He was born in Henryville, Indiana, where his father died when he was five. Since his mother worked full-time to make ends meet, Harland dropped out of school in the seventh grade to cook for and help take care of his family. But when his mother remarried a violent man who beat Harland, he ran away from home. He enlisted as a private in the army at sixteen, lying about his age. Later he worked a variety of jobs during his twenties and thirties, including steamboat pilot, insurance salesman, railroad fireman, and farmer.

By the time he was forty, Sanders owned a service station in Corbin, Kentucky, where he cooked chicken for his customers and passers-by. His savory meals became legendary, and he became head chef at a motel restaurant that seated 142 people. During the next nine years, Harland developed and perfected his secret chicken recipe in which he began using the very herbs and spices that are still used today by KFC. One of the first to use a pressure cooker to enhance flavor and speed up the cooking process, Sanders was made an honorary Kentucky Colonel in 1935 by Governor Ruby Laffoon. Hence the name Colonel Sanders.

All was going well until change and challenge knocked on the colonel's door. When the state decided to enlarge the Interstate 75 highway to run just adjacent to his property, he was forced to sell. Now, with no outlet for his food, Sanders lived off his social security checks and could easily have given up, but that was not the stuff that Harland Sanders was made of. Instead of backing down in the face of challenge and change, he took his now-famous chicken recipe on the road, driving from one restaurant to the next, cooking batches of chicken for the restaurant owners and their employees. If they liked his food (they always did), the owners paid him a nickel for each chicken meal sold, and in this way, he created new opportunities for himself. Confident of the quality of his chicken, the colonel devoted himself to creating a wave of franchises that took the country by storm.

Sanders's devoted work ethic and determination helped him transform his original small business into one of the largest and most recognizable fast-food chains in the country, while he became one of the most instantly recognizable people in the world. In 1964, he sold his company headquarters to a group of investors. He retired as head cook but retained the position of spokesman for the company for most of the rest of his life. In his final years, he created the Colonel Harland Sanders Trust and the Colonel Harland Sanders Charitable Organization, to aid other charities and fund scholarships. In 1980, he died of leukemia at age ninety. To this day, his trusts donate to groups such as the Trillium Health Care Center, where a wing of the facility was named after Colonel Sanders. ❧

This is one of my favorite success stories because Colonel Sanders's Core Story was one of extreme challenge. He didn't really start his career until he was in forties and it didn't take off until he was in his fifties. Sanders was dealt a major challenge and he found an open window. In the end, he lived life on his own terms, passionate about his talents and using his money to help others —all with no college degree.

UPHEAVALS AND CHALLENGES

During the last decade, along with major political and social upheavals, there have been gradual but steady lifestyle changes that tend to go unnoticed when they're happening—just as you hardly notice the constant change in your children growing up since you see them every day. Here are just a few examples of global changes that have occurred right before our eyes and affected us in a major way, whether we know it or not. Like any change, many of them have presented challenges, but all of them have brought some type of positive improvements to our lives.

Flying. After the 9/11 terrorist attacks, our travel experience has changed for good. Gone are the days we could get onto a plane with scissors, knives, and metal knitting needles. Today, we have to remove our shoes at security, discard bottles of unused water, and endure random searches. But although we

> # Day 10
> ## Pro-Active Action
> ASSIGNMENT
>
> Take a look at the challenges and changes in your life right now. Write them down in your journal. Are they causing you stress, anxiety, worry, and fear? In order to embrace challenge and change so you can find opportunities for growth, ask yourself these questions:
>
> 1. What do I want in this situation? What makes me anxious about it?
> 2. What opportunities could arise if I were willing to see this situation from a different perspective?
> 3. What can I do to create opportunities?
> 4. Am I willing to make the necessary change?

are inconvenienced by these extra safety precautions, we can travel more safely.

Cell phones. Remember when the term "blackberry" meant a fruit? Today, the Blackberry, the iPhone, and other high-tech tools are considered essential in the arsenals of corporate CEOs as well as soccer moms. We have become "reachable" no matter where we are or what we're doing. Although cell phones are sometimes annoying, they also can be a godsend in times of urgency, considering how fast-paced and spread-out our world has become. Technology, when used wisely, can benefit our quality of life immeasurably.

Texting. A sort of shorthand among peers and other groups (how R U?), texting has far surpassed phone calls and emails as the favored form of communication. These days we can communicate without having to engage in a full-on conversation. This is perfect for checking in when you are busy and unable to talk at that moment.

Google. Forget the Encyclopedia Britannica. We have Google, a form of instant gratification when it comes to doing research. It has become so popular that the brand-name noun has become a verb: we Google this or Google that. We can sit in our living room or office, never leave, and have the world at our fingertips.

Facebook. More than 300 million users log on to a website called Facebook to talk with their buddies, share photographs, and find long-lost friends. This service, originally created for Harvard students, has taken the world by storm. It has literally changed many people's lives, helping them stay connected and up-to-date with friends and loved ones on a daily basis without having to call each one individually every day. This is extremely helpful when it comes to remembering those birthdays.

Blogging: Everyone who has anything to say writes it on the Internet in "blogs." Believe it or not, there are more than 100 million of these Web logs discussing politics, health, redecorating, and what to eat for breakfast. Even though blogs can be negative and create information overload, they're a great way to build community and share ideas with people whom you would otherwise never come in contact with.

GPS. If you have a lousy sense of direction, it doesn't matter any more. You can have a GPS system in your car and on your phone that will guide you wherever you need to go in a calming voice that makes you feel secure. But you need to be specific about the address or you could end up in a city by the same name in a different state. Imagine if this sort of technology were available in other areas of our lives? Well, it actually is, and it's called divine guidance. If you learn to trust your intuition, you will be guided by your own internal GPS system. Your life will become a lot easier to navigate, allowing you to relax and enjoy the ride, knowing that you're on course and headed in the right direction.

Cameras. Remember when you took your film to the camera store or the drug store to get it developed? Today, even grandma has a digital camera and most cell phones have photographic functions. You just click the shutter, download the photos, and view them immediately. The challenge lies in learning how to use the device, but once you learn, it's instant gratification at its best. No more hoping you got the shot, praying that the camera is in focus, or getting irritated that Uncle George blinked again. You can keep on shooting until you get a flattering photo of Uncle George . . . or of youself! Just click and edit out what you don't like. If only the rest of life were this simple.

Dating. Internet dating has become the primo way to meet people. From youngsters to seniors, finding love on the Internet has outmoded going to bars or parties. What a wonderful way to become the co-creator of your relationships. No more waiting for Mr. Right to magically appear on your doorstep, no more dealing with geographical or social restrictions. While you must use caution with someone you have just met, Internet dating has broadened the horizon by giving you the opportunity to be more pro-active in choosing and finding a perfect mate. Be adventurous, open up to possibility, keep your eyes wide open, and, above all, enjoy the process.

Aging. From the clothes we wear to an international plastic surgery epidemic, few people look their real ages any more. It is in vogue to call forty the new thirty, fifty the new forty, and so on. But the good news is that the average U.S. life expectancy has risen from 75.4 years in 1990 to 77.6 years as reported in the July 2010 *Harvard Health Letter.* Given these encouraging statistics, why wouldn't we want to take pride in our appearance as we do our best to age gracefully? We just need to stay healthy and not go overboard in our lifestyle. The truth is that people are living longer and aging better.

Alternative medicine. Herbal supplements, acupuncture, and vitamin therapy have become mainstream. We've gone from treating a symptom to treating the whole person, focusing on prevention and changes in lifestyle like exercising and eating right. As skeptical as some may be about this new medicine and the extra effort it takes to be responsible for our own well-being, it has had an increasingly positive effect on our overall health. The trend toward awareness of lifestyle changes and natural remedies is a valuable addition to our overall health care and will continue to grow and affect us positively, both individually and as a nation.

Buying organic. With the onset of genetically modified foods and toxic insecticides, many of us are opting for organic produce. This trend is hailed by first lady Michelle Obama, who planted the first organic vegetable garden on the White House grounds. While organic produce costs a little more, its benefits are priceless. As public awareness grows and the health benefits of this trend become more widespread, the cost of organic produce will adjust, making an organic way of life more accessible to all.

Going green. We bring cloth bags to the supermarket, we use energy-saving lightbulbs, we buy hybrid cars, and we turn off lights when we leave a room. We are becoming conscious of over-consumerism and are trying to turn over a new leaf with sustainable gardens, natural textiles, and alternate sources for electricity. As sad as our environmental neglect has been, our new-found conscientious attitudes are wonderful ways to bring together families and communities. As a united force, we can reverse the damage caused by ignorance and show our kids we care about them and the planet they'll be inheriting.

THREE STEPS TO CONTROL YOUR FEAR

Some of my most potent opportunities have come from situations where I was challenged enough to *have* to do something. I was forced to face my fears and to change, which opened a door to an opportunity I'd never dreamed possible. My fear catapulted me to a whole new level of life experience as it urged me to open the door, look outside the box, and come up with some alternatives that were new and exciting.

Glen Hiemstra, our expert futurist, designates three actions that will help you control your fear in the face of challenge and change:

1. Get current with the latest technology. If you're not skilled technologically, it's time to learn some cool networking techniques that will help you connect to other people and the world at large. Then you won't have the sense that the world is leaving you behind.

2. Improve your personal communication skills. Nothing will get you further in life than being able to communicate clearly and directly. Then you can ask for what you want with no confusion.

3. Complexify yourself. This made-up word means that you need to discover your array of choices. Glen suggests you find a book on science fiction or management theory and read it. Or find a book on the history of the Great Depression and see how your ancestors coped during difficult times. Whatever attracts you, learn more and become a far more interested and interesting person.

People often say, "You know, I'd really like to do something important. I'd like to be part of something that matters."

If you fear the future, you will ruin your chances of making a difference because you will react to life with paranoia instead of hope. Like a tortoise hiding in its shell, people become so overwhelmed by fear, they are paralyzed, unable to move in any direction. There is a proven neurological response to fear that causes people to shut down at the precise moment when they need to make an important decision. Once the response kicks in, they either can't make any decision whatsoever, or they make the wrong one based on fearful projections about the future.

The challenge is to stay outside the boundary, Glen tells us, and find some alternatives to unfreeze yourself. You might engage in physical exercise like a hike or a bike ride to try to break up some of the stress. The point is that doing the three actions listed above can open you to change and the possibilities that come with it.

Most successful people do this on a steady basis. Glen regularly tells his groups, "The next twenty years are all about a mission. We've become more sustainable on a planetary basis, developing personal economies... that are maybe a little bit more modest but mostly just more sustainable, greener, and so forth."

At some time or another, we all must change the way we think, act, respond, and, most of all, the way we view the world and other people in it. It's time to stop the thought patterns that keep you stuck, like "I know it won't work." If that's your belief, then it won't. No excuses or reasons for not doing something, no matter how intricately thought out and expressed, can help you get what you want. Embracing challenge and change and turning them into opportunity is the solution.

> **Day 11**
>
> **Pro-Active Action**
>
> ASSIGNMENT
>
> Identify a change that is challenging you right now. Write about it in your journal. Ask yourself what you can do to turn this change into opportunity. Shift your thinking from fearful and re-active into pro-active. Only then can you find the open windows that will help you move forward.

Re-Active to Pro-Active Attitude Adjustments

1. RE-ACTIVE: I view change as loss, resulting in pain, fear, and panic that I'll have to let go of something or someone who represented safety and security to me.
   PRO-ACTIVE: I see change as an inevitable and exhilarating part of life. I accept that as I let go of my old, comfortable, familiar ways, I am creating space for new and exciting experiences to enter into my life.
2. RE-ACTIVE: I believe that my challenges are proof that life isn't fair. I am a victim of an unpredictable world.
   PRO-ACTIVE: I am embracing life's challenges as opportunities for my personal growth and development. I am the co-creator of my life. There is nothing that God and the universe have put in my path that I cannot handle.

3. **RE-ACTIVE:** I rush around in a state of desperation, anxiety, and panic, thinking that I'm responsible for fixing everyone and everything in my life.

   PRO-ACTIVE: I can distinguish between what is my responsibility to take care of and what is not. I can determine what is and isn't within my power to control and change.

THE Solution

CHAPTER SEVEN

The Art of Healthy Detachment

The tighter you squeeze, the less you have.

—Zen adage

An old man lived a quiet life, practicing equanimity and detachment. The poorest man in his village, he was resting peacefully under a tree when a wild horse, a beautiful white stallion, approached him. When the local villagers saw the horse standing next to the old man, they said, "Yesterday, you were poor. Today, you are no longer poor because you own a horse. You must be very happy for you are a lucky old man."

The old man nodded his head and said, *"Maybe so, maybe not."*

The next day when the old man woke up, he walked outside to find that the horse was gone. When the locals walked by and there was no horse, they said, "Old man, yesterday you were wealthy. You owned a horse. Today you have no horse so you are poor again. You are very unlucky and you must be very disappointed."

The old man nodded his head and said, *"Maybe so, maybe not."*

The very next day, when the old man sat beneath his favorite tree, the horse came back to him. But he was not alone. He had brought with him an entire herd of wild horses. Word spread in the village as they all gathered to watch the old man's herd prancing around. A woman said, "Old man, you are truly blessed. You are a rich man now and you must be very happy."

The old man nodded his head and said, *"Maybe so, maybe not."*

That afternoon, the old man's son was riding one of the wild horses in town when he fell and broke his leg. One of the villagers brought him home to the old man and said, "You poor old man. Your son had a terrible injury and he can no longer do hard work on your farm. How awful for you. You must be very angry at the horses. You are so unlucky."

The old man nodded his head and said, *"Maybe so, maybe not."*

The following day, a military recruiting agency visited the village and demanded that all eligible men be drafted into the war. When the recruitment officers got to the old man's son, they saw his broken leg and excused him from service. When the officers took their sons away, the villagers gathered around the old man. They said, "You are so lucky. Because your son broke his leg, he is still here with you and ours are gone. You are a very lucky man."

And once more the old man said,
"Maybe so, maybe not. You just never know."

The moral of the story: It's important to stay in balance when the rest of the world is doing its dance around you.

Just imagine how free and happy you'd feel if you could stay calm and poised, just like the old man in the story, no matter what is going on. How much physical, emotional, and mental energy would you save if you avoided upsets, anger, moodiness, fear, anxiety, worry, insecurity, and the unknown? Like the old man, it's time to practice inner equanimity and detachment. You *can* do it! You can learn the skill of under-reacting through healthy detachment. It's hard to see the big picture, and in many cases, maybe you aren't meant to. But you can learn something from whatever occurs. If you can develop enough detachment to recognize that the universe is at play for your good, you'll recognize the teaching in each event that comes into your life. To find inner peace, you must first gain some degree of inner detachment.

Ask yourself the following questions: Are you unable to let go of unhealthy relationships and destructive people? Do you feel needy and insecure in relationships? Do you turn to bad habits such as drinking, overeating, or sleeping too much when you feel down or depressed? Do you have a hard time staying in your personal strength when others are unkind to you? Do you lose your sense of self in the face of criticism and negative judgments? Are you unable to let go of irritation, anxiety, and unpleasant feelings after difficult or challenging interactions? Are you uncomfortable being alone? Do you overreact to stressful events or situations that come into your life unexpectedly? Do you buy into feelings of jealousy and insecurity? Are you someone who tries to "fix" people who have problems? Do you have abandonment issues?

If you answered yes to any of the above questions, then you have some work to do toward developing a healthy sense of inner detachment.

DEFINING DETACHMENT

I'd like to define detachment in terms we can all understand. But first let's look at how Buddhism defines detachment, which lies at the foundation of the most basic Buddhist teachings.

It is said that in ancient times, the Buddha found attachment and desire to be the source of all suffering. Buddhism defines attachment as exaggerated seeking and clinging to an object, person, or idea, viewing attached people as those who devote large amounts of energy to obtaining the objects of their desires. According to this definition, if we don't have *it,* whatever it is, we obsess about it, try to get it, and constantly mourn its absence. If we *do* have it, we fear losing it and desperately try to hold on to it. In this vicious cycle of grasping, our minds never rest. But the truth is that the more we grasp at something or someone out of desperation, the more we set ourselves up for loss and neediness. Our need becomes a self-fulfilling prophecy.

Healthy detachment is a state in which we overcome our cloying desire for things or other people. Dr. Ramez Sasson, teacher of positive thinking, defines healthy detachment as an inner state of calmness, or being uninvolved emotionally and mentally. But don't confuse healthy detachment with indifference. Indifferent people don't care about anything or anyone on a deep emotional level and often have a hard time with, or are incapable of, intimacy. Those who learn to detach in a healthy way, however, are compassionate and caring as they calmly accept the good and the bad equally. By the way, possessing inner detachment doesn't mean your life will suddenly be worry-free or that your problems will simply disappear. You'll still face disturbances, but your attitude will change, allowing you to act calmly and with common sense without catering to negative emotions, moodiness, or insecurities.

When it comes to intimate relationships, many of us tend to vacillate. We may be overly dependent on our partner, suffering from the "I can't live without you" syndrome. Or we may be suffering from the opposite, "I need space, you're smothering me" syndrome. Both are extreme. They cause anguish and suffering, leading to insurmountable problems.

The optimum position is the neutral, middle point of interdependence. A healthy interdependent relationship sees each person standing in his or her own light, creating a larger light that is the relationship. Take a look at the Relationship Continuum Scale below, and see where your relationships fall. (The numbered definitions are derived from the *Oxford Dictionary.*)

THE RELATIONSHIP CONTINUUM SCALE

DEPENDENT	INTERDEPENDENT/UNDEPENDENT	INDEPENDENT
1. contingent on or determined by 2. requiring someone or something for financial, emotional, or other support 3. unable to do without: *people dependent on drugs* 4. subordinate to another 5. a person who relies on another, esp. a family member, for financial support: *a single man with no dependent.*	Interdependence is a dynamic of being mutually and physically responsible to and sharing a common set of principles with others. This concept differs distinctly from "dependence" in that an interdependent relationship implies that all participants are emotionally, economically, ecologically, and/or morally free. Some people advocate freedom or independence as a sort of ultimate good; others do the same with devotion to one's family, community, or society. Interdependence recognizes the truth in each position and weaves them together. Two states that cooperate with each other are said to be interdependent. Interdependence can also be defined as interconnectedness and reliance on each other socially and economically.	1. free from outside control; not depending on another's authority; self-governing 2. not influenced or affected by others; impartial 3. not depending on another for livelihood or subsistence 4. capable of thinking or acting for oneself 5. not connected with another or with each other; separate 6. not depending on something else for strength or effectiveness; freestanding

DEPENDENT	INTERDEPENDENT/UNDEPENDENT	INDEPENDENT
On the left side of the Relationship Continuum Scale is the overly dependent person. This type of person gets enmeshed in unhealthy attachments that have an addictive quality to them. A woman, for example, might get so overly attached to a desired partner that she feels she cannot possibly live without him. She hands over her power to him, deifying him and believing that he is the source of her very survival. The partner she is attached to could be abusive verbally or physically, but she justifies her behavior by trying even harder to hold on to him.	At the center of the Relationship Continuum Scale is the healthy position of the interdependent. These people recognize that they need other people in their lives for love, comfort, and support. Their relationships are based on healthy boundaries and mutual respect. They know that love and connectedness are a very important aspect of life and that although they can spend time alone, they enjoy the rewards and benefits of close and loving relationships.	On the other end of the Relationship Continuum Scale is the overly independent person. Independence is a position often taken by people who are so afraid of becoming engulfed in a relationship and losing themselves that they keep a big distance between themselves and others. They convince themselves that they don't need anyone in their lives; that they are self-sufficient, without needs or wants. They are incapable of creating close, intimate attachments.

ARE YOU AN UNHEALTHY DEPENDENT?

Have you ever noticed how happy you feel when you get what you want, because it satisfies your most profound desires? But problems arise when you want something that only someone other than yourself can give you. In this case, you may try to entice a partner into giving you what you think you need. You imagine she has the power to give you a sense of security with yourself. In fact, she *does* have that power—because you handed it to her. You have attached yourself to another person's will, opinions, and actions, creating feelings of insecurity and fear of abandonment for yourself. And you never truly get what you want. Instead, you are crestfallen when your love interest doesn't act how you want her to or, worse yet, doesn't seem to care.

We all tend to develop unhealthy attachments to people when we become needy. We believe that certain people add value or security to our lives in such a powerful way that we just can't live without them. We may become dependent or even addicted to them and give them our power, but this is a very dangerous and vulnerable place to operate from. We can make bad decisions about relationships, parenting, and career choices, based on our inability to detach.

But you can overcome this cycle by engaging your reasonable mind. It's time to take a serious, honest look at yourself and your unhealthy attachments, especially to people. Take control over your overwhelming desire patterns (addictions) by convincing yourself that the other person does *not* have anything you can't get on your own. If you overcome your addiction to a person, that person loses authority over you. Then, as a healthy, functioning, interdependent human being, you can live life fully and attract others who are healthy.

Letting go

- isn't about not caring or cutting yourself off. It's about accepting the fact that you can't control other people's behavior. That would be a violation of their boundaries.
- isn't about enabling. It's about giving others the dignity of making their own choices. It's letting them learn from the consequences of their own actions and behaviors.
- isn't about taking control. It means surrendering to a higher power and trusting that the outcome isn't entirely in your hands.
- isn't about changing or blaming. It's about taking responsibility for yourself and making the most of the talents and gifts you were given.

- isn't about caring *for* someone. It's caring *about* someone and caring *for* yourself.
- isn't about fixing someone else. It's about being supportive while maintaining healthy boundaries.
- isn't about judging. It's about recognizing that we are all human with our own individual issues to work on and paths to follow. It's about allowing another person to be a human being.
- isn't about being protective. It's about permitting another adult to face the consequences of the life he or she has chosen.
- isn't about denying, nagging, scolding, arguing, or trying to change anyone else. It's about accepting people for who they are and doing the same for yourself.
- isn't about trying to adjust circumstance to meet your desires. It's about giving up the need to manipulate everything and everyone, taking each day as it comes, and cherishing yourself, no matter what happens.
- isn't about regretting the past. It's about utilizing the gifts and wisdom you got from past experiences, regardless of how painful they were. It's about turning your gaze toward a positive future.
- isn't about being selfish and not wanting to share with someone else. It's about becoming comfortable with being alone.
- isn't about avoiding intimacy altogether. It's about getting close to another person without losing yourself.
- isn't about detaching from everything. It's about learning the difference between healthy and unhealthy detachment.

DEVELOPING HEALTHY DETACHMENT

In her best seller *Codependent No More,* Melody Beatty calls healthy detachment an act and an art. She believes that "detachment can become a habitual response in the same manner that obsessing, worrying, and controlling become habitual responses—with practice."

Healthy detachment is about

- allowing others to be themselves.
- reversing the need to rescue, save, or fix anyone who is ill, dysfunctional, or irrational.
- reversing the need to be rescued, saved, or fixed yourself.
- giving other people the space to be themselves.
- disengaging from overly enmeshed or dependent relationships.
- being willing to accept that you cannot control other people or situations.
- developing and maintaining a safe emotional distance from someone to whom you previously gave away your power.
- establishing emotional boundaries between you and those who are overly dependent on you.
- feeling your own feelings when you see someone else falter, being neither responsible nor guilty.
- facing life with a healthy perspective.
- recognizing the need to avoid uncontrollable and unchangeable realities.
- exercising emotional self-protection to avoid emotional devastation.
- allowing your loved ones to accept responsibility for their actions as you avoid scolding them.
- avoiding being hurt, abused, or taken advantage of by others, especially those with whom you have been overly enmeshed.

Now you need to know *when* you should detach. Melody Beatty suggests we do it "when we can't stop thinking, talking about, or worrying about someone or something; when our emotions are churning and boiling; when we feel like we *have* to do something about someone because we can't stand it another minute; when we're hanging on by a thread, and it feels like the single thread is frayed; and when we believe we can no longer live with the problem we've been trying to live with."

A good rule of thumb is: *You need to detach most when it seems the least likely or possible thing to do.*

This is a very humbling but true realization.

Developing inner detachment is no different from developing any other skill. It requires an understanding of detachment and the desire to achieve it, which takes patience, practice and skills. Based on the research of Dr. Bruce Perry, a clinician, researcher, and internationally recognized authority on children in crisis, here are some powerful steps for developing healthy detachment from toxic relationships.

STEP ONE: Once you've identified your toxic people and areas of dysfunction from the list for your Day 12 assignment, spend time thinking through your responses to gain complete understanding about why you are in these toxic relationships and why it is so hard to detach.

STEP TWO: Identify irrational or false beliefs in your toxic relationship that stop you from detaching. Replace these beliefs with healthy, rational, honest ones.

STEP THREE: Identify why you feel hurt or threatened by the relationship.

STEP FOUR: Admit that the other person or situation is irrational, unhealthy, toxic, or addictive. No matter what you say or do, you cannot change or control this reality. But the one thing you can change is you. Stop imagining things to be better than they really are. Be honest about what the relationship really is or isn't.

STEP FIVE: Map out the reasons why there is no need to feel guilty over being emotionally detached from the relationship. Let go of the emotional "hooks."

Step Six: Affirm yourself as someone who deserves healthy, wholesome relationships. See yourself as a good person at home, at work, and in the community.

Step Seven: Seek support in therapy, from friends, and from support groups for letting go of your enmeshment in an unhealthy relationship.

Step Eight: Meditate and pray for the strength to detach from unhealthy people and situations.

Step Nine: Allow no one and nothing to affect your good feelings about yourself.

Step Ten: Practice, practice, practice the fine art of letting go. It takes time.

Step Eleven: Go back to Step One and go through the steps all over again.

Unhealthy attachments come in many different forms—not just to people, but also to the underlying belief systems that urge us to look outside of ourselves for strength and support. These beliefs tell us that we're not strong or capable enough to take care of ourselves. To some degree, within all of us resides a frightened child who still believes we need something or someone more powerful than us, or we could die. This unhealed, scarred child within is looking for a "magic pill"—a person who will take away our fear and vulnerability.

Below you will find examples of various types of unhealthy attachments. See if you can recognize yourself, but when you do, don't be despondent. Instead, tell yourself there is a light at the end of the tunnel, a light which is you, once you allow yourself to stand in the strength of your own light.

Day 12

Pro-Active Action

ASSIGNMENT

Make a list identifying the people from whom you need to detach. Then review the following symptoms of toxic relationships. In your journal, identify which people fit into the various categories:

- You find it hard to let go of someone because you feel addicted.
- A person is emotionally unavailable to you.
- A person is coercive, threatening, and intimidating.
- Someone is punitive or abusive to you.
- The relationship is nonproductive and creates feelings of insecurity.
- A partner is overly dependent on you or you are overly dependent on the partner.
- A partner has the power to impact your feelings about yourself.
- You are a chronic fixer, rescuer, or enabler.
- Your false sense of obligation and loyalty won't allow you to let go.
- You view this person as helpless, lost, out of control, or self-destructive.
- Your partner manipulates and cons you.
- You won't let go because of guilt.
- When you are with this person, you feel bad about yourself.
- This person scolds you.
- You start thinking that the person is right about your shortcomings.
- You feel fearful and anxious about losing this person.
- You fantasize that a partner will change into what you want him or her to be.
- You and your partner compete for control.
- You and your partner continue to bring up past hurts with no forgiveness.
- Your wants and needs are ignored in the relationship.

CATEGORIES OF UNHEALTHY ATTACHMENTS

Here are seven areas where detachment is necessary. Which are at play in your life?

1. Toxic unhealthy relationships. These relationships deplete vital energy and life force. You recognize them when you feel addicted to someone who is harmful to you, yet you still stay. You justify the attachment by thinking, "Maybe this is all I deserve. Maybe they're right about me, that I'm the one with the problem."

Perhaps you've attracted a self-centered, selfish, narcissistic partner who knows how to draw you back in. You stay, hoping the other person will change, but he won't. These relationships are highly toxic and hard to end, especially if you're needy, damaged, or have low self-esteem. This kind of relationship holds you hostage, occupying your mind with constant worry and concern, trapping you in a constant cycle of unrequited love and fear of abandonment.

Tina Turner

Tina Turner was eighteen when she began singing with rhythm and blues star Ike Turner in the late 1950s. Eventually they married and, along with their band, became known as the Ike and Tina Turner Revue. They became very successful, touring, recording, and making their name with a huge hit, "Proud Mary." But there was trouble in paradise. Tina had chosen a toxic partner who would bring her a great deal of pain and suffering until she could finally break free.

By the mid-1970s, Turner's personal life and marriage began to fail due to Ike's refusal to accept outside management, as well as the cost of maintaining his voracious cocaine habit. Touring dates declined and record sales dipped. In July 1976, Tina left Ike abruptly amid a violent argument and a history of physical abuse. Frightened for her life, she fled with thirty-six cents in her pocket and a gas station credit card, spending several months hiding out with friends. She cleaned her friends' houses and lived on food stamps, happy to be free from the abuse that had characterized her life for so long. Ike and Tina were divorced in 1976.

Tina found solace in the Nichiren Buddhist faith, finally gathering the courage to strike out on her own. Building a solo career and leaning on her newfound faith, she soon released her album *Private Dancer,* with the number one hit "What's Love Got to Do With It?" She appeared on the cover of *Rolling Stone* magazine, took home two American Music Awards, and won two Grammys. As American film critic Kurt Loder says, "After a quarter of a century, Tina Turner was an overnight sensation." ❧

2. External approval and validation. When you stop listening to your heart, your instincts, and your desires, you become preoccupied with trying to meet the needs and expectations of others. You become a people pleaser, with your self-esteem focused on what others think about you. This makes you a poor decision-maker, as you second-guess yourself and look to others for insight, validation, and self-worth. Your instincts have been overpowered by your need for approval; you fear that revealing your true self will result in rejection and abandonment. You also fear making a bad decision that could result in more anxiety or depression.

The truth is that approval and validation are inside jobs. You need to be your own biggest fan; affirmations can be helpful as you talk to yourself in positive ways, believe in yourself, and accept love. Drop your expectations of being perfect. We are all works in progress, constantly improving and growing.

Richel Rene "Chely" Wright

WHEN CHELY WRIGHT, AN AWARD-WINNING COUNTRY music artist, was growing up in rural Kansas in the 1970s, she knew she was "different." She also knew she was going to hell because she was gay. As an adult, she dated men and succeeded in keeping her secret from fellow artists (she dated Brad Paisley), fans, and even her family and friends, convinced that secrecy was the only way to maintain her career: "There had never been an openly gay country artist. I knew I had to duck and cover."

Eventually her carefully maintained facade crumbled. After a breakup with a girlfriend, Chely wound up in her Nashville home, determined to end her painful secrets and her fear that external judgments would derail her hard-earned career. She said, "I stared in the bathroom mirror with a 9mm gun in my mouth. When you have a weapon in your mouth, you kinda realize you're at the end of your rope. I felt like I was outside my body, watching this horrific experience go down. I couldn't believe how detached from myself I had become. How big this moat was between the different parts of myself and how completely unstitched I had become."

Chely didn't complete her suicide attempt. Instead, she decided to turn to her talents and write some new songs to heal her soul. It helped because the words she was inspired to write were truthful and uncompromising—words that forced her to reconnect to her most basic truth. "How can I talk about this album if I don't come out?" she wondered. "There are songs about a breakup and a broken heart. People are going to ask, 'What relationship were you in?' What'll I do? Make up a boyfriend from Buenos Aires?'"

First she told her collaborative songwriter, Rodney Crowell, that she was gay. Then she told everyone else and readied herself for the onslaught. But after her public disclosure, Chely began to feel lighter, as if her burden was lifted. "I feel incredible," she says. "Emotional and liberating. When I tell my story, I hear how incredibly sad it is—hearing about a little girl going to a horse pasture to pray three times a day to not be something she naturally was. It's sad to look back at the incredible charade I felt I was forced to endure. When you hold onto a lie, it becomes part of your future. When you admit a lie, it becomes part of your past. My lie, my secret, the admission of my truth is now behind me. I like that it can be part of my history. The future for me is truth."

3. Expecting a specific outcome or "how things should be." By being obsessively attached to a specific outcome, you don't enjoy the experience and you're not leaving room for a miracle. Obsessive thinking leads to second-guessing. You ask yourself, "Is it even possible? Do I really want it?" Or you say, "I need for this to happen so I can feel secure and validate my worth. I won't be happy until I get it."

Over-attachment to any outcome is unhealthy because paths change along the way and you need to stay open for a change that might lead you to a goal you never imagined. When you are the co-creator of your life, you're making room for a divine force that wants only your highest good, something hard to recognize from a limited earthly perspective. Of course you want to make plans and set goals. Go ahead, jump in, do the groundwork, and dream big. But don't forget to focus on the journey and enjoy getting there. Next time you're intensely focusing on the outcome of a relationship, a job, or anything else, ask for the outcome to be "this or something better for the greatest good of all concerned."

Neale Donald Walsh

Before Neale Donald Walsh wrote his best seller *Conversations with God* in 1995, he suffered a series of shattering events: a fire that destroyed his belongings, the end of his marriage, and a car accident in which he broke his neck. He was homeless for a year, living in a tent in Jackson Hot Springs, Oregon, and recycling aluminum cans to buy food.

He eventually landed a part-time job in broadcasting and worked his way into full-time employment as a syndicated radio talk-show host. Things were looking up, but this was not the way Walsh had expected his life to look or feel. When he awoke one night feeling empty and filled with despair, he wrote an anguished letter to God. "What does it take to make life work?" he scratched across his yellow legal pad.

Neale says that he heard a soft, kind voice answer that question and several more. In fact, he could hardly write fast enough to jot them all down. Some hours later, he laid down his pen and realized he had just been in a dialogue with God. It had felt like he was taking dictation. His original handwritten notes would become *Conversations with God.*

In his book *When Everything Changes, Change Everything,* Walsh describes how our sense of safety is threatened when our way of life is radically changed and nothing turns out like we thought it would. "Talk about feeling threatened," he writes. "I broke my neck in a car accident and had to stop working during months of rehabilitation while an insurance company was busy figuring out every possible way to reduce or eliminate compensation. All the while I was working through the pain of my separation from my life partner and our children. As my life dramatically changed course, I wound up homeless for a year living in the weather, walking the streets, panhandling for pocket change, and collecting soda cans and beer bottles to scrape together enough money to eat (some days it didn't go so well), with a sleeping bag and a tent, two pairs of jeans, three shirts, and a few odds and ends as my only possessions."

Today, Walsh is a spiritual messenger whose best-selling books and lectures profoundly touch the world. His books have been translated into twenty-seven languages and people say that he has inspired important changes in their day-to-day lives—an outcome that Neale had never imagined.

4. Material wealth alone. When you recognize that peace, happiness, and security come from within, you can detach from relying on the external environment and material success to bring you satisfaction. Money and material things offer validation of your worth and provide you with a sense of security. It's healthy and normal to strive for financial success, security, and material things—to a certain extent—but obsessive over-attachment is dangerous. There is always the potential for loss, and then what are you worth? If you determine your self-worth by your portfolio or the size of your home, you're setting yourself up for failure. It's fine to want nice things and financial security, but how attached are you to having these things determine your happiness? Find your passion and mission in life for they are the key to lasting happiness, security, and contentment.

Guy Laliberté

As a child in Quebec City, Canada, Guy Laliberté dreamed about traveling the world as a circus performer. In 1973, at age fourteen, he joined a folk music group and earned a modest living playing the accordion and harmonica on the streets of Quebec. Never focused on making money, he loved performing, telling stories, and listening to other people talk about their travels.

Four years later, he'd saved enough money to buy a ticket to London, where he fell asleep the first night on a park bench. Over a year, he traveled and met other street performers who taught him how to eat fire, juggle, and walk on stilts. Guy never missed an opportunity to ask friends about their experiences, ideas, and dreams, which he collected like precious stones. Considering these tidbits more valuable than money, Laliberté was gathering ideas and images for how his future shows would look.

In 1979, he did something revolutionary—he combined elements of dance, theater, and gymnastics, redefining the concept of the "circus." In 1984, he cofounded the Cirque du Soleil with a partner, Daniel Gautier. In three years, they gained a great reputation and Guy brought the circus to the Los Angeles Arts Festival, using every penny he could muster and beg from his troupe. All of this he did with no thoughts of making money. He was simply doing what he loved best. To him, nothing else mattered.

By 1991, the Cirque du Soleil had grown from 73 to 1,400 employees with offices on three continents. In 2000, Guy bought out his partner and doubled the number of employees over the next four years. In 2002, he was named one of *Time* magazine's most influential people. This man who started out walking on stilts for a handout ended up on *Forbes* magazine's list of billionaires. He said, "I am blessed for what I have, but I believed in it from the beginning. Today, the dream is the same: I still want to travel, I still want to entertain, and I most certainly still want to have fun." ❧

5. Controlling others. When you try to control other people's thoughts, feelings, or behaviors with "You have to, you ought to, and you should," you're engaging in codependent behavior. Attempting to control others will create anxiety and anger because you have no power over anyone else, even if it appears temporarily that you do. When you really examine the unhealthy attachment of attempting to control others, you'll see that nothing good can come from it.

Just let people be, accept them for who they are, or let them go. When you can detach with love and establish healthy expectations, you see people for who they are. You realize that you can't make anyone think like you, feel like you, or behave like you. Everyone has the right to choose how to live their lives, which creates an opportunity for you to learn the art of unconditional love.

Melody Beattie

Melody Beattie is one of America's most beloved self-help authors and a household name in addiction and recovery circles. Her father left home when she was a toddler. Her mother was a classic codependent; Melody recalls, "If my mother had a migraine, she wouldn't take an aspirin. She believed in suffering."

Beattie began drinking at age twelve, was a full-blown alcoholic at thirteen, and became a heroin junkie by eighteen, running with a crowd who robbed pharmacies for drugs. When she was caught, she was mandated, "Go to treatment for as long as it takes, or go to jail."

She continued doing drugs while in mandatory treatment until she had what she calls a spiritual epiphany. "I was on the lawn smoking dope," she says, "when the world turned this purplish color. Everything looked connected like a Monet painting. It wasn't a hallucination. It was what the Big Book of Alcoholics Anonymous calls 'a spiritual awakening.' Until then, I'd felt entitled to use drugs. I finally realized that if I put half as much energy into doing the right things as I had into doing the wrong things, I could do anything."

After eight months of treatment, Beattie married a former alcoholic who was a prominent and respected counselor. They had two children, but although she had stopped drinking and using drugs, Melody found herself sinking into despair when she discovered that her husband had been drinking and lying about it since before their marriage.

During her work with spouses of addicts at a treatment center, she realized that the very problems that had led to her alcoholism were still with her. She thought she was in pain about her husband's drinking and her inability to stop him, but she realized the problem was with her. What was she doing to herself when she tried to control her husband's behavior? The word "codependency" hadn't been coined yet, and she would be the one to do it.

Driven into the ground financially and emotionally by her husband's alcoholism, Melody turned her lifelong passion for writing into a career in journalism, focusing on the issues that had consumed her for years. Although the death of her twelve-year-old son Shane in a ski accident in 1991 almost destroyed her, Melody eventually picked up the pieces of her life again. "I wanted to die, but I kept waking up alive," she says. She began skydiving, mountain-climbing, and teaching others what she'd learned about grief.

Today, her twenty-four-year writing career has produced fifteen books published in twenty languages and hundreds of newspaper and magazine articles. A frequent guest on many national television shows, including *Oprah,* Melody is featured regularly in *Time, People,* and many other major periodicals around the world. ❧

6. Negative and obsessive thoughts. Once you understand the power of the mind, you'll see that you can choose how to interpret the circumstances of your life. Negative, depressing, self-defeating thinking is an unhealthy attachment—an addiction of sorts. Negative thinkers see themselves as victims of circumstance, unlucky, misunderstood, or just plain frustrated, quick to get caught up in negative, obsessive thinking to justify their unhappiness. Have you ever noticed that in a perverse sort of way, it feels good to wallow in self-pity and negativity? But only for a little while, since this kind of misery can lead to substance abuse or abuse of the people around you.

Depending on your perspective, you can see yourself as a helpless victim or a powerful co-creator of your life. The next time you are thinking or speaking negatively, stop and detach from your thoughts, let them go, and replace them with productive power thinking, which you will learn more about in Chapter 10.

Richard Carlson

STARTING AS A PSYCHOTHERAPIST IN CALIFORNIA, Richard Carlson ran a stress management center and published his first book in 1985. He was considered one of the foremost experts on happiness and stress reduction in the United States and around the world. Carlson's twelfth book, *Don't Sweat the Small Stuff—and It's All Small Stuff* hit the best-seller lists and stayed there for two consecutive years. *People* magazine named him one of the "Most Intriguing People in the World," and he was highly popular on the talk-show circuit, showing millions of people how to relax and not let the small stuff get the best of them.

Carlson, who died in December 2006 from a pulmonary embolism, had truly enjoyed his life. The following excerpt, one of my favorite ways to remind myself to under-react, is from *Don't Sweat the Small Stuff*:

> Whenever we're dealing with bad news, a difficult person, or a disappointment of some kind, most of us get into certain habits, ways of reacting to life—particularly adversity—that don't serve us very well. We overreact, blow things out of proportion, hold on too tightly, and focus on the negative aspects of life. When we are immobilized by little things—when we are irritated, annoyed and easily bothered—our (over) reactions not only make us frustrated but actually get in the way of getting what we want. We lose sight of the bigger picture, focus on the negative, and annoy other people who might otherwise help us. In short, we live our lives as if they were one great big emergency! We often rush around looking busy, trying to solve problems, but in reality, we are often compounding them. Because everything seems like such a big deal, we end up spending our lives dealing with one drama after another.

After a while we begin to believe that everything really is a big deal. We fail to recognize that the way we relate to our problems has a lot to do with how quickly and efficiently we resolve them. As I hope you will soon discover, when you learn the habit of responding to life with more ease, problems that seemed "insurmountable" will begin to seem more manageable. And even the "biggies," the things that are truly stressful, won't throw you off track as much as they once did.

Happily, there is another way to relate to life—a softer, more graceful path that makes life seem easier and the people in it more compatible. This other way of living involves replacing old habits of reaction with new habits of perspective. This new habits enable us to have richer, more satisfying, calmer lives.

7. Addictions to substances. When the pain gets too great, we believe that maybe something outside of ourselves will bring us comfort, strength, and relief. It's all too common to try to numb the pain with alcohol and drugs or stuff down feelings with overeating. You escape into a world where you think these things have the power to comfort you and make you feel better, at least temporarily. But the price of getting high is even higher because the more you use, the more you want to use, whether it's drugs, alcohol, or food. Everything becomes an excuse to eat, drink, or do drugs, whether you want to calm down, rev up, or mellow out. This attachment is both an emotional and a physical one.

The first step is admitting the addiction. The next step is deciding to abstain while you get help and support. Detaching from substance abuse will help you think more clearly, feel better, have more energy, sleep better, and feel better about yourself. How do you know when you have a substance addiction problem? It's simple. If you think you have a problem, you probably do.

Betty Ford

As a child, Betty Ford wanted to be a dancer, wife, and mother. But when her husband, Gerald Ford, was elected thirty-eighth president of the United States in 1974, she was catapulted into instant celebrity. Yet she had a terrible secret—she had been taking pain and sleeping medications since 1964, and she engaged in social drinking as well.

In 1978, Betty's family confronted her about her chemical dependency and she entered the Long Beach Naval Hospital for Drug and Alcohol Dependency. After her recovery, she became an advocate for drug and alcohol awareness, education, and treatment. In 1982, Ford and Leonard Firestone cofounded the Betty Ford Center in Rancho Mirage, California, for people with drug and alcohol dependencies. Today, it is regarded as one of the best treatment facilities in the United States, and Betty Ford is the chair of the center's board.

Now, at a time when she could be enjoying retirement, Ford works tirelessly to raise awareness about alcohol and drug addiction. She has been honored for her work related to cancer, arthritis, alcoholism, the disabled, women's rights, and women's health. In 1999, she and her husband received the Congressional Gold Medal for their dedication to public service and their humanitarian contributions.

UNDEPENDENCE

In her book *Codependent No More,* Melody Beattie explains that our inner child believes that we are basically unlovable and will never find the comfort we are so desperately seeking. Unfortunately, this false idea has become a deeply ingrained belief that results in seeing people as *not* being there, when in truth, they are. Our desperate need for help is blocking our ability to recognize and receive it when it arrives.

Why do we do this to ourselves? It is hardly ever deliberate, but most of us learned at a very young age that we needed someone else's love, approval, and emotional support to make our lives work. We thought we needed an external source of power for our very survival, and so we looked in all the wrong places for something that no one or nothing on the outside could provide. That's understandable and actually quite true for a child. But now, as adults, we're still letting our unhealed inner child run the show. Can you imagine letting a four-year-old choose your partner, your job, or how to spend your money? This is exactly what's taking place within us and it will continue to happen if we don't take the time and energy to heal this part of ourselves!

One of the themes here is to learn to be neither totally dependent nor totally independent. I like the term "undependent," coined by Melody Beattie. She believes that emotional security and our present level of insecurity are important issues to take into account when we are making decisions. Then we can strive to be undependent, if we so desire.

Here are six ways Beattie offers to achieve the liberated state of undependence:

1. Finish up business from childhood (your Core Story) as best you can. Grieve. Get some perspective. Figure out how childhood events are affecting you now as you refer back to your Core Story beliefs.
2. Nurture and cherish the frightened, vulnerable, needy child within. The child may never completely disappear, no matter how self-sufficient you become. Stress may cause the child to cry out. Unprovoked, the child may come out and demand attention when you least expect it.
3. Stop looking for happiness in other people. Your source of happiness and well-being is not inside others; it's inside you. Learn to center yourself in yourself.

4. Learn to be dependent upon yourself. Maybe other people haven't been there for you, but you always can be there for yourself.
5. Depend on your higher power, whatever name you have for him or her. Your spiritual beliefs can provide you with a strong sense of emotional security.
6. Strive for undependence. Begin examining ways that you are dependent, both emotionally and financially, on the people around you.

Healthy undependent people are those who

- allow for individuality.
- bring out the best qualities in themselves and others.
- maintain healthy boundaries with those around them.
- have a flexible attitude toward life and other people.
- are accepting and experience true intimacy.
- don't try to manipulate anyone else.
- know where they end and another person begins.
- ask honestly and directly for what they want.
- encourage self-sufficiency of others and recognize personal responsibilities.
- keep their side of the street clean.
- focus on their own lives, not on the lives of others.
- have differentiated and gained autonomy from their parents.
- are not addicted to any substance, object, or person.
- are neither dependent nor overly independent.
- recognize the need for emotional intimacy and close relationships, without becoming enmeshed.
- hold onto personal power and have high self-esteem.
- show care, compassion, and consideration with healthy detachment.
- accept and respect commitment.
- avoid trying to change or control others.

- accept limitations of themselves and others.
- feel free to state their beliefs, values, and thought.
- feel free to express their needs, wants, feelings, and to ask for support and love.
- engage in mutual problem-solving and decision-making.
- are assertive, not passive or aggressive.
- honestly share feelings without blaming and accusing others of causing them.
- start sentences with "I . . ." instead of "you made me . . ."

The joy of being an undependent person will be clear when you have tasted the freedom of releasing your desperation and being helpful to others. You get their support back, but you are ultimately relying on yourself.

Buddhist precepts consider all attachment as unhealthy, but for the purposes of this book, I'm using a broader definition of attachment, in which *healthy* attachments are a benefit to our lives. Dr. Bruce Perry defines attachment as the capacity to form and maintain healthy emotional relationships. He sees healthy attachment as a core strength that begins in early childhood. As infants being bathed, fed, rocked, and caressed, we are creating the roots of attachment, the capacity to form and maintain healthy emotional relationships. This includes the concepts of responsibility and commitment to yourself and others.

Establish a list of things, ideas, goals, and responsibilities to which you want to be healthily attached. Make the commitment to yourself and anyone else involved. Define what commitment means to you.

This particular chapter was quite humbling for me to write because I had to admit that I needed people, something I used to be afraid to do—until I learned the difference between unhealthy and healthy dependence. It is actually powerful and healthy to need others to some extent, but when does the need become an addiction?

Does a lack of need indicate narcissism? These are the questions you ask yourself when you admit to needing others.

The answers are in your heart. You know deep down when you're operating from an unhealthy perspective. Be honest with yourself so you can move to the next level of healthy living. It's all about finding balance and understanding the importance of being your own parachute. It's time to examine your life, your relationships, your attachments, and make some tough decisions to let go—so the universe will allow new and exciting people to enter your life. That's how it works. You'll see.

> *When you come to the edge of all the light you know*
> *and are about to step off into the darkness of the unknown*
> *(and let go), faith is knowing that either one of two things*
> *will happen: There will be something solid to stand on*
> *or you will learn to fly.*
>
> —BARBARA WINTER

Re-active to Pro-active Attitude Adjustments

1. **RE-ACTIVE:** I am attached out of fear to no-win relationships and situations, diminishing my self-esteem and causing me pain, anguish, and suffering.
   PRO-ACTIVE: I detach with compassion from unhealthy situations. In their place, I attract loving, enriching relationships that support my growing sense of self-worth and my vision for myself and my future.

2. **RE-ACTIVE:** I think I know exactly what's best for me. Being so attached to the outcome, I don't allow for the possibility of a miracle to occur.

PRO-ACTIVE: I detach from any specific outcome. I joyously open to divine guidance and the possibility of something truly inspiring entering my life that I never imagined possible.

3. **RE-ACTIVE:** I am so attached and controlled by external opinions and my need for validation that I lose sight of what makes me happy.

   PRO-ACTIVE: I detach from concern about what other people think or say about me or how I appear to the outside world. I honor what I consider truly important and valuable.

CHAPTER EIGHT

Lifelong Security

Too many people are thinking of security
instead of opportunity.
They seem more afraid of life than death.

—James F. Byrnes

I believe that there are two kinds of people in this world, the *haves* and the *have-nots.* Obviously the *haves* are people who *have* things such as lovely homes, nice cars, and great clothes. They take vacations, they are personally and financially satisfied, and they feel secure.

On the other hand, the *have-nots,* those who lack personal contentment and financial security, are people who do *not* have the things or the lifestyle they want. The *have-nots* have become really good at justifying why the *haves* are unhappy, selfish, and unworthy people. Over time, the *have-nots* become bitter and negative, denying their desires to have anything, often becoming pretentious since their value system is confused.

Which one are you? Are you happy with yourself? Are you satisfied with the rewards of your life or would you like things to be different? Do you feel that having things is bad, selfish, or materialistic? You just may be a victim of the *have-not* complex without even realizing it, preventing yourself from having anything you really want.

Are you justifying your personal lack by finding fault with the *haves*? There's nothing wrong with wanting and enjoying material things—unless "things" are all you care about. I know successful people, *haves*, who are also grounded, loving, and well-balanced. But I spent a great deal of my life as a *have-not,* envious of what others had. I felt out of place everywhere and inferior to almost everyone, since I knew for sure that my dad was a *have-not.* He envied other people's homes and beautiful things because he couldn't afford them, and he belittled what others had and found ways to insult them.

These messages were confusing to me. I knew I wanted a different life from that of my parents but I had no idea how to get it. Or if it was even okay to go for it. My parents were not role models because neither had become successful or had much in the way of material possessions. The worst part was that my father's negativity about the *haves* made me feel unworthy and guilty for wanting more. My self-esteem was gradually eroding until I didn't feel I had the right to shop in a nice department store. I imagined that the clerks would know how unworthy I was and they would turn me away. In my mind, I was discount store material, and besides, only pompous, insensitive, materialistic egomaniacs shopped at expensive stores. Or so I told myself.

According to Brent Kessel, author of *It's Not About the Money,* our attitudes about money started when we were three or four, when we watched a parent or an uncle behaving in a certain way. We may have decided right then and there that we would never be as greedy or tied up in the financial world as they were.

KESSEL: We felt the emotional pain of someone's absence or anger and somehow, in our young minds, we attributed that to money. We go through these formative, often painful experiences, and we decide, "I will always *blank* with money" or "I will never *blank* with money." It's different for everyone because we've all been through different conditioning.

BASSETT: I go to my own Core Story, and I really see the relationship between my personal fears and a sense of security that I wanted so badly. I grew up with a conditioned anger and jealousy toward the *haves.*

KESSEL: Right. It's interesting, because even the *haves* are *have-nots* on the inside. Everybody feels like they don't have enough, so the *haves* are buying the nice house, the nice car, the nice clothes to compensate for an internal feeling of not having enough.

BASSETT: So you're saying that even successful people are compensating for their fear of the bag lady syndrome?

KESSEL: It's not universal, but many are. Part of the reason my book is called *It's Not About the Money* is that I work with some of the most affluent people in society, as well as less affluent people in workshops, and there's no difference. The inner experience, I found, is very, very similar. The biggest fear for the *haves* is losing what they have.

BASSETT: The *have-nots,* their biggest fear is?

KESSEL: Basically, running out of money, having no choices, having to be financially dependent on someone else or on the government. Going without. I mean literally, "Do I buy groceries this week or keep the gas on?" Often, it's that primal sort of choice.

Remember that nothing is set in stone. This book can support you in unearthing those distorted ideas that have kept you stuck in your limiting belief-systems. As you read through this chapter, you are learning to leave behind your old identity of being a *have-not* and to enthusiastically step into your new role as being someone who can *have it all!*

DOERS AND DRIFTERS

Over the last twenty-five years, in my work with individuals and corporations, along with identifying the *haves* and *have-nots,* I've made an additional distinction between two types of people: doers and drifters.

Doers plan their lives and are strongly motivated. They know what they want, they get things done, they're goal-oriented, and they're willing to do whatever it takes to get where they want to be. These people are achievement-driven, moving along a forward path, dedicated to their financial freedom and prosperity since they were children, even if it was subconscious.

Drifters, on the other hand, just drift along with no clear sense of direction. They make no plans, they have no goals, they just go with the flow. Maybe they tried a few careers, wore a few different hats, and left their futures up to chance or chose the path of least resistance.

In his book *Keys to Success,* author Napoleon Hill uses the same terms that I came up with, doers and drifters, to describe the characteristics of these kinds of people:

Doers

- have a definite major purpose.
- manage circumstances and resources.
- examine every idea they encounter before they adopt or discard it.
- take risks and assume responsibility.
- learn from their mistakes.
- go the extra mile.
- control their habits.
- have positive mental attitudes.
- apply their faith to their own success.
- create mastermind alliances to expand their knowledge and experience.
- recognize their weaknesses and take steps to correct them.

Drifters

- have no goal in life.
- are controlled by circumstances and the lack of resources.
- flit from one idea about life to the other, depending on this week's fad or what the guy on TV said last night.
- run from opportunity and blame others for their lot in life.
- make the same mistakes over and over.
- do only what it takes to get by.
- let their habits control them.
- have negative mental attitudes.
- never do anything to improve their situation.
- learn all they want to know from that guy on TV.
- wouldn't know a weakness if it bit them.
- make excuses.
- blame others.
- are irresponsible.

The key is to determine which type you are and what you want and then ask yourself if you're happy. Are you content with your life as it is, or would you like it to be different? When we don't make a clear distinction, we leave our lives to chance, engaging in activities we don't really like, simply to achieve a false sense of security, both personal and financial. We fight our inner selves, wondering why we feel so dissatisfied and insecure. The solution is easy: We cannot be committed to that which is not in our hearts. Learn to be open and receptive to your heart's desires by paying attention to what ignites your inner flame. I'm referring to whatever excites you, energizes you, and makes you want to do anything and everything to make it happen.

FINANCIAL SATISFACTION

When I was a freshman in college, I shifted from being a *have-not,* feeling unworthy, into a woman who believed I could have whatever I wanted. It all started when a dear friend, Bill, invited me to New York to meet his parents. They were completely different from mine—worldly and sophisticated. I was in awe of their beautiful home and everything they did—eating at the finest restaurants and waltzing though Saks Fifth Avenue department store like they owned the place. I learned that it was okay to go right up to the counter and ask to see an article of fancy clothing, even if I didn't want to buy it. I could walk through the designer departments and say, "Just looking," and no one would throw me out.

During the time I spent with Bill in New York, I gave myself permission to aspire to a nice lifestyle, a level of financial satisfaction, and an attitude of achievement. He was the catalyst who motivated me to take risks and to open doors to new experiences about which I had only dreamed, helping me build a successful career and company. But it took time and patience to overcome my program of being a *have-not.* Below is more of my interview with Brent Kessel as he talks about learning to differentiate between the wanting mind's desire and heart-felt goals.

KESSEL: The wanting mind's desires are impulses that come up kind of quickly and dissipate kind of quickly if we don't satiate them. They've got a sense of impulsiveness and an impatience to them. The hallmarks of heartfelt desires, on the other hand, are a willingness to be more patient in getting them. Here's a key distinction: heartfelt goals benefit more than just ourselves. They tend to benefit a larger community of people—or animals or nature—whereas the wanting mind's desires really only benefit us. They're much more self-centered.

BASSETT: How do you suggest people become more balanced with their personal finances? Is there a simple formula so that people can begin to take control of their financial insecurity and really feel that they can move forward into the future?

KESSEL: The simple answer is to understand your Core Story (described fully in Chapter One) so you can also understand your unconscious tendencies with money. Then you can cultivate the opposite tendencies. If your tendency has been to spend money easily on things that bring you pleasure, start to cultivate pleasure from saving some of it—delaying gratification. If you tend to hoard and act like a tightwad, I encourage you to do some spending for personal pleasure. Also, try cultivating some generosity because that will make you happier.

FINANCIAL ARCHETYPES

No one is better equipped to describe a variety of financial archetypes than Brent Kessel. According to his research, we have all been conditioned to respond to money in particular and sometimes peculiar ways. Drawing on the work of various teachers, mentors, and philosophers, as well as on his own observations, Brent has described eight financial archetypes in his book *It's Not About the Money.* He sees these archetypes as energies within us, collective patterns that explain how we got the financial life we have today.

The following quiz, inspired by Kessel's book, will reveal your dominant financial archetype. More than one answer may apply so choose up to three answers that best describe you. Brent describes an optimal human being as a combination of all the archetypes.

1. Money primarily allows me to

☐ not worry	Guardian
☐ buy things and experience I enjoy	Pleasure Seeker
☐ create freedom for other pursuits	Idealist
☐ have a sense of security and balance	Saver
☐ feel important to and recognized by friends	Star
☐ have faith that things will work out for the best	Innocent
☐ care for others, perhaps at my own expense	Caretaker
☐ spend time and money to make a lasting impact	Empire Builder

2. With money, at my most extreme, I am

☐ avoidant and sometimes confused	Innocent
☐ self-abandoning and generous to a fault	Caretaker
☐ impulsive and pleasure-oriented	Pleasure Seeker
☐ frugal and undisciplined	Saver
☐ worried and anxious a lot	Guardian
☐ distrustful and mystified	Idealist
☐ grandiose and ambitious	Empire Builder
☐ hungry for attention and praise	Star

3. Over the last five years, my financial net worth has

☐ grown due to good saving and investing	Saver
☐ declined due to lack of focus, too many gifts	Innocent, Caretaker
☐ grown due to promotions, bonuses, stock options	Empire Builder, Star
☐ declined due to overspending	Pleasure Seeker, Star
☐ not stopped me from feeling anxious	Guardian
☐ I have no idea, it's not important	Innocent, Idealist

4. Which of the following "rules" describe your life?

☐ You can't take it with you, might as well enjoy it now	Pleasure Seeker, Star, Innocent
☐ It is better to give than to receive	Caretaker, Idealist
☐ A penny saved is a penny earned	Saver, Empire Builder
☐ Big corporations and government can't be trusted	Idealist, Empire Builder
☐ If I'm not vigilant, it could all fall apart	Guardian

5. Which of the following is true for you?

☐ I have been financially dependent on others	Pleasure Seeker, Star, Idealist, Innocent
☐ Others have been financially dependent on me	Caretaker, Saver, Empire Builder
☐ There are no dependencies either way	Guardian, Saver

6. What I have to show financially is

☐ a lot of stuff I've bought over the years	Pleasure Seeker
☐ I don't have investments	Innocent
☐ ownership in a business or real estate	Empire Builder
☐ investments like stocks, income property, mutual funds	Saver
☐ collectibles, art work, or academic work	Idealist
☐ family, friends who wouldn't have made it without me	Caretaker
☐ fixed income investments like CDs and T-bills	Guardian

Add up the boxes you checked and list the top three archetypes that best describe you. Then read about your type below to gain a better understanding of your relationship with money and finances, what you may be doing right, and what you may need to improve on to establish a firmer sense of financial responsibility.

1. The Guardian. Always alert and careful, Guardians live in constant terror that something is about to go terribly wrong. Their pitfalls are worry and anxiety; their gifts are alertness and prudence.

Their Core Story often involves a doomsday scenario including terrorism, global warming, or nuclear proliferation. While they may be highly effective with money, they have learned that the best way to deal with their anxiety is to save and be frugal.

You are a Guardian if you become paralyzed in the face of making a decision. Or you may be prone to excessive analysis. You mull over the what-if scenario and you abide by fear-driven rules such as never having debt and never living off your investment principal. Your emotional responses and worry levels are out of proportion to the situation at hand. You feel fear, anxiety, doubt, pessimism, uneasiness, obsession, and panic, certain that worrying about your finances will help you control the uncontrollable. You exhaust yourself to the point that you run out of energy to keep worrying—until the next time.

Advice for Guardians: Check your frenzied thoughts against reality. Stop the what-ifs: What if I get sick? What if I feel scared? What if I have an anxiety attack? What if I lose everything?

Learn that feeling unsafe is okay sometimes. Remember never to make financial decisions in the midst of intense emotions.

2. The Pleasure Seeker. These people prioritize pleasure and enjoyment in the here and now over all else. Their pitfalls are hedonism and impulsiveness; their gifts are enjoyment and fun. Pleasure seekers believe that the purpose of money is to enable them to enjoy life and go for sensory pleasures.

You are a Pleasure Seeker if you save very little money and tend to buy things that aren't necessary to your lifestyle. Generally, your debts exceed your assets and your investments fall under the categories of vacation homes, art collections, fine wines, and jewelry. You engage in "retail therapy" when you are feeling low, but spending money on luxury items creates tension in your relationships.

Advice for Pleasure Seekers: Break the pattern of satisfying your every wish by asking yourself whether this particular purchase serves your values. Find new ways to create pleasure in your life. Commit to one full day a week in which you don't handle money at all. Instead of going shopping, play with your child, get out in nature, dance to your favorite CD, or read a great book. Whatever you do, give it your full attention. Relish the world around you, as it is, in order to experience real pleasure that no one can ever take away. You can't spend every day like this, since life comes in when you least expect it, but do these pleasurable things whenever you get the time or the inclination.

3. THE IDEALIST. Idealists place great value on creativity, compassion, social justice, and spiritual growth. The pitfalls of these artistic types are distrust and aversion; their gifts are vision and compassion. Idealists tend to be prejudiced against money, feeling like outsiders in upper-class business or social circles. They feel shame and embarrassment regarding finances and believe that our system is corrupt, that money is the root of all evil.

You are an Idealist if you don't earn enough money to pay your taxes or you choose not to file at all since you believe the system is not your friend. As a result, you rely on others for financial support, and when you invest, you choose small businesses since you distrust big business. You only invest in well-screened companies that do no harm to the environment or are deemed to have fair business practices. As with many other archetypes, you use your idealistic convictions to avoid personal pain.

Advice for Idealists: Ask yourself if your deep-seated convictions are worth the price you are paying in your financial world. Get clear with your negative reactions to money. If you are in debt, instead of relying on others to bail you out, make a plan. But first call on the advice of an expert in your particular field. Be aware that your aversion to money is causing you undue stress and too much reliance on others.

4. The Saver. Savers seek security and abundance by accumulating financial assets. Their pitfalls are hoarding and penny-pinching; their gifts are self-sufficiency and abundance. For these people, money represents security, stability, protection, and nourishment. In crises, Savers believe that saving equals financial security as money takes on an inappropriate value. They have two possible orientations: a focus on reducing their spending or a focus on increasing their savings.

You are a Saver if you save more than 20 percent of your income, if you spend or give away less than 3 percent of your income, or if your net worth grows more than 5 percent from one year to the next. You experience a rush of good feelings after making a bank deposit or reducing your spending. But this is a temporary sense of relief since your mind is always looking for the next feeling of security. While saving is a good thing, over-saving can become a prison where the emotional costs outweigh the financial benefits.

Advice to Savers: Take a moment before you decide to alleviate your fears with reflexive saving. Instead of hoarding money, commit to a short period of self-reflection. Be aware of the discomfort you are trying to alleviate and slow down. If you need to get some input on saving vs. spending, call on a professional financial planner to help you see the big picture. With help in making your money decisions, you are more likely to break the death grip that saving has on you.

5. The Star. These types use their money to be recognized, to feel hip and classy, and to increase their self-esteem. The pitfalls of Stars are pretentiousness and self-importance; their gifts are leadership and great style. Star types tend to believe that money buys love. They spend excessive amounts on clothes and beauty treatments, prioritizing their physical attractiveness. They may also use charitable giving, their career choices, and their neighborhood prestige to impress others and garner social attention. But this habit of spending money for attention can lead to debt and a terrible feeling of emptiness.

You are a Star if you spend more than 25 percent of your income on clothing, hair, beauty, jewelry, and body image enhancements. You want to be seen as a giver (no anonymous donations for this archetype) and you have been known to alter your investments to keep up with the latest trends.

Advice to Stars: Before you blow your entire salary on the latest and greatest pair of ridiculously expensive shoes, figure out why you really want them. Will the overpriced pair of sunglasses make you feel more sophisticated? Are you overly invested in how others react to how you look and what you wear? Get clear with the lies you are telling yourself and give them up. It's time to step out of your comfort zone and try giving without expecting any one to praise you for it.

6. The Innocent. Innocents avoid placing significance on money. They hope and believe that life will simply work out okay for them. While the pitfalls of this archetype are avoidance and helplessness, the gifts are hope and adaptability. Innocents are not necessarily penniless, but they have difficulty attracting money or holding on to it. They are programmed to believe that they will never achieve an abundant lifestyle, and generally they do not possess economically based skills.

If you are an Innocent, you place little value on your attributes. You lack confidence in your ability to make money and when you do, you end up losing it because your unconscious mind has been programmed to create financial predicaments. Often a victim of abuse, addictions, and bad luck, you receive a lot of attention for your suffering and the "difficult plight" the world has thrust upon you.

Advice for Innocents: For most of you, this is not about money. Your currency may be creativity, compassion, activism, scholarship, or service. Rather than sacrificing your natural gifts to fit into an economic mold, formulate a plan that allows you to feel peace and abundance at your current level of income. Choose a reasonable amount of money to save each month, and write down how you feel about your finances, such as relief, confidence and freedom, or unworthy, uncomfortable, or unfamiliar.

7. The Caretaker. Caretakers give away and lend money to express their compassion and service. Their pitfalls are enabling and self-abandoning, while their gifts are empathy and generosity. These people use their money, time, and energy to assist their immediate family members and they extend themselves to help friends or the underprivileged in general. They generally work in the fields of health care and social work, while they keep their own lives in good order, seeing themselves as "other sufficient," meaning they will allow others to lean on them financially. Since we all need caretaking from time to time, the world would be a poorer place with the absence of Caretakers.

If you are a Caretaker, you spend more than 20 percent of your income on those in need, but you are not necessarily generous with yourself. You keep your investments liquid in case you suddenly need to rescue someone and you are quick to reach into your pocket when someone else needs help. You may have succeeded financially, but you feel a sense of responsibility to take on the role of savior.

Advice to Caretakers: Do a rigorous inquiry about your most innate intentions in spending money. Are you abandoning yourself to care for others? Are you exaggerating other people's needs in order to feel wanted? Is your generous approach empowering the people you help or is it stopping them from learning to take care of themselves? Make sure you understand what someone else needs before you offer your services.

8. The Empire Builder. These people thrive on power and innovation, determined to create something of enduring value. Their pitfalls are greed and domination; their gifts are innovation and decisiveness. Empire Builders are visionaries who believe they will only succeed when they achieve a task of great significance. Often, their ambition leads them to pursue careers in the political arena where they feel they can have a large-scale impact on the world.

You are an Empire Builder if your business or career occupies more than 75 percent of your waking attention. You avoid pulling money out of your empire, whether it is real estate, a business, or a single asset. You are aware of inflation and you know how much money you need to keep ahead of it. You make significant, lasting contributions to universities, charities, and art, in the process saving and improving countless lives. Often, having endured hardship when growing up, an Empire Builder seeks to alleviate difficult conditions in people's lives through philanthropy.

Advice to Empire Builders: You have much to be proud of and you also tend to be single-minded, holding a little too tightly to your pride and money. Focusing on your legacy can be great for others, but beware of the hidden costs of structuring your life so that your legacy is all that matters. You need a life beyond building an empire in which you can include activities and states of being that will feed your own heart and soul.

As you ponder which characteristics you embody, you may find you fall under several categories. Don't become embarrassed, self-critical, or filled with shame about the state of your finances. When you review the eight archetypes listed above, you'll see that people can develop many different relationships with money. No archetypal relationship is better than another when taken to extremes. When you act out due to a faulty belief system that has been in place since childhood, you're placing your sense of satisfaction and security at risk. The solution to overcoming your negative relationship with money is to reprogram these outdated belief systems. If you have a positive relationship with money, sit back and enjoy reading about Paula Deen. You and she might have a few things in common.

PAULA DEEN: EMPIRE BUILDER

Paula Deen, an award-winning restaurateur from Savannah, Georgia, is an Empire Builder, but she did not come into her own until late in life. She had a really tough start. She was born in Albany, Georgia, in 1947; both her parents died before she was eighteen. After she graduated from high school, she married a local tugboat captain, Jimmy Deen, but the relationship ended in divorce. Now she had two boys and less than $200 in her bank account. Plagued by panic attacks and agoraphobia, unable to leave her house, Paula became proficient at southern cuisine. When she finally felt well enough to leave home and go to a job, she took a bank teller position before she made a decision to expand her cooking experiences. She created a catering business she called The Bag Lady, making sandwiches and other meals for office workers, which her two sons delivered in paper bags.

Quickly outgrowing her small kitchen, Deen opened her own restaurant, The Lady & Sons, in downtown Savannah in January 1996. It became an instant success since her food expertise was widely lauded. At the age of fifty, in spite of struggling with anxiety and agoraphobia, Deen was starting over. Making a huge splash with her home-style southern cooking, she gained national attention and landed her own cable TV show in 2003, proving that it's never too late to go for your dreams.

Paula appeared on *The Oprah Winfrey Show* in 2002, sparking hundreds of letters from women who said they took control of their lives after watching Paula tell her rags-to-riches, panic-to-power story. Today, Paula Deen owns a cooking empire and is the proud recipient of two Emmy awards, one for Outstanding Lifestyle Host and another for Outstanding Lifestyle Program for her popular show, *Paula's Home Cooking*. She's come a long way from housebound single parent to one of the best-known gourmet cooks on television.

Did Paula go to a fancy culinary school, earn a degree in hospitality, or have the perfect mother who loved to cook? No! Driven by her passion for cooking, she went after her dreams in spite of her fear and anxiety. In fact, I'm certain that a good part of her motivation came from her desire to be able to support herself and her family so that she would never feel financially insecure or dependent again.

There are multitudes of ways to achieve your goals, but all of them require clarity of desire, a plan, and, of course, a willingness to take risks and do the necessary work. Drop the excuses that you're too old and it's too late. Neither is true. Think about Paula Deen, who didn't come into her own until she was fifty. You can emulate her or anyone else you choose as a role model, but first you will have to understand what money means in your life. What is your relationship with money? This requires that you look not only at today, but also into the future at the upcoming changes and trends.

WORST-CASE SCENARIO

In a conversation with Brent Kessel about fear of losing money, he suggested a process that I tried with him. "It's about going back to your Core Story," he said. "It's extremely important for people to get comfortable with their worst-case scenario."

"But how can a person get comfortable with that?" I asked him.

"Let's try," he suggested.

So I said, "Growing up in a brown-shingled house at the end of a dead-end street, we literally had to divide up our Friday night dinners to make sure we all ate. We could never have anybody to our home for dinner because there wasn't enough food. That's how I grew up. I've told my daughter this, that I'm afraid that we're going to go back to that."

Brent asked me to describe a very specific scene of this unwished-for future financial scenario, my "bag lady" syndrome. "You need to tell it," he said, "as if I was a movie director. I want to know exactly how many actors I need to cast, what scenery I need to build behind them, and what the specific shot will look like."

(As I tell my story here, as scary as it sounds, I ask the reader to do this, too. That means you need to think hard to envision your own biggest financial fear.)

I told Brent that my biggest fear was bankruptcy. "I've just lost everything," I told him. "I have no checking account and when I try to use my credit card by inserting it into the ATM machine, a warning on the screen says, 'Sorry, I can't accept this credit card.' I try another and the ATM won't accept that either. Now I can't retrieve money on my credit card and I can't write a check because there's nothing in my checking account."

Brent asked me to sit back, close my eyes, and stay quiet for about five minutes as he led me through a guided process.

"We want to make this very specific," he said. "Just one scene. I want to put you back there for a moment."

You may be wondering why in the world I would ask you to imagine your worst-case scenario. "Isn't that the same as manifesting it?" you may ask.

The truth is that your worst-case scenario is already in your subconscious. So take a good look at what is already there. What do you see for yourself in this unwished-for financial situation? What do you see yourself doing or not doing? What do you hear yourself saying or not saying? What do you feel in your body in this situation? Brent told me, "As you look out of your own eyes, in the middle of this scene, what's going on around you? How does all this make you feel? What is the belief that you're telling yourself in this situation—*I am* . . . what?

"Now imagine this scene receding out of the main frame," Brent continued, "almost as if the scene begins spinning round and round, going out of focus. Maybe it's rising above your head, spinning faster and faster. Now it starts to slow down and descend. As it comes into focus, you notice that everything is exactly the same. You're in the same financial situation, except for one thing: you're coping. You're bringing your absolute best self to the situation. You're being resourceful. Now, as you see yourself responding, what do you see yourself doing differently? What do you see yourself saying, or not saying? What do you hear others saying, or not saying? What do you feel in your body now that you are coping, bringing the very best of yourself to this terrible situation? What do you believe about yourself? Try saying, *Now that I'm being so resourceful, I am . . .* "

Brent asked me to take a deep breath and open my eyes. He said, "Come back to the room you're in." He suggested I write in a journal about my belief about myself at the end of the first half of the exercise and compare it to my belief at the end of the second half. "Breathe this new self-belief into your body, and then journal a little bit more," he advised. He told me I could draw a picture or paint something that represented my new belief about myself.

Here is how I experienced it. When I first went to that insecure place, I felt scared, anxious, panicky; I was disturbed by a spinning sensation. Since I'm a type A personality, I thought, *Oh my gosh, what am I going to do?* But then I backed up, left the room, and said to myself, *You're handling it.* I saw myself confident and strong, in control and taking over. I recalled a time in my life when that was exactly what had happened. I had to step in there, be strong, and take control, regardless of the situation. I knew that I had resources and I could get through it. For me, that was the beauty of the exercise.

Brent said, "Fear is always worse than the reality. When we are jumping into the future, our minds play all kinds of nasty tricks on us."

CREATE AND LIVE WITHIN A BUDGET

A budget is a great start in helping you address the causes of your financial stress. It will help you stop second-guessing whether or not you can afford something. The idea is to eliminate surprises, so when your taxes are due or if a pipe suddenly bursts in your home, there is money already set aside to care of these things. Then, when you *do* buy something, you won't feel guilty and you will eliminate what I call a "leaky budget," when your bank account balance is creeping lower than you expected. I suggest you record all your expenses into a log for a month. Add them up and decide if you want to keep buying these things, or if you need to minimize your expenses for the sake of your financial security.

By the way, if you're making minimum payments on your credit card, you're spending a great deal more on your items than they cost. Pay off your credit cards each month. If you can't, you're spending too much, plain and simple. Brent Kessel suggests that you try talking with a financial consulting service and move into a "cash flow system" for a while. Paying cash for your purchases will really be an eye-opener for you.

Here is another excerpt from the terrific interview I did with Brent, as he explained his cash flow system.

BASSETT: For the average person, do you have any quick tips on things they can do to manage their money better?

KESSEL: Yeah. One thing we've found is that people who spend only cash tend to spend 10 to 20 percent less. Go to the bank, take out enough cash—however much you can afford—for your next three days or a week's worth of expenses, and only use cash. That won't be possible necessarily with the rent or the mortgage. If you can, then do it that way. I mean literally just get the cash. That's one thing.

Another thing is there's a great website called Mint.com. It takes five to ten minutes to set up. Literally, once you've set it up, right then, in that same ten-minute session, you'll be able to look at the last ninety days of your spending, assuming it's spending that you've done out of your checking account or credit card accounts. You can see where the money is actually going. I mean everybody's sort of like, "Well, where have I been spending the money?" You can actually see it on Mint.com: here's how much is going to entertainment, here's how much to restaurants, here's how much to travel, here's how much to gifts, blah-blah-blah. That's a great tip I found for people. The other thing is if you've got enough to save a little bit, set up a savings account that's automatic so that it automatically sweeps a little bit of your paycheck, every single time you make a deposit, over into the savings side of the equation.

BASSETT: That's a good idea.

KESSEL: It doesn't matter if it's $10 a paycheck or $100 a paycheck, whatever you can afford, have that money go out first. I mean it's a cliché and most of the self-help personal finance books have already said it before me so it's not my idea, but making things automatic really helps. It's like an automatic opt-in 401(k) plan that's so much better, where you're automatically enrolled unless you choose to opt out, because you don't really miss the money.

Day 13

Pro-Active Action

ASSIGNMENT

Choose a power partner, perhaps a family member or a friend, a mentor whom you respect and admire and who really wants you to accomplish your goals, someone who can help you define your financial goals and dreams that you have written down in your journal. This person can help you stay within your budget, reminding you when you might be overspending or impulse buying when you should be saving and focusing on moving toward the things that matter to you. Often, spending is a compulsive habit that can effectively distract you from something you really should be focusing on to achieve your goals.

YOUR FINANCIAL FORECAST: IMPULSE BUYING

I've already explained how important it is to look at the big picture when you're working on a financial plan. That means taking the past, the present moment, and the future into account to create your financial forecast. This is a long-term vision of what you believe to be financial security for you and your family. There is no set menu here because each of us is different and we value different things. Your financial forecast may mean breaking free of credit card debt, saving up for a great family vacation, or creating a college fund for your kids. Whatever your forecast is, the clearer you can visualize it, the easier it will be to achieve.

Try this. While you're walking away from that new pair of shoes or the flat screen TV you've been lusting after, imagine wiggling your toes in the warm sand and relaxing with your family on the beach in the tropics—that vacation you've always dreamed about. This is something you might be able to save for and actually achieve, if you stop your compulsive buying. As good as the instant gratification feels when you engage in impulse buying, just imagine the feeling of freedom when you pay off your credit card debt. Or when you go to your son's college graduation.

It will all make sense—saving and choosing where to put your money—when you're working toward your personal financial long-term forecast. Are you willing to remain stuck in a self-limiting, risk-avoiding lifestyle, to avoid the anxiety that often accompanies the unfamiliar? So many of us complain that we need to change, while, deep down, our real desire is to stay in our comfort zone. But if we don't take some risks and make a decision to change, we can't move forward in life.

The truth is that we all want to enjoy our lives, our careers, our families, and our relationships. We want to feel needed and important, appreciated and useful. We want our lives to have value so we can feel like we're making a difference in the world. We want to be financially secure and independent. We want to go to bed at night feeling content and peaceful, and in the morning, we want to feel confident about the day ahead. We want to have control over our lives and know that our families are safe and well cared for. In short, we want personal and financial satisfaction, and we can have it.

FINANCIAL SATISFACTION GUIDELINES

Use the following guidelines to establish a sense of financial responsibility and financial satisfaction:

1. Write a paragraph about the "things" you want. Be specific. What kind of home have you always dreamed about? Is there a car that catches your eye when you see it speeding by? Who is your favorite designer and what kind of clothing would you most like to own? Try to keep within your most realistic financial potential. If you cannot provide these things for yourself, how can you see yourself as worthy and capable of getting what you want?
2. Write a paragraph about your preferred lifestyle from a financial perspective. How do you like to spend money? What would you like to do less often? Would you like to get a massage, live in a bigger apartment, or get a new wardrobe? Make a realistic budget that will support your preferred lifestyle. How can you best achieve it? When you retire, what kind of money do you need to live well? Look into retirement or investment seminars. There are countless classes, books, and Internet information that can show you healthy ways to invest your money for the long term.
3. See yourself as someone who enjoys life and experiences and give yourself permission to be whoever you want to be.

It's all right to enjoy what you have and to work to have more. Understand that you are financially capable, and use your creativity and imagination to find new ways to make money. Once you determine what you want for yourself personally, professionally, and materially, it becomes easier to determine what you need financially.

BILL OF RIGHTS FOR FINANCIAL SATISFACTION

- You have the right to want and enjoy money.
- You have the right to enjoy material things.
- You have the right to choose the lifestyle you want.
- You have the right to a better life.
- You have the right to be anywhere and to fit in everywhere.
- You have the right to feel motivated and driven.
- You have the right to a simple life.
- You have the right to want nice things without feeling guilty.
- You have the right to feel secure.

Re-Active to Pro-Active Attitude Adjustments

1. **RE-ACTIVE:** I'll never be financially secure enough to afford the things I desire. When it comes to finances, I'm unlucky and incompetent. I might as well accept being a *have-not.*

   PRO-ACTIVE: Nothing can stop me from being a *have.* I am capable of attracting and achieving a satisfying, enriching life, full of financial abundance and security. I am using my wealth to improve the quality of life for myself, my family, and the world at large.

2. **RE-ACTIVE:** I feel there is no point in dreaming. I have never amounted to much or achieved anything meaningful with my

life. I just drift along aimlessly from one thing to the next with no purpose or direction.

PRO-ACTIVE: I am a visionary, a planner, and a doer. I know my life's mission and I can see my right direction and exactly what it will take to get me there.

3. **RE-ACTIVE:** I have a terrible relationship with money. It is the cause of most of my worries as well as my feelings of being out of control.

   PRO-ACTIVE: I have an enlightening and liberating new perspective of how I relate to money. I have the ability to consciously choose how to use my money to enhance and enrich my life experience.

You have the right to feel secure. You have the right to enjoy your life. You are capable, talented, and creative. You know what you want and you know how to get it. You create abundance in your life. You feel safe with yourself because you know you're in great hands—your own. You know what matters. Life is an adventure and you're up for it.

You are a joy magnet. You are also a money magnet. Money flows effortlessly into your bank account while your income grows every day. You are an excellent money manager and you respect your own abilities to work to your full potential. You always have what you need and you are a confident, successful businessperson. You use your prosperity wisely and you have the resources to manifest whatever you want. You are organized, talented, intelligent, and innovative. You are smart and savvy, debt-free and powerful, able to accomplish your personal and financial goals with ease.

CHAPTER NINE

Vital Living

If you don't take care of your body,
where will you live?

—Dr. Mary S. Harris

Many of us treat our cars better than we do our bodies. After all, we wash our cars regularly, we wax them, and we make sure their engines are in safe working order. We get them checkups when they're due and we take them to the "car doctor" at the slightest hint of a problem.

Do you do the same for your body? How well do you take care of yourself? Do you exercise or are you too lazy or tired? Do you grab food on the fly? Do you raise your energy level with soft drinks and caffeine? How do you sleep? Do you turn to alcohol or medication in an attempt to calm yourself down?

The truth is that these days, a large number of people are *not* dying from natural causes. Rather, they are dying from their own bad choices. Some may be stress-induced, others may be affected by the environment, but much of our bad health and many of our premature deaths come from the processed foods and additives we put into our bodies. We just don't take good enough care of ourselves.

Did you know that your ability to cope with stress is directly related to your health, dietary choices, exercise, and your ability to sleep? If any one of these four elements is out of balance, your emotional and physical health will not be stable and your life may be shortened. If your goal is to feel good, to be healthy, and to live a long life, you have to take responsibility for the whole package. It's not only about how positive you are or how clearly you think. It's also about what you eat and drink and how you take care of your body.

It is time to let go of excuses for not feeling good. There are some easy, life-changing solutions in this chapter that will help you feel better immediately. They will help you get more sleep and have more energy during the day. You can take control of your health and feel better physically and emotionally. Remember, when you don't feel well, it doesn't matter what kind of car you drive, where you live, or where you go on vacation. If your health is poor, you won't want to drive or go on vacation, no matter how much money you have.

The bottom line is that money cannot buy health. But if you feel good, you'll have the stamina to reach for the stars. You'll be able to do your job efficiently, keep up with your kids, and still have enough left over to enjoy an evening out. You really have a lot more control than you might think. I encourage you take responsibility for your own good mood, good health, and great attitude. These are things you can control right now. If you choose to be less affected and more effective, being physically fit can make all the difference in the world.

Start right now. The smallest change, even though you think it won't make a difference, really will matter. The results may not initially be obvious on the outside, but on the inside, dramatic changes are occurring. From calming your mind to losing a few unwanted pounds, these small changes can have a significant effect on your self-esteem and vitality. Congratulate yourself for taking that first step, precisely what you need right now to stay motivated and inspired along your path toward optimum health.

A MAN NAMED JACK

A fifty-seven-year-old engineer named Jack lost his wife a few years back. He still had his children and several grandchildren, but something vital had changed when he saw the doctor for his annual checkup. For the first time, his tests revealed high cholesterol and high blood pressure, and his energy and his humor were fading. Jack just wasn't the happy guy he used to be, and he was showing his advanced age. He had gained thirty pounds, mostly around his waist, and he was heading toward obesity and diabetes. He had dropped his lunchtime walking routine (he hadn't walked in six months), and he had no motivation to cook the healthy, fresh foods that his wife had always prepared for him. He was showing the effects of unhealthy living as he consumed processed fast foods.

The doctor put Jack on two different blood pressure medications, but his blood pressure still went up ten points in the next year while his cholesterol jumped to 280. A flight of stairs left him gasping for breath, he felt sad and tired, he had very little sex drive, and he had no will to exercise. Around this time, Jack stopped hanging out with his friends and he didn't spend as much time with his kids or his grandkids either. The doctor was so concerned that he put Jack on an antidepressant. The question was, Was Jack open to hearing about healthier options?

The doctor said to him directly, "Hey, Jack, do you want to fall apart, feel bad, continue to age rapidly, and probably die at an early age from some unnecessary disease? Or would you rather feel ten years younger, be trim and fit, have more energy, and get your good mood and your life back?"

"Are you kidding?" Jack said. "Of course I want to feel better, but I don't want to work as hard as I used to."

"Remember when you used to come in here and tell me one joke after the other?" the doctor reminded Jack. "I know your wife died and that you've been grieving. But you loved your job, you enjoyed your work, and you loved your life. What happened to you?"

Jack looked at the doctor without saying a word. He was wondering the same thing himself.

"I'm concerned about you," the doctor went on, "but if you're willing to make some behavioral and lifestyle changes, you can look and feel ten years younger. Will you listen to me before it's too late?"

Jack hesitated. Would he have to work hard to change his lifestyle? He'd lost his wife so he had an excuse not to be happy, didn't he? The doctor asked him about his grandson's soccer team, which Jack used to brag about. Now, he just sat there, frowning and shrugging. He hated to admit that he hadn't been to a game in a long time.

"What do I have to do?" he finally asked reluctantly.

The doctor gave Jack a shopping list for healthy, vital foods and some new recipes. "I want you to clean out your cupboards and get rid of everything that isn't on this list." He put Jack on an exercise regime for an hour a day and he advised him to plan at least two social events a week. "People need people," he told Jack, "so I want you to connect back to your family and friends. You need to feel loved in order to get over your loneliness and depression."

One month later, Jack literally came bounding into the doctor's office with a big smile on his face. He was ten pounds thinner, his muscle tone had greatly improved, his blood pressure had dropped twelve points, and his cholesterol level was down to 220. All in one month! Within six months, he was holding hands with a new girlfriend, he looked ten years younger, he had lost twenty more pounds, his blood pressure was normal, and his cholesterol level was at 170.

The best part was that he was free of all medications, he had lots of energy, and he was excited about life. As you can see, it's never too late to turn your life around. ❧

In order for Jack to return to a vital lifestyle, he needed the help of a doctor who understood the importance of healthy living and could teach Jack how to achieve it. I did an interview with this very man, Dr. Steven Masley, physician, nutritionist, former medical director of the Pritikin Longevity Center in Miami, Florida, and author of the book *Ten Years Younger.* Currently the medical director of the Optimal Health Center and assistant professor at the University of South Florida, Dr. Masley points out the two most common ingredients that are toxic to the human system and therefore detrimental to your health.

BASSETT: What do you consider the perfect meal?

DR. MASLEY: Some wild grilled salmon with dill and lemon juice sprinkled on top. I'd also have some steamed asparagus in an orange vinaigrette over wild rice with garlic, onion, and herbs and a glass of red wine. For dessert, chocolate mousse.

BASSETT: Some people would rather have a steak, a baked potato with butter or sour cream, and maybe some corn on the cob—with a beer or a glass of Scotch. Do you have a problem with that?

DR. MASLEY: The question is, how do you feel after that meal? I'd be hard-pressed to get out of my chair. I want to feel energized after I eat, filled with vitality. When you reach for a cheeseburger, French fries, and ice cream or pizza, you feel bad and you are on a downward spiral. And you gain weight, too.

BASSETT: You deal with work, financial problems, relationship issues, emotional issues, and family problems. You sit and you worry while you drink coffee, eat junk, sugar, have a

> hamburger, eat a steak, have a glass of wine or a beer, and you don't exercise. *Maybe I'll get to it tonight,* but before you know it, it's 11 o'clock and you're lying in bed thinking ugh, I feel so bad. Empowering yourself from a health standpoint starts with a strong base—healthy eating. It's important to start becoming conscious of what and when you eat.

Dr. Masley points out the two most common ingredients that are toxic to the human system and, therefore, detrimental to your health.

The first is fructose corn syrup, a metabolic toxin that disrupts the way the body makes energy. You find it in Twinkies, donuts, and soft drinks. Some juices have high fructose corn syrup and it's in a lot of packaged foods. Eating it is like pouring dirt into your gas tank. Your body has to store this toxin as liver fat so it's as if you're making a pâté out of yourself, raising your triglycerides and clogging your insulin pathways.

The second substance is hydrogenated oil, found in dairy-free coffee creamers, French fries, frozen entrées, cakes, cookies, margarine, and most fried foods. Imagine putting oil in liquid cadmium, heating it, and pumping in hydrogen gas. That is exactly how they create hydrogenated oil. It's like making plastic and then eating it! It will drain your energy, cause weight gain, and stiffen your tissue, leading to high cholesterol and the risk of cancer.

Dr. Masley believes that diet sodas have no redeeming qualities. We used to think they were the answer to consuming fewer calories and losing weight—until we learned that the brain knows something is wrong with the chemicals in diet sodas and it feels ripped off. It thinks, *You keep telling me I'm getting something sweet but there are no calories to show for it. I better give you a bigger appetite so you can make up for those calories I'm missing.* "Drink noncaffeinated green tea," he adds. "It's good for you.

WHAT CAN I EAT?

Dr. Masley has realistic suggestions for healthy eating that can set you on the right track. Although it would be beneficial, it isn't necessary to buy everything organic. What really matters is that you eat *real* food like fruit and vegetables, lean protein, nuts, and whole grains. He calls them "vitality foods," which rules out getting your protein from processed foods, cheeseburgers, and hot dogs. Instead, try lean cuts of protein like turkey breast, fish, and beans. If you eat red meat, choose sirloin, which is the leanest cut.

Stress is a given in our lives. Dr. Masley actually likes stress because it gives us purpose and challenge. "But if you don't manage it," he adds, "you'll feel poorly and it'll tip the inner balance. When you add healthy food and you feel better, you can manage your stress better."

Berries are a nutritious food that slows down the aging process. But when you add stimulants such as caffeine, soda pop, and sugars, you are escalating your stress and your anxiety. The pigment in green leafy vegetables like romaine lettuce or organic red and green mixed lettuce is very beneficial. Go for whole-grain brown rice rather than refined white rice.

If you need to make these changes slowly over the course of few weeks, that's perfectly okay. For me, the solution was to start each week with a new promise to myself, *to give up one negative thing* that was draining me of my vital energy and zest for life, or to take up something positive, such as an activity or ritual that would reinforce and support me in improving my health, well-being, and happiness.

A HEALTHY ATTITUDE: A HEALTHY DIET

I'm so worried and anxious, I can't sleep. Does this sound familiar? Do you get up and have another glass of wine in an attempt to relax, or do you take a sleeping pill? We all want something to take the edge off, to take the pain away, to stop the worry, the anxiety, and the feelings of uncertainty that accompany high stress.

The trouble is that you can't find peace of mind and good health in a bottle or a pill jar. You have to take responsibility for your diet, your exercise, and the way you think. Are you an emotional eater? When you're stressed and nervous, do you reach for the ice cream? When you feel lonely, do you go for the box of cookies? Emotional eating acts like a temporary antidepressant, so when you sit down to that bowl of ice cream or a plate of pasta in cream sauce, you may feel better for a short time, but very soon you'll be feeling a whole lot worse as your insulin levels rise, then drop, and you crash.

We are living in a diet-conscious culture: we see fast-food restaurants adding low-calorie, low-fat choices, and we have begun to watch our portion sizes. There are many reasons to stay away from fried foods, not the least of which are the saturated fats that clog your blood vessels and cause long-term damage to your heart and brain. You need to become aware of the difference between feeling stuffed and feeling satisfied. We laugh about the old quip, *I can't believe I ate the whole thing.* If you'd stopped when you felt satisfied, you would have consumed about one-third less when you were finished.

The truth is that when you get accustomed to eating the right amount and the healthiest choices, stuffing yourself with fried foods will not be appealing and they won't even taste good. I used to crave M&M Chocolate Peanuts. I just couldn't get enough of them, but now when I'm stressed and anxious, I reach for a banana and some almonds instead. The last thing I do is eat sugar because I know how it'll make me feel.

What can you do to feel better? Instead of a glass of wine at night (I know how tempting it is), try a cup of stress-reducing decaffeinated tea. Instead of going for ice cream, try munching some sweet baby carrots. I start my day with a healthy smoothie which I highly recommend. In a blender, put:

1 scoop protein powder
1 banana
handful of blueberries
1 teaspoon peanut butter
1 fresh peach, sliced
1 cup skim milk

Add ice and blend it all together for a great breakfast. I feel good when I finish it and I have lots of energy.

I suggest that you eat a light dinner early in the evening to avoid feeling bloated before you go to bed. Try some high-fiber carbohydrates like broccoli, cauliflower, tomatoes, and other vegetables that don't contain much sugar. Pair them with high-quality, low-fat proteins, but you don't need a huge amount of protein. Avoid meats that contain hormones and pesticides. The idea is to eat more fresh fish, free-range organic chicken and turkey, and lots of vegetables and salads. Keep away from mashed potatoes, white breads, and pastas, and gravitate toward whole grains and whole wheat.

Dr. Masley suggests that we eat the colors of the rainbow. He's talking about naturally colored fruits and vegetables that contain *phytochemicals* or *antioxidants* that prevent aging, stress, dementia, and heart disease. Some of my favorites are dark-colored fruits like blueberries, strawberries, cherries, mangoes, and purple grapes. Dark-colored vegetables include eggplant with the peel, sweet potatoes, beets, red cabbage, and spinach. Skip the iceberg lettuce as it has no nutritional value whatsoever. The more your plate resembles a rainbow, the better for you, so eat your colors.

Here are some other foods that will increase your health and fitness:

- Broccoli, Brussels sprouts, and cabbage contain vitamin C, vitamin A, calcium, and fiber, which help fight cancer.
- Organic nonfat skim milk gives you fat-free protein and also protects your bones.

- Nuts are wonderful too, since they taste so good and they help fight heart disease, curb your appetite, and contain omega-3 fatty acids, which are also found in fish and flaxseed.
- Fresh fish helps your heart and improves blood sugar regulation and brain function. But eat tuna and swordfish only a couple of times a month since they have a high mercury content.
- Beans lower your bad cholesterol (LDL), raise your healthy cholesterol (HDL), and suppress hunger while helping to stabilize your blood sugar levels. They're also loaded with cancer-fighting compounds.
- Soy products lower cholesterol and blood sugar levels. My son loves soy hot dogs and burgers, which are packed with cancer-fighting compounds like fiber, antioxidants, calcium, and anti-aging nutrients.
- Whole grains like barley, buckwheat, wild rice, and oats are tastier than processed grains and can help prevent weight gain and diabetes.
- Flaxseed fights cancer and heart disease. Shake some on your cereal or add to your smoothie.

As mentioned in Chapter Three, natural remedies that help you feel better emotionally and physically, sleep better, and have more energy can be included in your healthy diet regimen:

- *chamomile:* used as an anodyne, anti-inflammatory, antispasmodic, stomachic, tonic, and vasodilatory; has a mild tranquilizing effect that can ease spasms and discomfort in the digestive tract
- *5-HTP (hydroxy-tryptophan):* an amino acid that helps to raise serotonin levels
- *folic acid:* a B vitamin that builds muscle and produces essential chemicals for the brain and nervous systems; aids with digestion, helps the body utilize protein

- *gingko biloba:* enhances memory, increases blood flow to the brain and extremities, decreases depression, anxiety, headaches, macular degeneration, and hypertension
- *jujube seed:* used for treatment of insomnia and anxiety as it relieves nervous tension and apprehension while it prevents damage to nerve cells.
- *L-tyrosine:* supports mood balance, stress management, and thyroid function
- *passionflower:* a woody vine for mood and sleep difficulties
- *peppermint:* acts as a muscle relaxant, particularly in the digestive tract; reduces inflammation of nasal passages and relieves muscle pain; useful in fighting stress and controlling asthma
- *rhodiola rosea:* provides support during periods of heightened mental and physical stress, relieving occasional anxiety and panic, mild to moderate mood changes, and a depressed mood caused by everyday stress
- *SAM (S-adenosyl methionine):* an effective natural depression treatment with good tolerability; increases the availability of serotonin in the brain; sold as SAM-e
- *schizandra:* rich in minerals, vitamins, and essential oils, used for insomnia, irritation, palpitations, and dyspnea
- *St.-John's-wort:* a relaxing herb with long-lasting tonic effects on the nervous system, often used as an antidepressant
- *valerian root:* known for stress reduction and help with sleep
- *vitamin B-12:* aids proper nerve function
- *vitamin C:* also known as ascorbic acid, effective in healing wounds, improving memory, fighting chronic fatigue and the effects of aging

SET A GOOD EXAMPLE WITH DIET AND EXERCISE

As a general rule, your kids will eat what you eat. If you expose them to fish, vegetables, salad, and tofu, they will learn to appreciate them. And so will you. If you eliminate caffeine and alcohol while you eat natural foods every three to four hours, you will experience a whole new energy level, improve your attitude, and fall asleep much more easily when you want to.

In order to inspire your family to follow in your healthy footsteps, Dr. Masley suggests that you go into your pantry and discard the junk food. Since we eat what's in front of us, replace bad food with healthy natural choices. Now that you know what's good for you, look for recipes that utilize these foods. Always read labels in the grocery store, concentrating on the back of the package since food companies cover the front with false promises. If you have your children cook with you, they will learn how to prepare foods that are good for them. And if they help cook it, they are likely to eat it.

A key element in taking care of your body is exercise. In fact, Dr. Masley says, "Not exercising is not an option." Research has proven that people who exercise feel better, sleep better, have more energy, and live longer. But you don't have to join a gym. Walking for thirty minutes a day will hugely benefit your body and your brain, and you can do it for free. It will help stabilize your blood sugar, increase your endurance, build muscle, burn fat, and make you stronger.

From a physical point of view, exercise will help prevent heart disease, strokes, and cancer. From an emotional point of view, exercise can reduce depression, anxiety, and stress by raising the endorphin levels in your brain. It will make a difference in your mood, too, which has important implications for your relationships. If you don't like walking alone and you can't find someone to walk with you, consider getting a dog. My dog is big, she has lots of energy, and she forces me to get out and walk every day. When I don't walk her, she gets hyper and stressed out—just like me. After a walk she lies down; she's relaxed and more comfortable—just like me, too.

I keep some light weights in my car that I can use while I'm waiting for the kids at school or picking them up from practice. Try walking instead of taking elevators and look for activities like gardening and housework. If you want your family to join you, walk, bike, or play ball together. Plan active vacations like hiking, cycling, or skiing.

ALL I WANT IS A GOOD NIGHT'S SLEEP

Sleep is a huge concern for many people. Either they can't fall asleep or they sleep for two hours, wake up, and can't get back to sleep. Your morning caffeine, no matter that you drank it so many hours ago, is one of the main offenders. Lack of exercise is another. When your body doesn't get tired, it's harder to fall asleep. But exercising right before bed can be too stimulating and can contribute to insomnia.

> **Day 14**
>
> **Pro-Active Action**
>
> ASSIGNMENT
>
> Do this assignment in bed before you go to sleep. Starting at your feet, working your way up to your head, tense and then relax each large muscle group – your calves, your thighs, your buttocks, your abdomen and chest. As you release these muscles, tell yourself that the tension is draining away and that each part of your body feels heavy, relaxed, and rested.

If you're depressed, you may sleep too much or too little, as your sleep clock may be turned upside down. Sleeplessness often occurs in women between the ages of fifty and fifty-five, due to hormone changes. But when you correct your underlying chemical imbalances with exercise and proper nutrition, your sleep quality can improve significantly. I suggest you keep your bedroom completely dark, because the tiniest amount of light, like the green LED readout on your digital clock, is enough to interfere with sleep. This means blocking out the morning sunlight in some parts of the country at certain times of the year when the sun rises early.

Make sure you have a really good bed, and don't watch TV in your bedroom. In fact, you really shouldn't do anything in your bedroom apart from making love and sleeping. I also suggest you do your planned worry time in the evening. Write down what you're worried about and come up with a plan of action to solve your problems. With a selection of choices already in your head, sleep will come a lot easier. I often meditate or do some light yoga before I go to sleep. Repeating a positive mantra can help you feel calm, and a hot bath before bed will loosen your muscles.

It is important to take a moment to recognize the things that you already do to support yourself in a healthy, vibrant lifestyle. It's easy to be hard on yourself and say, "I can't do this perfectly or even well enough, so what's the point?" This is the time you need to give yourself a pep talk, some encouragement from your toughest critic, you, to stay focused on the big picture. The point here is to take baby steps, never losing sight of your goal—creating a healthier life style for yourself, one that will support you both mentally and physically so that you can reap the rewards of a life well lived for many years to come.

Day 15

Pro-Active Action

ASSIGNMENT

Try the following visualization technique when you go to bed: Imagine yourself in your favorite calming spot. Let's say your spot is off the shore of Hawaii. See yourself snorkeling in the blue water, walking in the white sand, and taking in the colors of the fish at the reef. Imagine the rhythmic sound of the tides, lulling you to sleep. Use this visualization or create your own. Where is your favorite stress-free place in the entire world?

A QUICK REVIEW

The following lifestyle changes will help you feel better, look better, sleep better, and have more energy.

- Become familiar with family patterns of bad behavior and change them.
- Do everything in moderation.
- Keep a food journal for a week and write down *everything* you eat, including late-night snacking.
- Change your unhealthy diet. Eat raw, colorful foods; avoid fried foods.
- Eliminate junk foods and alcohol. If you think you are addicted, get help.
- Cut down on soft drinks and caffeine.
- Exercise every day.
- Try some homeopathic remedies to enhance relaxation and sleep.
- See your doctor at least once a year for a physical and make sure you get your routine blood work, mammogram, pap smear, and colonoscopy.
- Avoid negative people and negative stimuli.

It's easy to get overwhelmed by all the advice out there about diet and nutrition. But don't give up before you start. The point is that doing even a little bit of something that's good for you will make a big change in your life. If all you do right now is eliminate sodas and take a half-hour walk a few days a week, you'll feel better, which will motivate you to do more.

As you become aware of how to help yourself and you start making healthy, rational choices, you'll find out that you have more control than you ever imagined—over how you feel, your good health, the fuel that goes into your body, and how well you sleep at night. You need to take total responsibility for how you feel in every way, both physically and emotionally. For optimum health and well-being, along with your supplements, try giving yourself a daily dose of self-acceptance and unconditional love. This will calm your nervous system, soothe your soul, and generate an inner radiant glow that will surround you. It's time to reclaim your power and feel better than you've ever felt in your life, starting right now.

Re-Active to Pro-Active Attitude Adjustments

1. **RE-ACTIVE:** I ingest unhealthy substances, such as fatty and sugary foods, excessive alcohol, caffeine, or drugs, to stuff down frustration, worry, and anxiety.

   PRO-ACTIVE: I honor my body by consuming healthy, nutritious food and beverages that support my emotional and physical well-being. As a result, I stay clear and focused on what I'm trying to achieve.

2. **RE-ACTIVE:** I make excuses for not sticking to a healthy exercise routine. I believe deep down that I really don't have enough time.

   PRO-ACTIVE: I recognize regular exercise as an integral part of a healthy regime that promotes good physical health and raises my self-esteem. This helps me cope with stress and anxiety, as well as feelings of depression.

3. **RE-ACTIVE:** I take care of other people's needs before my own. I neglect myself and put myself last.

   PRO-ACTIVE: I am following the age-old airline advice of putting the oxygen mask on myself first, before taking care of others. I do this by staying well-nourished emotionally, physically, and spiritually, in whatever form suits me.

You enjoy feeling good. Your health is extremely important to you. You radiate positive energy. You take care of yourself and others notice. You look healthy. You feel radiant. You are physically fit and strong. You have high energy and you enjoy your daily activities. You appreciate every breath and you understand that each day is an opportunity to live fully.

You appreciate good, healthy food. In fact, you crave it. You make healthy choices for yourself. You fall asleep easily at night and you wake up refreshed. If you happen to awaken in the night for any reason, you can go right back to sleep. Every minute, every breath, every step you take is a gift.

CHAPTER TEN

Power Thinking

The man who has no imagination has no wings.

—Muhammad Ali

See if you relate to the following list:

Negative thinkers

- tell themselves they are not good enough
- are confused about what they want
- don't value or accept themselves
- have no purpose or mission in life, since they feel inferior and talentless
- have no belief in themselves
- fear they will fail
- see themselves as victims, not victors
- fear change and hang onto the past, even if it was painful

- neglect themselves and their needs
- view themselves as powerless before their negative emotions
- act out in inappropriate ways
- allow fear to prevent them from taking action
- demean and denigrate themselves
- play small
- feel limited and talk down their accomplishments
- feel hopeless and are shy, insecure, and withdrawn
- focus on the past and don't take responsibility for their lives
- beat themselves up and put themselves down
- harbor blame and resentment toward others
- act miserly toward themselves
- lack compassion and judge everyone harshly, especially themselves
- waste time focusing on what "could or should have been"
- feel they have nothing to contribute
- have no gratitude
- don't take risks and anticipate the worst
- are easily disturbed by their external environment
- indulge in negative projections and expectations
- are rigid and closed-minded
- have deep regrets and obsess on "if only"
- lack a spiritual support system
- are passive, ineffective, and indecisive
- procrastinate and are noncommittal
- have trouble knowing what they're really feeling
- don't consider the consequences of their actions
- feel undeserving and fail to ask for appropriate support
- look for validation from external sources
- take everything personally
- try to control what is not within their ability to control
- think they don't deserve to be happy
- don't believe in hope or possibility

- have no trust in their intuition
- are envious of other people's accomplishments
- don't believe in miracles
- feel all alone in the world
- don't know that they are negative thinkers

Thinking negatively affects your attitude about your future and the kind of people you attract. It also affects the opportunities you can draw into your life, so changing the way you think may be the most powerful skill you can acquire and teach to your children. If you teach your children how to be positive, optimistic, hopeful, and how to think from a place of empowerment, it can change the whole family dynamic as well as your children's future.

If you're a positive power thinker, the following list will resonate:

Power thinkers

- feel worthy and deserving of good things
- have a sense of purpose and a clear vision for their future
- love, accept, and value themselves
- believe in their unique gifts and talents
- believe they can achieve anything they set their heart on
- give themselves permission to fail, reframing failure as a learning experience
- see every situation, whether difficult or easy, as an opportunity for growth
- see themselves as important and a necessary contribution to the whole
- do not negate, abandon, or neglect themselves
- express their full range of emotions in healthy and appropriate ways
- know that they are not responsible for other people's choices and behaviors
- do not demean or denigrate themselves

- take big risks
- are optimistic and enthusiastic
- see themselves as having limitless potential
- feel the fear and do it anyway
- believe the world is full of infinite possibility
- think, speak, and act with self-confidence
- take responsibility for their lives and focus on the future
- celebrate their accomplishments, no matter how small
- learn to distinguish old negative thought patterns
- let go of blame, resentment, and regrets and are generous with themselves
- are compassionate toward themselves and others
- do not judge or criticize themselves or others harshly
- see themselves as powerful, open, and inquisitive
- do not waste time focusing on what "should" or "could" have been
- stay calm and centered regardless of their external environment
- take risks and anticipate the best outcome
- refrain from indulging in negative projections and expectations
- are inspired and inspiring
- do not try to control and manipulate others
- see themselves as victors, not victims
- are motivated and excited by life
- accept the fact that pain, change, and loss are a natural part of life
- appreciate what they already have and believe in the law of attraction
- are productive, effective, decisive, and task-oriented
- consider the consequences of their choices
- know what they want and recognize what works and doesn't work for them

- ask for appropriate support
- know they deserve to be happy and content
- are inspired by other people's accomplishments
- trust their feelings and intuition
- know that self-worth, peace, and happiness come from within
- do not take things personally
- recognize what they can and cannot control
- know that they are not alone in the world
- are open to the possibility of miracles

I'm not suggesting you always have to be excessively cheerful, in a perpetual Pollyanna state, with a fake smile painted on your face, denying and suppressing your frustration when life doesn't turn out the way you think it should. Rather, you need to maintain emotional awareness about your true feelings when you get stuck in a downward spiral of obsessive negativity.

We live in a dualistic world, filled with opposites and extremes, where we get daily doses of the highs and lows of life. But we can choose which side to focus on—positive or negative. Ask yourself, "Am I looking for what's right about this? Or am I looking for what's wrong?" All I know for sure is that you *will* find what you're looking for.

We all have a powerful gift that we can use to make ourselves and other people feel good, safe, loved, secure, understood, strong, and capable. I'm referring to the gift of communication, specifically what we say and how we say it. Our words are one of our most intimate and pure sources of communication. But we abuse this gift all too often with a lack of compassion for ourselves and others.

THE CALL FOR COMPASSION

Compassionate communication is any message you give yourself (or someone else) that makes you or someone else feel good, confident, relaxed, capable, loving, energetic, peaceful, or motivated. Simply by saying the right thing, we can transform other people's moods, lighten their day, or maybe even their entire life. So why do we hold back from giving this most precious and powerful gift?

We all need to feel loved and accepted, but the world today spins around too quickly, offering us very little security or validation for being who we are. Actually, the world seems to offer validation for just the opposite. We're led to believe that who we are is simply not good enough. We think we should be prettier, smarter, thinner, flashier, more aggressive, more laid-back, and way more successful. Our teeth should be straighter and whiter, our breasts should be larger and firmer, and our stomachs should be flatter. We are not allowed to grow old or get depressed, and if we're unhappy, we're not supposed to talk about it.

Have you ever been with a child who feels different or challenged for one reason or another? A loving and inspirational word or two can work wonders with a sensitive child. A gentle touch, a smile, a compliment, a warm look that implies "Hey, you're okay and you're loved" can make a huge difference. And it works great with adults, too.

So how do we learn to be compassionate? The people who are best at being compassionate toward others have learned to be compassionate with themselves, first. Someone who talks lovingly to himself or herself excels in speaking loving words to others, and the opposite is true. If you verbally beat yourself up as a habit, you will tend to be negative toward other people, too.

Ask yourself the following questions:

- Do I tend to see the negative side of a situation?
- Do I find fault easily?
- Do I enjoy "putting others in their place"?
- Do I feel uncomfortable when someone expresses painful emotions to me?

- Do I complain a lot?
- Do I have negative friends?
- Do I often feel misunderstood?
- Do I make fun of others and then tell them I'm just kidding?
- Do I feel uncomfortable around people who are challenged or different?
- Am I judgmental?
- Do other people accuse me of being insensitive?

If you answered "yes" to two or more of the above questions, you have some work to do on your compassion levels. Maybe your lack in this area explains why you have a hard time making friends or being in intimate relationships. If you have family or marital problems, compassion is most likely a skill you really need to learn. After all, it will make you a better friend, lover, and parent.

We all know the pain of pouring out our hearts to someone who is either nonresponsive or, worse, slams us with cynicism or sarcasm. When my family and I first moved to California, we had no friends or relatives here. Several months passed, and while our kids were making friends and fitting in, I was lonely. I wanted a close girlfriend. Eventually I met a woman I'll call Barbara whom I really liked. She was smart and inquisitive and had a quirky sense of humor that appealed to me.

We began to spend some time together, but I soon started to see a cynical side of Barbara. She got sarcastic and brash from time to time, and she showed very little sensitivity or compassion. I realized that she was not emotionally sensitive and she was extremely unhappy. My husband had been onto her from the start. He'd noticed that Barbara was selfish and cynical, but it took me longer to recognize these traits since I wanted a friend so much. When I tried to discuss our relationship with her, Barbara didn't want to hear about it. There was little I could do except pull back and, sadly, end our friendship.

Are you someone who has a hard time with compassion? If so, this is the place to begin. Let's discuss a very important topic called self-talk.

SELF-TALK: THE KEY TO HEALTHY SELF-ESTEEM

Thinking negatively is a bad habit. It took us years to perfect it, and now it comes naturally, but we needn't despair because we can change it. Many of us see ourselves as positive thinkers, but it's not necessarily true. It's hard to maintain a positive outlook when the media bombards us daily with negative messages, violence, and vulgarity. Just turn on your computer or your television set and there it is—a load of terrifying reports on just about any topic you can think of.

How much negative TV do you watch? Negative thoughts are contagious, so when you think and talk negatively, when you sit and worry with your spouse or your friends, you feed off each other's negativity. In the end, although the negative messages may start on the outside, they take up residence on the inside and will lead to sabotage on every level of your life. This is what Dr. Shad Helmstetter, whom we are about to meet in this chapter, calls "programming gone wrong."

As a result of this kind of programming, the average person probably has more than 250 negative thoughts in a given day. When you break that down, you are beating yourself up verbally at least once every two and a half minutes. These thoughts come in a steady stream: I'm fat, I don't feel good, I don't want to go to work, I hate my hair, it's raining, I'm exhausted. Do these sound familiar? I just wrote six thoughts in a few seconds. How long do you think it would take to get to 250? Most of us are a lot more negative than we realize. But this condition is easily remedied once you become conscious of your old thought patterns and behaviors that, until now, have been skewing your perspective toward the negative.

When I work with anxious clients, I try to convince them that they are thinking in a negative way, which is creating their anxiety in the first place. I use the word "convince" here because most people believe they have healthy attitudes when, in fact, they don't. They just don't realize how badly their negative thoughts affect their attitudes and their life.

So what do you do? I interviewed Dr. Shad Helmstetter, renowned author, lecturer, and behavioral researcher in the field of motivation. One of the most respected "people programmers" of our time, he is chair of the Life Coach Institute, an organization that develops self-talk programs for schools and businesses around the world. In the following excerpt, you can see how special and unusual this man is.

BASSETT: Welcome, Shad. So what's your mantra today?

DR. HELMSTETTER: I'm in tune, in touch, on top, and going forward. I'm organized and in control today especially. Today's my day and let's do it.

BASSETT: Wow. Do you always start your days out like that?

DR. HELMSTETTER: Yes. Attitude is everything because life happens to all of us in many different ways. It gets down to the difference between people who cope well and those who don't cope so well. We're all given the same choices but some of us make the wrong ones.

BASSETT: How does that programming happen and when?

DR. HELMSTETTER: It starts on the way home from the hospital when you're an infant. Every single message you've ever gotten, everything ever said to you, everything you've ever seen or experienced, everything you've ever said or thought has been typed into your brain, your mental computer, through your five senses. We all hear a lot of negative messages around us all the time. The part of the brain that stores them is like a computer disk—it doesn't know the difference between things that are true or false or bad or good or right or wrong or positive or negative. The programs you get the most often—that's who you end up becoming.

BASSETT: Is it ever too late to reprogram yourself?

DR. HELMSTETTER: No, it's *never* too late. Until the day you pass on, your brain is constantly looking for new information and is busy rewiring itself no matter your age. That means there's hope for all of us.

BASSETT: You're a great example of someone who reprogrammed yourself and went after your dream. If you can do it, people reading this book can do it. How would you define positive self-talk?

DR. HELMSTETTER: Positive self-talk is the foundation, the bedrock of all our attitudes, beliefs, and opinions.

BASSETT: What makes you good at positive self-talk and how do you begin to reprogram yourself?

DR. HELMSTETTER: Practice. The secret of self-talk is based on replacing the old counterproductive, negative messages that hold us back with the opposite, since our programming is based on repetition, repetition, repetition. You need to practice these new kinds of pictures of yourself, new kinds of attitudes. At the moment you start thinking you don't look good, you reverse that by saying, "I look great every day." Eventually your brain says, "I get it. You want to look great. That's how I'll help you be."

BASSETT: Why is it so difficult?

DR. HELMSTETTER: Behavioral researchers say that the programs in the average person who's living a pretty okay life are as much as 76 to 77 percent negative and counterproductive. That may seem like an impossible barrier, but you can get past the negatives with repetition.

My Positive Self-Talk Story

I once received an offer to appear on a national TV talk show whose host had a great reputation. The staff promised me the whole hour if I would bring in some of my clients who were presently working with stress and anxiety. A few clients agreed to be there and to tell their very sensitive stories. As long as they could talk to me on the air, they said, they felt comfortable being open about their struggles. After clearing this with the show's producer, I assured my people that I would be sitting with them onstage for the entire hour and they could address their conversations to me.

I felt pretty secure but when I arrived at the studio, I noticed that the staff was treating my guests harshly and showing very little respect. Then, when the host came to meet me before we went on the air, she said that I would be sitting offstage in the studio audience while she talked with my clients. This was not the agreement I'd made. I was concerned about my people who needed my support to be courageous enough to tell their stories on television.

Luckily, I'd done a lot of work on my self-esteem and positive self-talk, so I was not afraid to speak up. I told the host, "Let me make something clear to you. This is my call." At this point, I pointed my finger at her. "I am responsible for these people so you do it my way or not at all. If your producer had told me I was not going to be onstage with my people, I never would have agreed to do this."

Becoming irate, the host screamed "This show is canceled!" and ran to her dressing room. Within seconds, I took control of my thoughts with positive self-talk. *I'm okay,* I told myself. *The host was trying to intimidate me, but she can't hurt me or negatively affect my life in any way. This is no great loss since we all got a free trip to New York. This woman has no power over me.*

In the next moment, the host came back to me and negotiated. I had gained her respect for standing up for myself, and the show went on—with me onstage.

IT'S ALL ABOUT YOUR ATTITUDE

If you have a smoking problem, you're probably going to make a conscious effort to break it by using the patch. If you have an overeating problem, you're probably going to monitor your food intake. If you have an anger problem, you may take an anger management class or see a therapist. And so, if you have a negative thinking problem, why not make a conscious effort to break that, too? When I feel negative or despondent, I often say to myself, *When it's dark enough, you can see the stars.* When I repeat this mantra, I think about a dark sky at night full of beautiful twinkling stars, and I'm inspired to see the positive in everything around me.

Changing the way you think is arguably one of the most powerful skills you can acquire and teach your children. Your attitude can determine a multitude of things, from whom you marry to what you do for a living. But transforming your attitude from negative to positive is a skill that most of us never learned.

Bad habits are fueled by chemical addictions. The pathways in the brain get used to these chemicals and the nerve receptors send messages that they require more of that chemical to stay stimulated. The brain responds by searching its memory bank for memories that will trigger the feelings associated with that chemical. The brain may instruct your senses to seek circumstances outside yourself to trigger the desired reaction. That explains the cycle of addiction, whether it's smoking, overeating, or being negative.

I've heard countless people say, "I'm not a negative person. I have an optimistic attitude." I understand this tendency. I said the same thing when I started getting help for my anxiety. But when I really thought about my life, I got in touch with my guilt, anger, bitterness, and blame.

I sometimes lead seminars for the heads of such large corporations as Chrysler, AT&T, and McDonald's. One time, I asked the supervisors to describe the most valuable traits of their best employees. Here are the words they used: pleasant, dedicated, positive, energetic, creative, motivated, hardworking, responsible, good with people. I asked them, "Did you know that the number one reason people do bad work, have problems with their coworkers, and are dissatisfied with their job is poor attitude?"

They agreed that attitude is not only important for those who manage people and work in large companies. It also makes all the difference in leading a successful, contented life. It's all about how you approach obstacles, how you feel about yourself, your life, and your future. Here I refer once again to my interview with Dr. Shad Helmstetter:

BASSETT: What do you think about the future of the world with regard to attitude? Do you think the world is an optimistic place?

DR. HELMSTETTER: A shift is taking place in the way people think. They're getting tired of the old way. They're saying, "We've had enough of this, people hating each other and going to war." People are figuring out that they actually have some control in the matter. And next, it's happening with the kids. I'm so excited about the generation of teenagers and younger kids and even infants because they're starting to hear things in a different way. When I wrote my first book, people thought programming meant brainwashing. Then science took over and we got to look inside the human brain and see that—oh my gosh—we're controlling a lot of our health, our anxiety, and our fear.

BASSETT: We're certainly creating it.

DR. HELMSTETTER: That's what we're doing.

BASSETT: You feel that the world is embracing the change and becoming more open to the possibilities of being in control of our thoughts and our surroundings?

DR. HELMSTETTER: You've got it. We've been around long enough doing this and people are finding out it works. Their health is getting better. Their weight is balancing without a diet. People are changing their programs.

Since living a life with a negative attitude creates limitations in finding satisfaction and success, let's see how your attitude rates. Take the following checkup to see if you have any limitations to work on.

ATTITUDE CHECKUP

ANSWER YES OR NO TO THE FOLLOWING STATEMENTS.

1. I really need to feel in control. ____
2. I am easily disappointed in myself and others. ____
3. I don't trust people and I tend to avoid high risk situations. ____
4. I like familiarity; I don't like trying new things, odd food, unusual clothing. ____
5. I don't like people to be angry at me and dislike me. ____
6. Sudden life changes make me uncomfortable. ____
7. Happy people get on my nerves. ____
8. I feel that certain people take advantage of me. ____
9. I am not content with my life, but it would be too difficult to make a change. ____
10. I haven't had any real fun for quite a while. ____
11. I think the world is changing for the worse. ____
12. I think that success for other people is about luck. ____
13. I feel guilty and I cry easily. ____
14. I feel tired and unmotivated a great deal of the time. ____
15. If I want something done right, I feel I have to do it myself. ____
16. I have trouble controlling my anger. ____

SCORING
If you answered yes to 1, 2, and 15, you may be a control freak and a perfectionist.
If you said yes to 1, 2, 3, 6, and 14, you have unrealistic expectations.
If you answered yes to 6, 9, 10, 11, and 14, you have a victim attitude.
If you said yes to 2, 3, 8, 12, and 13, you may be a skeptical person.
If you said yes to 4, 5, 6, 7, and 10, you're not a major risk taker.

People with success-oriented attitudes think like this:

- The sky's the limit!
- Anything is possible!
- Sure I can!
- Watch me!
- So what if . . .
- Don't tell me it can't be done!
- It's never too late!
- Try, try again!

A study done at Harvard University found that when people get the job or the promotion, 85% of the time it's because of their positive attitude. A study in the *Journal of Psychosomatic Medicine* says that keeping a positive attitude is just the right medicine to fight disease. The study reports that people with a positive attitude are energetic, happy, relaxed and are less likely to catch colds or more serious diseases than those who are depressed, nervous, or angry.

MOST INFLUENTIAL "POSITIVE THINKER" IN MY LIFE

I have a wonderful friend named Bruce, a successful personal wealth manager in Los Angeles, managing portfolios worth billions of dollars. At the age of thirty-five, Bruce was at the top of his game:

handsome and successful, with a great family, and looking forward to the rest of his life. But he complained to his doctor about quirky, jerky little movements in certain parts of his body. His doctor suggested a pinched nerve, but Bruce was dissatisfied with that diagnosis so he decided to see a specialist. And so, in the midst of a hectic day, Bruce received the mind-boggling diagnosis of a lifetime: He had Parkinson's disease.

As he tells it, he went straight to a bookstore, thinking, in his typical fashion, that he would take control of whatever this was and get on with his life. But he was stunned to read the prognosis. Parkinson's disease is a chronic, degenerative neurological disease believed to be caused by deterioration in the brain cells that produce dopamine. It occurs generally after the age of sixty. Characterized by tremors and muscle rigidity, it is extremely debilitating and there is no cure.

Bruce got busy. He became an advocate for people with the disease, and to this day he is working to find a cure. In addition, his business has continued to thrive. The disease has progressed significantly, yet Bruce, now in his late forties, is the most positive person I know. He truly lives in the moment. On some days he literally can't get off the floor, but he gives himself a shot, gets up, and gets going.

He came into my life about three years ago when I badly needed someone to remind me that life is about not looking too far into the future (you have no control over it anyway) and staying happy in the moment. Bruce taught me how to be here now and focus on the positive. He is a wild man, passionate about playing the drums, his family and friends, and living life to the fullest. He has a shining presence and people love to be around him because he makes them smile. He makes people stop and think about how lucky they are just to be alive and healthy. His upbeat attitude stems from a positive perspective.

One day I asked him, "How do you do it? How do you stay so upbeat considering what's going on with you?"

"I live in the moment," he told me. "I live for today because I don't know what tomorrow's going to bring."

I just love to be around his energy, his humor, and his attitude toward life. It really is contagious and humbling. He is extraordinary because he has every reason to be in despair, to be bitter and angry about the hand fate has dealt him. He has every reason to be scared and worried about his future, but he isn't. He has every right to sit around depressed, anxious, and fearful, but he chooses to live in the present and to enjoy his life. He's successful, passionate, optimistic, and a whole lot of fun to be around. He is a gift to everyone in his circle and has had a powerful influence on me.

BECOMING A POSITIVE, PRODUCTIVE POWER THINKER

If you want to be like Bruce, you have to learn the skill of positive thinking. As Dr. Helmstetter says, you have to practice. Once you admit to yourself that you are a negative thinker, you've won half the battle. The following five steps will help you recognize the negative thoughts that are sabotaging your potential for success and happiness.

STEP ONE: For one week, carry a small pad of paper with you and jot down every negative thought you have. Include thoughts such as, "I'm too tired, I feel like a bad mother, I feel fat, I feel like such a hypocrite." Write down any thought that makes you feel sad, bad, unattractive, exhausted, lazy, weak, insecure, depressed, overwhelmed, unloved, angry, and annoyed. They may be hard to pinpoint at first, but the more aware of your thoughts you become, the more you'll find ways to turn them around.

STEP TWO: Write positive replacements for each negative thought on the page. Counteract each negative thought with a positive one that relates to the issue. Here are some examples:

Negative: I feel hurt that my daughter yells at me in front of her friends.
Positive: All teenagers go through this. I'll tell her how much it bothers me. If she doesn't change, I'll take away some privileges until she learns to respect me.

Negative: I feel like such a failure. I can't do anything right and I'm afraid.
Positive: It's okay to be scared. Everybody gets scared sometimes. I'm strong, capable, and proud of myself. I'm working toward improving myself. That's a little scary but it's also healthy and exciting.

Negative: I hate to fly. It's dangerous. And today there's a heavy wind. What if there's turbulence?
Positive: It's okay that I don't like flying. A lot of people don't. If there's turbulence, the plane is built to withstand it. I know the pilot will do his best to avoid it.

STEP THREE: Recognize your negative thought pattern as a bad habit and commit to breaking it. Breaking a habit, especially this one, takes time, practice, and unconditional self-love. As you track your negative thoughts, you'll become aware of how negative you really are. Amazing, isn't it? You'll also become aware of how negative others are. When you become more positive, you'll have less tolerance for negative people.

STEP FOUR: Block your negative thoughts and replace them with comforting, realistic, empowering thoughts. In order to become a positive, productive, power thinker, you need to change your negative thoughts as soon as you have them. Ask yourself, "What can I say to make myself feel better right now?" And then say it. As with all skills, the more you practice, the better you get. The idea is to make the positive replacement become an automatic response. Here are a few examples for replacing disempowering negative thoughts with positive, affirming thoughts.

Negative thought: I'm tired and overwhelmed. I don't feel good about myself right now.
Positive replacement: Of course I'm tired. I've been through a lot. I need to exercise, eat better, and talk with friends who can offer support. I'll feel better tomorrow.

Negative thought: I'm worried about money.
Positive replacement: It's fine to be concerned about my finances. It makes me look closely at how I spend and save. I am responsible and place myself in the best possible position I can financially, and then I let go of the worry and enjoy the moment.

Negative thought: I'm lonely.
Positive replacement: I'm really good at personal relationships. I just choose to be alone right now. I am working on being more social and putting myself in situations that give me more opportunity to meet people. But being alone is okay, too.

Negative thought: I'm so angry, I can hardly see straight.
Positive replacement: Anger used to control my life, but not any more. I am learning to control my anger so I am less stressed and more peaceful and enjoyable to be around.

STEP FIVE: Take every opportunity to act in a positive way toward others. Every action begins with a thought, which creates an idea, which creates energy, which leads to an action. When was the last time you told your loved ones how much you really care? Or how wonderful they are? Do you compliment your spouse regularly for being a great lover? Have your told your close friends lately how amazing they are and how they make your life better? Have you complimented your coworker or even your boss lately? Positive thinking feels good, it's contagious, and it doesn't cost a penny!

Here are some positive statements that will help you feel strong and capable:

- I love life. It's stimulating, exciting, and unpredictable, and that's okay since it keeps things interesting.
- I'm a positive person with an optimistic outlook. I'm comfortable accepting the fact that nothing is easy or perfect.
- I like myself. I like who I am and how I look. People enjoy being around me because I'm an interesting person.
- I can achieve any goal when I put my mind to it. I am creative and capable, and nothing can stand in my way.
- Risks are exciting and productive, and I enjoy taking them.
- I am talented, loving, sensitive, and compassionate.
- I solve problems easily by looking for solutions and focusing on the positive potential in any situation.
- I am working to control my anger by underreacting instead of overreacting.
- I am physically strong, healthy, and energetic.
- I am sincere and comfortable with my weaknesses and strengths.
- I am happy in my life right now and I'm looking forward to my future.
- I am calm, content, and in control of my emotions.
- I know I can't please everyone. I don't want to or need to. I pick my friends carefully.
- I do not let other people's negative energy affect me. I hold my own power.
- Today is a wonderful day, full of pleasure. I feel lucky to be alive and healthy.

Think Like an *A*

A friend of mine who attended a university was waiting to take her final exam. She was very nervous and one of the girls standing beside her said, "One of the things I've learned in my drama class is to act like I'm an *A*. When I feel myself having *A* energy, I usually end up getting *A*s on my tests." My friend decided to do the same thing that day and she ended up getting an *A*, too. So act like an *A*. Fill yourself with an attitude of achievement.

I work with a wonderful coworker who is a great example. When we have a really intense work schedule, no matter how thing are going, he walks into my office with a big smile on his face and he finds something positive to say, like "We're doing great today. We're going to make it and it's going to be fabulous." I like being around him because he always chooses to focus on the positive—that everything is going to work out.

People like being around others who are positive and upbeat. They're so much more fun than people who are negative. By the way, negative attracts negative in the same way that positive attracts positive. Those with a bad attitude will reinforce your own negativity, so be very careful choosing whom you want to hang out with.

> **Day 16**
>
> **Pro-Active Action**
>
> ASSIGNMENT
>
> Write down three goals which you can achieve acting like an *A*. Imagine how you will approach each one with a positive attitude and positive self-talk. You just don't know what you're capable of doing until you stretch yourself. Do this for the next thirty days and watch your life begin to change.

Here's more from Dr. Helmstetter:

DR. HELMSTETTER: It's hard to get people to choose to make the change. That's where it begins.

BASSETT: You have to make a conscious choice. First of all, you have to accept the responsibility that you're choosing to be negative. You have to say to yourself, "I'm going to choose a different path and I'm going to make a choice to be positive," but it's going to take time. That's what I hear you saying. It's going to take persistence. It's going to take practice.

DR. HELMSTETTER: You become like the friends or the people you hang around with most. They're programming you all the time with everything they're saying to you. Every time they call and complain, you listen. So you need to use positive self-talk to make positive choices. When you do, you feel better, even if the crisis is not resolved yet. When you speak kindly to yourself, you feel better about everything you choose.

BASSETT: We can come up with a million reasons why we have the right to be miserable, tired, negative, and sorry for ourselves. But we can say, "I choose to see this in a positive light." I've seen how contagious negativity can be, so if we're choosing to be negative, we're passing that on to our family, friends, and coworkers.

DR. HELMSTETTER: Just say, I choose ...

BASSETT: I choose to be happy. I choose to enjoy the present moment.

DR. HELMSTETTER: When I speak all over the world, instead of trying to get people to change their lives, I explain how self-talk works, how programming works, and what they can do. Then, instead of suggesting they try it for a year, I ask them to try it for ten minutes or an hour. Many people have told me, "I did it one day and then I did it for another day and then I thought, 'Why have I been beating myself up, beating up everybody around me, making my life terrible, and not wanting to be here? Why did I live that way when I could have stopped at any time and turned it around?'" There's an instant shift with positive thinking. I've come to the conclusion that in addition to the words "I love you," the four most important words any one can say to someone are "I believe in you." I wouldn't just say it once. I'd say, "I believe in you. I believe in you. I believe in you. I believe in you," and most important, "I believe in you." It works.

BASSETT: If I asked you for some positive closing self-talk phrases or replacement empowerment statements for people to use right now, what would they be?

DR. HELMSTETTER: My life is good. I'm glad to be here. I'm glad to be me today and I'm going to make this one count. I can't wait to do it again tomorrow.

You are so much more powerful than you give yourself credit for. Even if it occurs subconsciously, you are fashioning your life to support the image of who you think you are. If you see yourself as a helpless victim, you will attract events and scenarios to support the story of "Poor me, why does this always happen in my life?"

It happens because you create it. The universe is simply doing its job of giving you what you say you want. Maybe on an unconscious level, you enjoy the negative attention that being a victim brings, and if you convince the universe that you are a victim, the universe will deliver. Isn't that a good enough reason to change your negative, self-defeating thoughts into those that exude power and possibility? Let that victim role go, and start thinking of yourself as a magnificent, powerful, and courageous being. Then sit back and enjoy the gifts that the universe showers on you. These new, fresh experiences will reflect your healthy, empowered vision of yourself.

In my case, once I let go of the "Why me?" syndrome and the "I feel like a victim" syndrome, the chaotic, negative events that had constantly plagued me started to settle down. And my life experiences began to change for the better. I truly began to understand the saying *Your outer world is a reflection of your inner world.*

Re-Active to Pro-Active Attitude Adjustment

Take three of the positive affirmations at the end of this chapter and remember your initial re-active attitude. Now replace each reaction with a pro-active attitude adjustment. For example:

1. *Affirmation:* You are able to see sunshine and rainbows in your future and you have the ability to solve problems.

   RE-ACTIVE: That isn't me. I can't see the light and my problems overwhelm me.

   PRO-ACTIVE: Of course that's me. I'm a happy person and I know how to solve my problems.

2. *Affirmation:* You have confidence in what you do, no matter what someone else tells you.

   RE-ACTIVE: Everyone knows I am not worthy or capable. I know it too.

   PRO-ACTIVE: I do believe in myself. I know that I am an amazing, capable, talented person, regardless of what anyone else may say.

3. *Affirmation:* You like a lot of things about yourself, and you speak to yourself with compassion and kindness.

   RE-ACTIVE: I don't like myself because I'm not good enough. I'm too fat, too stupid, too old, too wrinkled, and too pathetic. No one will ever love me.

   PRO-ACTIVE: I like myself. In fact, I love, accept, and cherish everything about me, just as I am. I love my strengths and my weaknesses and I embrace myself in my entirety.

You always think of something beautiful. Your feelings are your own and you create your own experiences. You often feel happy, and you think of others with warmth and caring. You have confidence in what you do, no matter what someone else tells you. You see how much you've grown because you recognize your doubts as signs of strength, not weakness. You maintain a strong commitment to improving yourself, even though you believe that you are already a really good person.

You like a lot of things about yourself, and you speak to yourself with compassion and kindness. You are patient with yourself and you care about others. You take pleasure in your home and your family. You are able to see sunshine and rainbows in your future and you have the ability to solve problems. You see open windows and a joyous future. You are self-confident, strong, and loving and you surround yourself with positive people. You have a pervasive sense of well-being and great self-respect.

CHAPTER ELEVEN

An Action Plan
for Immediate Manifestation

In preparing for battle I have always found that plans are useless, but planning is indispensable.

—Dwight D. Eisenhower

When I first arrived in Los Angeles, I began recording our *Life Without Limits* program in a Hollywood studio. Each morning, I got up early and drove my minivan through my neighborhood to the Hollywood 101 freeway on-ramp. One morning, a woman I knew waved at me and called out, "Hey, Lucinda, where are you going?"

"To Hollywood!" I called out the window, waving back.

"Hollywood?" she asked me.

"Yes, Hollywood," I yelled over my shoulder.

She smiled, shook her head good-naturedly, and I drove on, amazed that I, a girl from a small midwestern town, who had an alcoholic father, could be on my way to a recording session in a Hollywood studio. It wasn't possible, and yet here I was doing it.

Have you manifested your dream? If you can be really honest with yourself, when you figure out what you really want, you will also get in touch with what may be blocking you from getting it. It might be your belief system—the way your mind works to create or destroy all that you want for yourself. You can make your dreams come true. It's absolutely possible.

In order to determine your personal belief system, write down the answers to the following questions:

- Who are you?
- What kind of person are you?
- How far can you go?
- What potential do you have?
- What do you like to do?
- What are your capabilities?
- What talents do you have?
- What would other people say is special about you?

It really doesn't matter who you are, your age, your nationality, what you've survived, the wounds you carry, the extent of your education, or how long you've been anxiety-ridden. What matters is this:

If you believe you can, you can.

When I first started creating the Attacking Anxiety and Depression program, I had no idea how to do it. I just knew it had to be done, there was a call for it, so I got busy. I had the used computer David had bought me, so we purchased a simple recording device and began recording the people that Dr. Fisher, our medical director, and I were working with in a group format. As I recorded them and their personal experiences, I created the program and the workbook. After all, I'd already helped hundreds of people who went through our groups. There was no reason why I couldn't help people in different parts of the country. I just needed a way to get to them.

Secure in the knowledge that people really needed this material, it came pouring out with passion and a strong conviction about my mission. It took a couple of years and a lot of trial and error. But I'm happy to say that I succeeded. Today, millions of people—doctors, teachers, housewives, corporate salesmen, plumbers, and psychologists—are using the skills I created to help themselves and their loved ones. The payoffs for me are the letters, emails, and calls I get from all over the world, thanking me. I have my attitude of achievement to thank for my ability to manifest what I want, and you can have the same attitude, too, if you can stay focused long enough to see the results. You just need to be clear about what you want and why you want it. Then you can figure out how to get it.

THE ART OF MANIFESTATION

The art of manifestation rests on using the universal law of attraction to benefit your life. I see it as the law of attraction in action—the process of doing something in order to achieve a specific purpose. When you say things like "I can't afford that" or "That isn't for people like me," you are generating a climate in which you truly can't afford it so it isn't for you. Instead, try saying "I always have plenty of money for everything I need and want." Now you are generating energy that will put you in control and help you prioritize your decisions based on abundance, not lack.

The idea is to act like the thing you wish to manifest is already your reality. Just keep in mind that everything takes time and that your circumstances today are a direct result of your past thoughts and beliefs. If you start thinking and acting differently now, if you give the new habit time to set in, you will reap different results in the future. The universe is just waiting for you to take action. So don't underestimate the power of taking one step at a time. It doesn't matter how big or small your actions are. Any action in the general direction of your new reality is enough to get the ball rolling.

Using deliberateness in the art of manifestation is crucial. You will be successful when you

- Are specific about what you want.
- Use the present tense in your expressions. (I *am* making more money instead of I *will be* making more money.)
- Affirm your desires all day long.
- Understand the changes you are asking for.
- Have faith in the end result.
- Be flexible.
- Use the power of daily meditation and prayer.
- Get in the habit of expressing gratitude.

There are several ways I've found to shift my overall patterns of manifestation: affirmations and visualizations as well as active meditations and prayer. Readers of this book are already familiar with affirmations as I have ended most of the chapters with a long list. The purpose of affirmations is to increase your intention and desire, thus inviting the magical experience of manifestation to occur.

The second choice for manifesting is the use of visualization. The images you visualize can be as simple as a single snapshot held in your mind. But when it becomes more dynamic, such as a detailed image of a life change or a place you'd like to live, there will be added power in your action. You will be creating a "vision board" later in the chapter to aid you in visualization manifestation.

If you want to be even more focused, I suggest you create a daily mantra that will help you affirm the way you want to live. Dating back thousands of years, mantras are words or sentences that affirm the way you want to live your life. In order to create your own personal mantra, make a list of three things you want to change in your life. Write them in this form:

I am . . . stressed, debt-ridden, exhausted.

Don't think too much. Just write them down as they arise in your mind. Then, for each item, write down the opposite idea in the same form:

I am . . . at peace, financially secure, well-rested.

String together these positive thoughts in a pleasing order, such as in this form:

I am at peace and well-rested and my world is financially secure.

Write down your mantra on an index card and post it where you will see it often during the day. Make multiple copies, one for your car, your office, your bathroom. Repeat this mantra throughout the day, whenever you think about it and especially before you go to bed.

ATTITUDE OF ACHIEVEMENT

One day when I was in my early twenties, I was driving through a wealthy section of town with my friend Laura. The homes around us were gorgeous and I stopped in front of one of them to admire its beauty. "Laura," I said, "look at that one. I'm going to have a house that beautiful someday."

Laura stared at me a moment and said, "You know, I look at that house and wonder what people do to afford such a wonderful home. But never in my wildest dreams do I imagine I could end up with a place like this. I just assume I won't. I guess that's the difference between you and me. You assume you will."

She summarized it perfectly. I'm the kind of person who decides what I want and commits to it totally. I have learned to set my attitude to support me, not to thwart me. I see now that I'm halfway there when I believe in myself and adopt a positive attitude. Of course, I'm human and there is a part of me that says, *What if it doesn't happen?* But the more secure I get, the more I tell myself *I can.*

It gives me a powerful feeling to approach the various obstacles in my life with an achievement attitude. I ask myself, *What am I supposed to learn from this?* and then I usually find myself on the right path. If you're being tested right now to see how badly you want something, remember this:

The more you practice the attitude of achievement, the more certain you will become.

That is where the magic begins. I know this because I've been knocked down many times. In fact, I've been knocked down more often than I have gotten the brass ring. But I learned that focusing on the brass ring would keep me vital and allow me to keep on getting back up and maintaining a positive attitude.

Whatever you want to accomplish in life, whether it's financial success, peace of mind, or being able to get on a plane without having a panic attack, you must believe in yourself. And it doesn't get easier when you get more successful. Sorry to say, it often gets harder. Survivors are not necessarily the ones who stay on their feet during challenging times. Rather they are the aikido masters, the ones who know how to fall, get up, and try again. These people are the picture of resilience. They are in control, not over what happens, but over their *attitude* about what happens.

If you want to be happy and successful, set your sights on exciting goals that you can achieve. You'll be amazed to discover how far you can go and how much joy you will have, when you commit to an achievement attitude.

DEFINE YOUR DREAMS

Achievement means different things to different people. If you are challenged with anxiety, for example, it means being independent and panic-free. It means being able to control your racing thoughts and staying clear about your dreams and goals. However you choose to define success and achievement, once you learn to control your fears and uncertainty, your goals will change. You will broaden your horizons and dream bigger dreams. Your goal of overcoming simple limitations you believe you have will stretch into overcoming bigger limitations and moving toward new and exciting opportunities such as starting a new job, opening yourself up to new relationships, or taking great trips. This is the bottom line:

Your ability to define your goals and desires will help to alleviate your anxiety.

Once, when I was leading a seminar for a large corporation, I said, "Pretend I'm a magic fairy. When I tap you on the head, your most desired dream will immediately come true. Is it going back to school or starting your own business? How about owning a cabin on a lake or a golf course? Do you dream about taking ice skating lessons or flying to Europe? Take a minute or two to think and then write it down."

A very sad thing happened. While some of the people in the room started jotting down their dreams, a large percentage of my participants had nothing to write. They had so lost touch with their dreams that they couldn't conjure up anything. They just sat there, dumbfounded. So where did their dreams go? Had they settled into an uncomfortable "comfort zone" where they didn't want to be and where they had given up their dreams?

Didn't we all have dreams when we were young? But the reality of making a living took over when we had to pay our bills, rent our apartments, raise our families, and take care of others. We sacrificed our dreams, repressed them, or delegated them to the background until they were so far away that we forgot they ever existed.

A woman with three children once came into the Midwest Center, depressed and overweight. She felt very bad about herself, and when we did the "What's your dream?" exercise, she recalled her previously hidden dream—she always had wanted to work in the health-care industry. She decided to take steps to make this dream come true. She reported all her news to our group each week, and it was stunning to witness what happened.

She began by working in a hospital. She was making very little money, but she was learning new skills and her depression lifted quickly. Within a few months she was doing public speaking and having a wonderful time. A year later, she had lost thirty pounds, she was wearing hip clothing, and she'd started traveling. She had changed her attitude, discovered a newfound respect for herself, and was making her dreams come true.

ACHIEVE YOUR DREAMS

The more passionate you are about what you do, the more energy you are dedicating to the manifestation of your dreams. In fact, without passion, you will never manifest anything. That is because all works of creation are generated by love—your love for yourself and for what you are creating. The love with which you imbue your work and your life in general will touch the hearts of people who come in contact with you.

The following suggestions will help you get in touch with your dreams:

ALLOW YOURSELF TO DREAM AGAIN. If I were your fairy godmother and I could sprinkle fairy dust on you and grant you one wish, what would it be? It's time to stop talking about not having a dream and start figuring out what it is and how to achieve it. Be your own fairy godmother.

Be specific. If you want a new home, what does it look like in detail? How many rooms are there? What color is it and what is the style of furniture? Who will live there with you? Will you be there all the time or only in the winter? How many decks does the house have and how big a garden? Is there a fountain at the front entrance? Does it have a swimming pool? These choices are all yours, so be specific. Focus on visualizing this dream, make it a reality in your mind, and give it everything you've got.

Give yourself a timeline. When can you make your dream happen? In two years? In five years? Are you saying something like "I'd really like to go back to school but I have three young children"? Change the "but" to an "and": "I'd really like to go back to school *and* I have three young children." Doesn't that make it feel more like a possibility? Just put a timeline on achieving your dream, because without one, it probably won't happen. When you timeline your goal, you begin taking action in your life to move toward that goal, and you begin saying "no" to whatever is diverting you.

Make a plan of action. Excuses will do nothing to move you toward your goal. Only taking action will work. If you need to go back to school, sign up for one course to start with. If the university is forty miles away, get in your car and start driving. The sooner you take positive steps in the right direction, the more real it becomes. If you want that home on a beach somewhere, go to a real estate agent and discuss it. The strength of your commitment and your belief in yourself will create the end result. If you need financing, start looking now. Go to your local bank and discuss the possibilities. Or talk to people who have already done it. If they did it, so can you!

Take action. Do it now. Take the first step, and remember to surround yourself with people who lift you up, help you fly, and then stand back and watch you soar. Gayle King, lifelong friend to Oprah Winfrey and editor at large for *O* magazine, said in the June 14, 2010, issue of *People* magazine, "I celebrate Oprah's success. I'm not in her shadow—I'm in her light."

> *And those who were seen dancing were thought to be insane by those who could not hear the music.*
>
> —FRIEDRICH NIETZSCHE

Let's take a look at someone who made a plan of action work for him in a really big way.

Raymond Albert Kroc

BORN IN 1902 IN CHICAGO, RAYMOND ALBERT KROC created the McDonald's billion-dollar restaurant chain franchise we know today. The chain was based on the concepts of his original plan of action—controlling the quality of the food and creating uniformity in its preparation.

How he learned to do this is not evident in his background. He was born to Czech parents and served in World War I as an ambulance driver. He eventually tried his hand at a number of trades, such as selling paper cups, playing the piano, and working at a radio station. But none of these jobs satisfied him and he had to decide what he really wanted. When he dreamed up the idea of working in the food industry, the first step in his plan of action was to get a job in one of Ray Dambaugh's restaurants (a known gambler and friend of Jimmy the Greek) to learn the restaurant business.

For his next step, Kroc created something that had never been seen before—a machine called the Mult-A-Mixer, designed to make five milkshakes simultaneously. He made a decent living selling these machines to other restaurants until he decided to extend his plan even more. Partnering with two brothers, Mac (Maurice) and Dick (Richard) McDonald, who had purchased his mixer for their drive-in restaurant, he presented them with the idea of franchising their initial restaurant, maintaining the quality control, and utilizing a standardized menu and assembly-line production of hamburgers. French fries were made in-house, quality beef was used, and milkshake mixture ratios were perfected. His action plan included training seminars for franchise owners and managers that emphasized automation and standardization. Kroc bought the golden arches symbol from the McDonald brothers and made it recognizable worldwide.

Since Kroc's plan involved expanding widely, for his next step, he sold his successful Mult-A-Mixer company and, within six years, used his profits to open 228 McDonald's restaurant franchises. He eventually bought the brothers out, and, with his plan of action working so well, he became responsible for the fast-food revolution that continues to this day. At the time of his death, in January 1984, there were 7,500 McDonald's restaurants worldwide, making it the world's largest food-service retailer.

HOW MUCH DO YOU WANT IT?

Have you told the people around you about your new plan of action? Have you described what you have in mind and what you intend to do? Did they build you up or try to drag you down? If they tried to drag you down, it isn't that they don't believe in you, although it may feel that way. Rather, it's because your dream and your commitment to go after it triggers their fear. Seeing someone else step out will make them question themselves, so they'd prefer to say that it can't be done.

It's up to you *not* to believe negative messages. When I was in the midst of moving from the Midwest to California, just about everybody lectured me on how irresponsible I was being. But I felt that I was being responsible for myself and my family, for our happiness and my success. My answer was, "I'm 100 percent certain that I'm supposed to move there. I'm going to follow my intuition and my goals." And that is exactly what I did.

Believe in yourself! Have faith in your abilities!
Without a humble but reasonable confidence
in your own powers, you cannot be successful or happy.

—NORMAN VINCENT PEALE

CREATING YOUR ACTION PLAN

Are you ready to create your action plan? If you're ready to stop worrying about your future and start planning for it, you'll need to identify your goals as well as the steps needed to achieve them, just like Raymond Kroc did. This involves prioritizing your tasks, making lists, giving yourself a deadline, and having a contingency plan when things go differently than expected. Remember that an effective plan of action will include a concrete timetable and a set of clearly defined steps.

Unless you have definite, precise,
clearly set goals, you are not going to realize
the maximum potential that lies within you.

—ZIG ZIGLAR, *best-selling author*
& motivational speaker

Don't procrastinate. When you complete something, no matter how arduous or how much focus you needed, you will feel instantly lighter and filled with good self-esteem. Once you start an activity, don't stop until you have completed it.

Day 17

Pro-Active Action

ASSIGNMENT

Write out your action plan in steps. Be clear about what you want and follow the steps. When you have achieved your goal, reward yourself with something wonderful.

For an example, let's look at the following steps that the University of Kent, in England, lays out on its website:

1. **Have a clear objective.** A goal must be challenging enough to be stimulating but not so difficult it becomes demoralizing. Try reaching just outside your comfort zone, stretching but not being stressed.
2. **List the benefits you would gain by achieving your goal.** These are the things you want deep in your heart that will give you the life you deserve.
3. **Begin with what you are doing *now* that could help you get to your goal.** What point would there be to start in six months?
4. **Clearly define the steps you intend to take.** This answers the question *How do I get there?* Break down large steps into smaller components.
5. **Identify an end point for each step.** Reward yourself for achieving it! This could be a meal, clothing, anything that is good for you and makes you happy.
6. **Put the steps in logical order and set a date for beginning each one.**
7. **Map out several paths to your goal.** If one plan gets blocked, make sure you have an alternative ready. Remain flexible.
8. **Review your progress.** Keep a diary or blog of your activities and record your progress as it happens.
9. **Create a support network of positive people who have positive energy and keep you motivated.** Nothing will thwart your plans faster than being around people who are negative.

YOUR BILL OF RIGHTS

In order to stop sitting on the sidelines and waiting for someone else to call the shots, try solving your own problems and making your opportunities happen. You have the right to a good life and to make the best decisions for yourself and your loved ones. I call these "entitlements" so let's see how these statements feel:

- You have a right to ask for what you need, for attention, reassurance, appreciation, and affirmation.
- You have a right to make mistakes.
- You have a right to say what you are feeling.
- You have a right to your opinions.
- You have a right to say no without an explanation.
- You have a right to express your anger.
- You have a right to feel off-kilter, ill, or unsociable.
- You have a right to feel insecure.
- You have a right to feel confident.
- You have a right to question things you don't understand.
- You have a right to be happy.
- You have a right to feel good about yourself.
- You have a right to loving relationships and friendships.
- You have a right to pick your friends.
- You have a right to spend time with your friends.
- You have a right to ask for help.
- You have a right to peace of mind.
- You have a right to spend time alone.
- You have a right to rest.
- You have a right to dream.
- You have a right to follow your heart and go after your dreams.
- You have a right to do what's fun as long it doesn't hurt anybody.
- You have a right to feel good physically.
- You have a right to feel sexy and to enjoy sex.
- You have a right to feel beautiful.

- You have a right to be smart.
- You have a right to spend time on self-discovery.
- You have a right to seek spiritual awareness.
- You have a right to play and have fun.
- You have a right to your emotions.

Always remember that you are special and capable of greatness. With so much newfound confidence and determination, you can't help getting what you want!

CREATING A VISION BOARD

Many people find it difficult to visualize their dreams with passion. But in order to manifest anything, you need to have a sense that you have already achieved your dream. This is where a vision board can be extremely helpful. And it's fun to make one! A vision board is a collage of pictures and written words, collected from books, magazines, and the Internet, that represents what it is that you envision for yourself and your future. The pictures you choose will work like affirmations, providing a visual representation of the future toward which you are striving. A colorful and vibrant visual aid, your vision board will inspire in you a depth of feelings and emotions that will boost your ability to manifest what you want.

Day 18

Pro-Active Action

ASSIGNMENT

It's time to create your vision board so you can manifest your dreams with passion. Before you begin, I suggest you sit quietly and set your intention. Ask for what you want with kindness and then sit with your desires. You may hear a one-word answer or images may come into your head. You are taking this time to let your ego step aside a little bit so you can get a clearer picture of your desired vision. Play some soft music in the background that will help you quiet your mind and allow you to concentrate on the project in front of you.

1. Browse through books, magazines, and the Internet for images and words that appeal to you, excite you, inspire you, and trigger your most hopeful feelings.
2. Print them out or cut them out or write them down. Lay them on a white poster board. As you place them on the board, let your intuition guide you. Perhaps you'll decide to designate a corner for each part of your life, such as career, relationships, health, and spirituality. Or you can blend the different areas to represent an integration of the various aspects of your life. There is no right or wrong way to do this as long as you are following your heart.
3. Glue the images and words onto the board. If you want to, you can draw words on your vision board with a colored marker.
4. Leave space in the center for a personal photo. Select one in which you look radiant and secure and glue it onto your board.
5. Hang your vision board in a place where you'll see it often. Remind yourself of the feelings attached to the pictures. Carry

these feeling with you throughout the day and release them to the universe through your actions. Then watch your vision start manifesting into reality.

I hope you are beginning to understand the power you hold. You have the power of your own dreams and desires. But you must be clear and have a plan. You must also believe in your ability to manifest what you want. And you must be willing to do the work to make these things your reality. You can't just sit and "think it" in order for it to happen. You need to MAKE IT HAPPEN. Manifestation occurs when your thoughts create action that creates opportunities that create your dream.

I want to end this chapter with an excerpt I keep in a frame on my desk that does a beautiful job of summarizing the power of manifestation and universal energy.

Until one is committed, there is hesitancy,
the chance to draw back, always ineffectiveness;
Concerning all acts of initiative (and creation) there is
one elementary truth, the ignorance of which
kills countless ideas and splendid plans;
That the moment one definitely commits oneself,
Then Providence moves too.

All sorts of things occur to help one
That would never have otherwise occurred.
A whole stream of events issues from the decision,
raising in one's favor all manner of unforeseen incidents
and meetings and material assistance,
which no man could have dreamed would have come his way.
I have learned a deep respect for one of Goethe's couplets:
Whatever you can do, or dream you can, begin it.
Boldness has genius, power, and magic in it.

—W.H. MURRAY

Re-Active to Pro-Active Attitude Adjustments

1. **RE-ACTIVE:** I'm too overwhelmed and confused to even start thinking about putting together an action plan. I have no idea where to begin.

   PRO-ACTIVE: I'm excited to start designing my plan of action. I see it will guide me through the necessary steps toward manifesting the life of my dreams.

2. **RE-ACTIVE:** I loathe confrontations. I'd rather bottle up my thoughts and feelings and keep the peace so everyone will like me.

   PRO-ACTIVE: I share my truth in a respectful, assertive manner. It doesn't have to lead to confrontation but if it does, I can handle it just fine.

3. **RE-ACTIVE:** I can't visualize anything. I have a terrible imagination and I have no idea what I want my future to look like. My dreams died a long time ago.

   PRO-ACTIVE: I can relax and focus on whatever will bring me the greatest pleasure and sense of fulfillment. My mind naturally fills up with images of those exact scenarios and I am visualizing my outstanding success!

CHAPTER TWELVE

The Best Is Yet to Come

The power to fulfill our dreams is within each of us. We alone have the responsibility to shape our lives. When we understand this, we know that nothing, and no one, can deny us greatness. We are the ones pushing ourselves forward or holding ourselves back. The power to succeed or fail is ours alone.

—Unknown

LIVING A BALANCED LIFE IS SOMETHING WE ALL STRIVE TO achieve. We want great things for ourselves and our loved ones and we want some degree of control over our lives. We want to be able to take what life throws at us and thrive as we learn and grow from each and every life situation. But many of us have not yet learned how to do that. In fact, a large majority of people believe that the notion of a balanced life is a myth.

That's because when there's too much to do and no time to do it, we live in constant stress and anxiety. But with the help of this book, we are learning another way. There is a path that can help us find a better sense of balance in our personal and professional lives, in our spiritual interdependent self, and in our relationships. But we must understand how balance works and what it means to each of us individually. That's the only way we can create the life we want.

DEFINITION OF BALANCE

We all would agree that balance is an essential component of happiness. The dictionary defines balance as *a stable mental or psychological state; emotional stability; a harmonious or satisfying arrangement or proportion of parts or elements.*

I liken a balanced life to a four-legged chair. Each leg represents a component of your life, such as mental, emotional, spiritual, and personal. The idea is to keep the legs of the chair the same length so your life won't become lopsided. For example, if you work excessively and you don't make time for your family, the personal leg of the chair will be too short and your life will feel shaky, because you'll be off-balance. If the legs of the chair don't match—if one part of your life is ignored or given short shrift—no matter how much energy you give to the other legs, you'll still have to battle stress, anxiety, and depression. But when the legs of your chair (the parts of your life) are equally nurtured and strengthened, you will feel strong, in control, and up to handling whatever hand life deals you.

Leading a balanced life requires a very personal determination, according to life coach Jerry Lopper. He maintains that what feels like balance to one person may feel way off balance to another. But essentially, lack of balance in any area will cause you to be overwhelmed, whether in your career, your family life, or both. It feels as if something is missing, as if there's a void in your center and you have no idea how to fill it. Lopper believes that this kind of existence lacks meaning and purpose, and as a result, you may feel depressed, lethargic, or deeply sad that "this is all there is."

By contrast, Lopper says hopefully, a balanced life just feels right, as if things are exactly the way they should be. Despite the normal ups and downs in an average day, when your life is balanced, you are an active participant, fully engaged, and finding meaning in all that you do and in who you are. Lopper has designated "the five P's" as the fundamentals of life:

1. **Purpose**—finding your mission in life
2. **Passion**—finding what you love to do
3. **Powers**—exercising your unique strengths and abilities
4. **Principles**—discovering what you value
5. **Perspective**—discovering what you believe

CLARIFY YOUR PRIORITIES

"Would you tell me, please, which way I ought to go from here?"
"That depends a good deal on where you want to get to," said the cat.
"I don't much care where," said Alice.
"Then it doesn't matter which way you go," said the cat.

—LEWIS CARROLL, from *Alice in Wonderland*

In order to get where we want to go, we need to know where we are going. If we don't know what we want, how can we create a plan of action to get it? If we don't know our priorities, how will we know where and how to spend our time? In order to prioritize the value of our life activities and goals, author Alex Blackwell suggests we do the important things first. He believes that distractions such as email, text messages, and mind-numbing television keep us from focusing on what really matters. He lists the following five productivity tips and encourages us to spend time on activities that will help us keep our lives in balance:

1. Take at least one hour of email amnesty each day. Shut off your email one day a week.
2. Get up at least fifteen minutes early to get a head start on planning your day.
3. Make a mental or, even better, a written list of what you need to accomplish that day.
4. Stay on alert for time-killing behaviors, like TV or unnecessary phone calls.
5. Know what you value most in life and spend more time there.

THE LIFE PRIORITIES PIE (A PLAN OF ACTION)

In order to pinpoint areas of your life that need more attention, it is imperative to look more closely at what screams out as lacking. You probably already know which areas they are, but in order to achieve balance, let's do the following "slice of life" exercise.

Below is an illustration of the Life Priorities Pie. There is only so much time in your day and in your life, as there is only so much pie on the pie platter. Once it's gone, it's gone. How do you want to divide up your life, your pie, so you can get the most out of it?

Your Life Priorities Pie is divided into eight "slice of life" categories for you to assess. Each slice has an internal rating scale of 1 to 5 for you to color in.

1. Indicates that you spend very little or no time in this area of your life.
2. Indicates a modest amount of time.
3. Indicates a moderate amount of time.
4. Indicates a considerable amount of time.
5. Indicates that you spend a great deal of time in this area of your life.

Review the slices and color them in appropriately, according to how much time you spend in each, beginning at the center of the pie and coloring out toward the edge. Notice how much time you spend in each area.

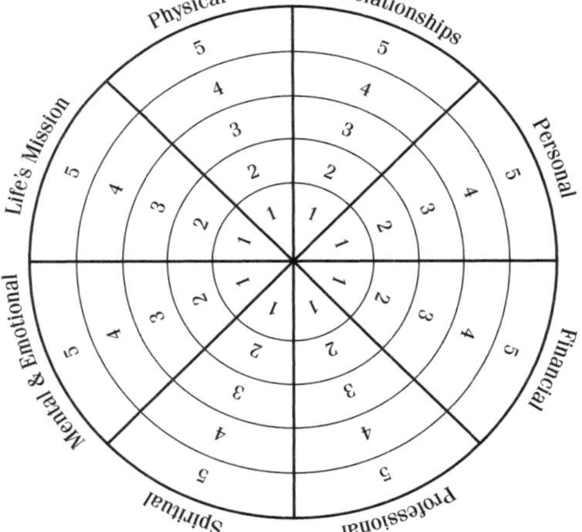

Now, as you look at your completed pie, which of the pieces are the least colored in? These are clearly the areas of your life that are neglected, possibly causing you to feel off balance. Assessing the various "slice of life" categories below, check the specific areas of that category you want to work on.

PHYSICAL

____ Appearance
____ Good health
____ Exercise
____ Healthy diet

RELATIONSHIPS

____ Partner/spouse
____ Romance and physical affection
____ Children
____ Parents
____ Siblings
____ Friendships

PERSONAL

____ Enjoyment and fun
____ Trips and vacations
____ Time for myself
____ Pleasant home life
____ Sense of community

FINANCIAL

____ Improving financial security
____ Good credit
____ Living within monthly budget
____ Current savings
____ Long-term investment strategy
____ Managing spending and debt

PROFESSIONAL

____ Enjoying career
____ Growing professionally
____ Financially rewarding

SPIRITUAL

____ Spiritual growth and education
____ Prayer and/or meditating
____ Spiritual community

MENTAL AND EMOTIONAL

____ Personal growth
____ Relaxed self time
____ Eliminating unhealthy addictions—smoking, alcohol, drugs
____ Living with gratitude
____ Feeling loved and supported
____ Managing emotions—worry, anxiety, fear, depression

LIFE'S MISSION

____ Giving time to others in need
____ Donating time to causes
____ Making a difference in some positive way
____ Clarity in my life's mission and purpose

WHAT CHANGES WOULD YOU LIKE TO HAPPEN?

Now that you've rated each slice of life and indicated in which specific areas you need work, refer to the Life Priorities Chart below for more clarity in defining your plan of action for a balanced life. Get creative and open your eyes to new possibilities. Don't limit yourself by deciding why something can't happen or who's standing in your way. The sky *is* the limit and miracles *do* happen when you take the initial step toward transforming your vision into your reality. The key is to hold onto the clear image of your success as if it has already happened, because, in truth, somewhere out there in the universe, it already has. For your part, writing it down and creating an action plan will create synchronicity, which will help you draw in what you want.

For clarification, take a look at the sample chart below. The four columns indicate the area that needs improvement, your goal for that particular area, the action steps to achieve your goal, and the cost of neglecting to make the changes needed to improve that particular area of your life.

LIFE PRIORITIES CHART
SAMPLE 1

AREAS TO BE IMPROVED	MY GOAL FOR THIS AREA	ACTION STEPS TO ACHIEVE MY GOALS	THE COST OF NOT ACHIEVING MY GOAL
#1 PHYSICAL	To lose 10 pounds and begin to eat a healthier diet	I will begin to buy organic healthy food, and I will join a gym and begin an exercise program	My self-esteem suffers and I feel tired and unattractive, and unhealthy
#2 FINANCIAL	Becoming more responsible about spending and creating a budget	I will talk to a financial adviser and put together a weekly budget for myself and my family	I will continue to spend every penny I earn, and not feel in control of my finances

SAMPLE 2

AREAS TO BE IMPROVED	MY GOAL FOR THIS AREA	ACTION STEPS TO ACHIEVE MY GOALS	THE COST OF NOT ACHIEVING MY GOAL
#1 PROFESSIONAL:	Job satisfaction and sense of security. Start a new business of my own	I will create a business plan and talk with people who can give me advice who own the type of business I want to start	Lack of career fulfillment, feeling of dissatisfaction and lack of security
#2 SPIRITUAL	To develop a deeper connection to my Higher Power	I will buy spiritual books recommended by friends; I will join a church or spiritual support group or attend a few workshops	Separation and a feeling of being alone in the world. No sense of higher power to connect with

SAMPLE 3

AREAS TO BE IMPROVED	MY GOAL FOR THIS AREA	ACTION STEPS TO ACHIEVE MY GOALS	THE COST OF NOT ACHIEVING MY GOAL
#1 RELATIONSHIPS	To improve my relationship with my spouse	I will begin to spend more time with certain people, focusing on positive experiences and physical affection	That there will be no passion between my spouse and myself
#2 MENTAL/ EMOTIONAL	To work on my issues with worrying, low self-esteem, and Core Story false beliefs	I will begin to use worry reversal and the skills in this book to control and manage my worry and fear	That I will continue to be plagued by feelings of insecurity and unworthiness and continue to make excuses for not being happy and not achieving my goals

Now, take a moment and fill in your own Life Priorities Chart below. *A reminder:* the categories are…

COLUMN #1: Areas that need improvement.
COLUMN #2: Your goal for that particular area.
COLUMN #3: Action steps to achieve your goals.
COLUMN #4: The cost of neglecting to make the changes needed to improve that particular area of your life.

LIFE PRIORITIES CHART

AREAS TO BE IMPROVED	MY GOAL FOR THIS AREA	ACTION STEPS TO ACHIEVE MY GOALS	THE COST OF NOT ACHIEVING MY GOAL
# 1			
# 2			

Don't be afraid to ask for help from people whom you trust and respect. Now that you've defined your particular areas in need of attention, why not study the choices, actions, and behaviors of those who are successfully doing what you want to do? Turn to experts in your field for support, guidance, and some suggestions. Whether you want insight on a personal, spiritual, financial, or professional level, there is nothing more valuable than a support system to make sure you're moving in the right direction. Whether it's a friend, a counselor, or a support group, positive encouragement from others will keep you motivated and on track.

LIVING IN THE MOMENT

The secret of health for both body and mind
is not to mourn for the past or
worry about the future,
but to live in the moment,
wisely and earnestly.

—BUDDHA

Shann Vander Leek, a respected life coach, has written a powerful piece on being present and living in the moment. He believes that there are three kinds of people: those who dwell in the past, those who thrive in the moment, and those who prepare for the future.

"We all hop from one reality to the other," he tells us, "but most of us, as creatures of habit, tend to live mainly in one form of reality or another. When we realize that we are special, unique, and worthy of great accomplishments, we no longer need to reside in the back story, what we call the Core Story. We can start experiencing today by letting go of any attachments to our past. Forgive, leave the burden behind, allow for positive change."

In other words, we will begin to establish a new, healthy proactive perspective of ourselves that allows us to become our own biggest fan with a highly developed sense of security and worth. By letting go of the past and living in the moment, we focus on who we are and what matters right now.

Vander Leek goes on to say that no matter where our thoughts travel, the time is always NOW. "Not yesterday," he stresses, "last week, last month, last year. It is not tomorrow, next week, or next year. Time is always RIGHT NOW. Choosing to be in the moment allows us to maximize the opportunities of Today."

He reminds us that at some point in each of our lives we are meant to figure out that life is about the journey and that our experiences along the way form our reality. Best-selling author Eckhart Tolle agrees with him. In his blockbuster book *The Power of Now,* Tolle says, "to break your old pattern of present moment denial and present moment resistance, make it your practice to withdraw attention from the past and the future whenever they are not needed. Step out of the time dimension as much as possible in everyday life. If you find it hard to enter the 'Now' directly, start by observing the habitual tendency of your mind to want to escape from the 'Now.' You will observe that the future is usually imagined as either better or worse than the present. If the imagined future is better, it gives you hope or pleasurable anticipation. If it is worse, it creates anxiety." Tolle adds, "All negativity is caused by an accumulation of psychological time and denial of the present. Unease, anxiety, tension, stress, worry are all forms of fear. Guilt, regret, resentment, grievances, sadness, bitterness, and all forms of non-forgiveness are caused by too much past, and not enough presence."

◆◆◆◆◆

Begin right now to move out of the past and into the moment. It's a great place to be if you choose to be happy because, ultimately, happiness is a choice. I recently drove to the airport to pick up a friend, but I hadn't called ahead to check whether the plane was on time. When I learned it was going to be delayed for an hour and a half, I parked the car, sat in the baggage claim area, and engaged in one of my favorite activities—people watching. I focused on a heavyset man with a Santa Claus beard entering the baggage claim area, dressed in tattered clothing, worn-out tennis shoes, and carrying a cane. He limped along, and from outward appearances, he looked destitute and ill. But there was also something fascinating about him.

He took a seat near me and began chatting with someone sitting beside him. I could hear the conversation and he was laughing, speaking tenderly, and articulating his words beautifully. He had a powerful and lively presence, despite the way he looked on the outside. Several other people were pacing and looking at their watches, clearly frustrated, and some were angry, but the bearded man was actually enjoying the moment and I found myself wanting to talk to him. *How interesting,* I thought. *What makes him so happy? I wonder who he's waiting for. I bet they'll be really glad to see him.*

Is that the way people feel around you? Is that how you feel about yourself?

THE RIGHT TO HAPPINESS

I hope that by reading this book, you will realize that happiness is not a set of situations or positive outcomes. Rather, it is a state of mind that has nothing to do with outside circumstances. We have all felt some degree of serenity and peace in our lives, even if it was a fleeting moment. It does exist within our experience, and in order to access it and allow it into our lives, we must understand who we are and how we function.

The Dalai Lama says in his book *The Art of Happiness,* "I believe that the very purpose of our life is to seek happiness. That is clear. Whether one believes in religion or not, whether one believes in this religion or that religion, we all are seeking something better in life. So, I think, the very motion of our life is towards happiness."

He also says, "But isn't a life based on seeking personal happiness by nature self-centered, even self-indulgent? Not necessarily. In fact, survey after survey has shown that it is *unhappy* people who tend to be most self-focused and often socially withdrawn, brooding, and even antagonistic. Happy people, in contrast, I generally have found to be more sociable, flexible, and creative and able to tolerate life's daily frustrations more easily than unhappy people. And, most important, they are found to be more loving and forgiving than unhappy people."

We all know that a good deal of effort is required to achieve anything worthwhile, but when it comes to happiness, you really don't need to search for it. In fact, there's no way to get there by searching. You have only to go within yourself to find a sense of innate good health, peace of mind, and balance. It's about learning to flow as you stop *trying* to be happy and you start simply *being* happy. You can reach your inner sense of contentment when you truly embrace the fact that happiness comes from inside of you, not outside. Then you are living *from* happiness, rather than living *for* it.

Your Bill of Rights for Happiness

Happiness is more than a wonderful gift. It is your inherent right and anything else is going against the grain of what life is meant to be. With this in mind, I have created a bill of rights for happiness:

You have the right to be excited about your life.
You have the right to create an attractive, comfortable home.
You have the right to live wherever you choose.
You have the right to have healthy, rewarding relationships.
You have the right to feel attractive and healthy.
You have the right to be proud of who you are.
You have the right to spend time on yourself.
You have the right to find your own spiritual path.
You have the right to have a career.
You have the right to enjoy your life every day.
You have the right to change things in your life whenever you desire.
You have the right to set goals and go after them.
You have the right to make your own decisions.
You have the right to be proud of yourself and your accomplishments.
You have the right to earn and enjoy money and material things.
You have the right to choose your own lifestyle.
You have the right to feel motivated and driven.
You have the right to live a simple life.
You have the right to choose how you spend your time.
You have the right to feel secure.
You have the right to be the best that you can be.
You have the right to eliminate chaos from your life.
You have the right to feel calm, satisfied, and content.

Day 19

Pro-Active Action

ASSIGNMENT

Create a gratefulness section in your journal. At the end of each day, list the things that occurred for which you feel grateful. I'm talking about time with your children, laughing, playing or talking, good health, your ability to walk, run, work out, relationships, lovers, friends, spouse, your job, or a beautiful sunset. How about a good movie, a great meal, or physical intimacy with someone you love? These are all wonderful things not to be taken for granted. It's a known fact that grateful people enjoy better physical health, are optimistic, exercise regularly, and feel happier about their lives than those who aren't. Bethany Hamilton, in the story given here, exemplifies gratitude in the face of great challenge.

Bethany Hamilton's Challenge

Born to surfer parents in Kauai, Hawaii, Bethany Hamilton was eight years old when she won her first surfing award in the "Push and Ride" division of a Quicksilver surfing contest. It was logical then, that she would dream about becoming a professional surfer and she began competing more seriously when she was nine. But the best-laid plans often go awry, something that Bethany was about to learn.

By the time she was twenty, she had a sponsor, *Rip Curl,* and she was gung ho, competing in the National Scholastic Surfing competition. Then, on October 31, 2003, Bethany went for an early morning surf along Tunnels Beach, in Kauai, with friends. The water was crystal clear and calm that day and she was relaxing on her board, her left arm dangling in the cool water, while she waited for the next wave to roll in. Her friends were floating not too far from her, all of them looking out to sea, when Bethany suddenly spotted a flash of gray.

In the next moment, she felt severe pressure on her left arm, a couple of fast tugs, and Bethany watched a shark bite off her arm to the shoulder. The water around her turned bright red and she managed to say in a loud but not panicked voice, "I just got attacked by a shark." As she paddled the half mile back to shore with the help of her friends and her good right arm, one thought was repeating in her head, "Get to the beach. Get to the beach."

Once out of the water, Bethany lapsed in and out of consciousness while a friend made a tourniquet for her arm stub from a surfboard leash and a T-shirt. By the time they reached Wilcox Memorial Hospital, Bethany had lost 60 percent of her blood and the pain, which had been nonexistent at first, began to catch up with her. She was wheeled straight into the operating room and she remained in recovery for the next seven days.

At first she thought she might never surf again. But nothing had ever made her happier than surfing. Although the initial sight of her shoulder without an arm nearly caused her to faint, she was determined to keep on doing the thing that brought her the most joy. When she told the doctor she'd decided to get back on a surfboard as soon as possible, he made her promise to wait until her stitches were removed. She agreed.

She got back in the water about one month later, on Thanksgiving Day, 2003, and in July, 2004, Hamilton won the ESPY Award for Best Comeback Athlete of the Year. She won a Special Courage Award at the 2004 Teen Choice Awards and in 2005, with one arm, she won first place in the National Scholastic Surfing Association Championships, a goal she'd been trying to achieve since before the shark attack. She appreciates the awards which she continues to win, despite her disability, and she loves competing against some of the best women surfers in the world. But most of all, Bethany is satisfied with her life because she continues to do the thing that makes her happiest — surfing.

THE POWER OF PRAYER

I have never found a more effective method for clarifying desires and finding happiness than prayer. Prayer helps me to define my problem and to be honest with myself. Then I can analyze a situation from a more humble, less worldly perspective.

Prayer is a means of sharing the burden, which relieves pressure, as you tell your worries and concerns to someone who will listen and won't judge, no matter what you say. Praying is like handing the problem over to someone else as you talk it out. Then you can tune in for guidance and a different perspective that will exude heartfelt energy. When you pray, you are exposing your real self and extending sincere, loving energy to yourself. It doesn't matter if your words are fancy or plain, and there is no way to do it right or wrong. Prayer is about opening your heart and being sincere.

Prayer can connect you with your higher power, enabling you to ask for a miracle as you connect to God and the universe. I see it as universal communication on the highest level since through prayer, you can find the spiritual wholeness that most of

Day 20

Pro-Active Action

ASSIGNMENT

This action assignment is called *Become Your Own Hero*. Start by identifying a person who has achieved some version of what you're striving for. Now list two qualities you most admire about that person.

Each morning, claim those qualities as your own by consciously breathing them in with a deep conscious breath. When you have finished your breaths, tell yourself, "If I can recognize generosity in that person, it already exists within me." "If I can recognize courage in that person, it already exists in me."

In this way, you are becoming your own hero.

us are looking for. It is a form of communication with God and with yourself as you explore your deepest desires and needs.

If prayer is new to you, let me share some suggestions that have worked for me:

- Acknowledge your higher power; speak directly and be humble.
- Be grateful.
- Be honest.
- Don't judge yourself. No one is perfect and we all make mistakes.
- Don't wait. There is no perfect time to pray.
- Pray often. Small prayers throughout the day will make you feel better.
- Pray when you're happy, not just when you want something.

Just as there is no right or wrong way to pray, there is no right or wrong place to do it. You don't have to be on your knees in a church. Your backyard or your bedroom is just as effective a place as a chapel or synagogue. All that matters is that you go to a quiet, private place and be sincere. It will strengthen you and give you the courage to keep on moving toward your goals. You can pray in the day or the night, and you don't have to use specific words. It's like meditating in that you become quiet, go deep inside yourself, and ask God to help you increase your faith so you can go deeper.

YOUR MISSION

In considering the importance of your Core Story, it's important to realize that much of what you went through in your life was in preparation for a mission. Is your mission clear to you yet? Maybe you're already a teacher, a therapist, a minister, or a doctor. These people generally knew what they wanted at an early age and went for it.

Day 21

Pro-Active Action

ASSIGNMENT

It's time to create your personal talisman. The dictionary defines a *talisman* as an object, such as a stone, that is believed to have special powers to reject evil and bring good fortune to its wearer. The word itself has roots in the Arabic word *tilasm* and the Greek *talein*, which both translate to "initiation into the mysteries." The talisman has a long history in religions and societies from ancient times. Traditionally, a talisman was seen as an object marked with magic signs, supposedly capable of conferring on its owner supernatural powers, protection, and success. I see a talisman as something that reminds me of who I am and what marvels I'm capable of creating. Your talisman can be a stone, a crystal, a key chain, or a favorite bracelet, and you can have more than one. Each time your see it, it will remind you to stay focused on a positive vision for yourself and your future.

My talisman is a key chain with two simple silver hearts, one large and one small, which my daughter Brittany gave me years ago. The keys hanging on the chain have changed over the years, but the hearts have not. Every time I look at it, it reminds me of our bond as mother and daughter. It also reminds me of Sammy, my son, and of my entire support system that includes family and friends. It always gives me a lift.

For a second talisman, I cherish the watch that my husband gave me before he passed away. It is warm and heavy and reminds me of him – his energy, his support, and his love and belief in me. It's almost like he's with me again.

Since this is your personal talisman, you get to choose it, but more often than not, it chooses you. It just shows up and feels right and you want to keep it on you or near you to remind you of what is important. You may already have a talisman without even knowing it.

But for many of you, the mission wasn't so obvious. Far too many people go through life unaware of their own suffering and much more focused on helping others. After all, we all want to be here for each other. But whether your life has been one of struggle or not, you still have a mission. You are here to give. As a result of your life experiences, both good and bad, you can take your unique talents and share them with others to make the world a better place.

Nothing gives a person more pleasure, keeps them more humble, and sets a better example for children, than giving. Especially giving time—to listen, to reassure, to comfort, to teach, and to play. Time is our most precious commodity, so when you give it to someone else, that is quite a special gift. Some people call this your mission.

Maybe your mission is to be a musician because you had music in your life growing up, and you enjoy playing or singing for others. Maybe, through your desire for growth, you've attended workshops, read self-help books, and you're good at talking people through tough times. This is an amazingly powerful gift or mission. Maybe, as a result of something in your Core Story, you are patient with children, understand their frustrations, and you can give them good advice. If you're good with money, maybe you're running your own business and you can help friends who don't understand finances. Maybe you're good at taking things lightly, something you can teach by example. Or maybe you're good with death and dying because you've lost so many people in your life that you're able to help others who are going through this type of loss.

Do you see all the ways you can "minister" to others by doing your personal mission? You will inevitably find several ways to reach out and give back. Or you may even be doing it now and not realizing it. Take a moment and think about who you are and what you have to give in order to make the world a better place.

In his book *A Purpose Driven Life,* Rick Warren talks about everyone's personal ministry. He believes that you use your experiences to determine your purpose, and he names five categories of experiences from the past that have helped mold you and imbue your potential for service:

Family: What did you learn growing up in your family?

Educational: What did you learn in school?

Vocational: What have you learned from your work experience?

Ministry: How have you reached out to others?

Painful Experiences: What problems, hurts, and trials have you endured that have provided you with insight and tenderness toward others?

It is this last category, Painful Experiences, that Warren believes God uses to prepare each of us for our personal ministry. He believes that our greatest ministry will come out of our greatest hurts. "After all," he says, "who could better minister to the parents of a Down syndrome child than another couple facing the same situation? Who could better help an alcoholic recover than someone who fought the disease himself? Who could better comfort an abandoned wife than someone whose own husband left her for another woman?"

Warren urges us to try to embrace a powerful truth: The very experiences you resent or regret the most, the ones you try to hide and forget, are exactly what God wants you to use to help others.

That *is* your ministry! But to use these experiences, you must be willing to stop covering them up and instead to share them—your faults, your failures, and your fears. People who need support are more encouraged when you admit your weaknesses than when you brag about your strengths. The truth is, Warren tells us, that your weaknesses increase your capacity for sympathizing with other people. And so the things you are most embarrassed about, most ashamed of, most reluctant to share, are the very tools God can use most powerfully to help you help others.

If you're wondering when you should give to or serve someone else, I believe in doing it spontaneously, perhaps in a shared moment of emotion. Or any time you feel like someone needs your support. Whether you do it all the time, occasionally, or when the opportunity arises, just do it. Reach out and give of yourself and your time. I have seen, time and again, that happiness and enjoyment arise from being of service in simple ways.

In *A Purpose Driven Life,* Rick Warren also says, "At some point in your life you must decide whether you want to impress people or influence them. You can impress from a distance, but to influence someone, you must get close to them. When you do, they will be able to see your flaws, and that's okay."

Happiness is only available with total acceptance of who you are, including all your fears, worries, and anxiety. It will be there for you when you can see your own inner beauty. You cannot achieve happiness without using your past, your Core Story, your flaws, insecurities, and imperfections in a positive way. It is about letting go and detaching from unhealthy people, ideas, and lifestyle choices, and replacing them with interdependent, pro-active ways of thinking and responding.

Are you beginning to see how it all ties together for your good? Do you realize that you hold the key that can unlock your life's potential? Are you looking at things from a new and more optimistic perspective? Do you acknowledge now that you are capable of great things when you change your attitude and take responsibility? If so, congratulations! You have found the Solution. *Now go live your life.*

ACKNOWLEDGMENTS

I want to thank my agent, Margret McBride, for being such an incredible friend, as well as an amazing businesswoman. Time spent with you is always a humbling, eye-opening learning experience. Thank you so much for always believing in me and my message.

A very special thanks goes to my collaborator, Andrea Kagan, for helping to make the journey of writing this book joyful, fun, and "almost" painless. You are such a sensitive, tuned-in professional. You make my job easy.

And a warm hug and big thank-you goes to Del Adey Jones, my incredible researcher and teacher, but more importantly, one of my dearest friends. You have been such a gift in my life in these past few years. What would I do without you and your loving support? Thank you for being such a giver.

And of course, my children, Brittany and Sammy, thank you both for believing in me, but mostly for believing in yourselves.

Here's to the future.

INDEX